$28.50

THE WOLF SHALL LIE
WITH THE LAMB

THE WOLF SHALL LIE WITH THE LAMB

THE MESSIAH IN HASIDIC THOUGHT

Shmuel Boteach

JASON ARONSON INC.
Northvale, New Jersey
London

This book is set in 11 point Garamond by Lind Graphics of Upper Saddle River, New Jersey, and printed at Haddon Craftsmen of Scranton, Pennsyvlania.

Library of Congress Cataloging-in-Publication Data

Boteach, Shmuel.
    The wolf shall lie with the lamb: the messiah in Hasidic thought
/ by Shmuel Boteach.
        p. cm.
    Includes index.
    ISBN 0-87668-339-1
    1. Messiah—Judaism.   2. Messianic era (Judaism)   3. Hasidism.
4. Habad. I. Title.
BM615.B6   1993
296.3′3—dc20   92-28697

Manufactured in the United States of America. Jason Aronson Inc. offers books and cassettes. For information and catalog write to Jason Aronson Inc., 230 Livingston Street, Northvale, New Jersey 07647.

Dedicated to the Lubavitcher Rebbe,
Rabbi Menachem M. Schneerson,
whose magnificent vision and inexhaustible enthusiasm
for the messianic coming
serve as an inspiration to anyone brave enough
to accept its challenge.

In the merit of the millions of people whose lives he has touched in every corner of the globe, may the Almighty grant him renewed health and energy to complete the greatest undertaking in the world's history—the transformation of the earth via a messianic awakening!

CONTENTS

II
The Belief in the Resurrection of the Dead

III
What Will Happen in the Messianic Era

ACKNOWLEDGMENT

This book is based on forty-four years of hasidic dialectic on the subject of the Messiah and the era he will usher in, by the Lubavitcher Rebbe Shlita, Rabbi Menachem M. Schneerson. Much of the material, which is of encyclopedic proportion, was condensed and systematized by the great contemporary hasidic scholar Rabbi Yoel Kahn, to whom I am eternally grateful. Rabbi Kahn also serves as Rabbi Schneerson's chief *hozer*. The need for a *hozer* (literally, one who commits the Rebbe's lengthy discourses to memory), arises from the fact that the rebbe's public addresses usually take place on the Sabbath and Jewish festivals, when the use of audio recording devices is prescribed by Jewish law. The breadth of Rabbi Kahn's hasidic knowledge, and the lucidity with which it is conveyed, has inspired thousands of young students to search for the infinite depth contained within hasidic thought, with myself not least among them.

I would also like to thank the many student members of the Oxford University L'Chaim Society, whose volunteer work in our offices enable me to find time to write, and whose challenging questions in all areas of Jewish thought, particularly in the difficult areas like the messianic era, cause me to think more deeply and thoroughly into the essential principles of Judaism.

I thank my wife Devorah, whose selflessness and dedication to me, my work, and our three daughters knows no bounds.

ix

Finally, I humbly offer thanks to the Master of the Universe for guiding me along a path in life, where I discovered the beauty of a hasidic life-style and to be a student and teacher of Judaism. I can think of no greater honor.

INTRODUCTION

In what has become one of his most celebrated and well-known works, Maimonides, in his commentary on the *Mishnah,* compiles what he refers to as the *Shloshah-Asar Ikkarim,* the Thirteen Articles of Faith, compiled from Judaism's 613 commandments found in the Torah. The Thirteen Articles of Jewish faith are as follows:

  1. Belief in the existence of the Creator, be He blessed, who is perfect in every manner of existence and is the Primary Cause of all that exists.
  2. The belief in God's absolute and unparalleled unity.
  3. The belief in God's noncorporeality, nor that He will be affected by any physical occurrences, such as movement, or rest, or dwelling.
  4. The belief in God's eternity.
  5. The imperative to worship Him exclusively and no foreign false gods.
  6. The belief that God communicates with man through prophecy.
  7. The belief that the prophecy of Moses our teacher has priority.
  8. The belief in the divine origin of the Torah.
  9. The belief in the immutability of the Torah.
  10. The belief in divine omniscience and providence.

11. The belief in divine reward and retribution.

12. The belief in the arrival of the Messiah and the messianic era.

13. The belief in the resurrection of the dead.

It is the custom of many congregations to recite the Thirteen Articles, in a slightly more poetic form, beginning with the words *Ani Maamin*—"I believe"—every day after the morning prayers in the synagogue. In his commentary on the *Mishnah* (*Sanhedrin,* chap. 10), Maimonides refers to these thirteen principles of faith as "the fundamental truths of our religion and its very foundations."

Maimonides' intention in composing the thirteen rules was not for the Jew to accept the validity of these thirteen principles and reject the rest. A Jew is obligated to believe in every single word and every letter of the Torah, whether it be the Written or Oral Law, and he who does not believe in even the smallest aspect of the Written Torah is halakhically branded a *kofer* (heretic). This principle itself is included by Maimonides as part of the fifth principle of faith. He writes, "We are obligated to believe that this entire Torah, which was given to us through our master Moses, of blessed memory, emanates entirely from the Almighty. This means that the Torah, in its entirety, was given to us by God." Thus, it is clear that he who rejects even a single letter of the Torah is halakhically defined as a *kofer*, a heretic.

Having said this, however, the question arises as to how the Thirteen Principles differ from all the other rules in the Torah? If one must believe in the entire Torah, what makes these thirteen rules so special, and how do they differ from any other Torah law?

Maimonides explains that the Thirteen Principles form the very foundation on which all of Jewish belief and practices rests. A rejection of any of them is not only a rejection of a single tenet of Judaism, but a rejection of the entire structure of Jewish thought.

For example, the Talmud maintains that there are seven heavens. If one were to reject this statement of the Oral Law as being implausible, he would be considered a heretic, not because of his rejection of the existence of *seven heavens,* but because he is rejecting the *truth* of the Torah. By disputing the Torah's claim as to the number of heavens, one is thereby rejecting the fact that the entire Torah is true. The belief in the truth of the Torah constitutes one of the Thirteen Articles of Faith.

There is not a single statement or utterance of the Torah that is not in turn related to, and supported by, one of the Thirteen Articles of Faith. Thus, when one rejects even a seemingly insignificant point of the Torah, the severity of one's action is related to the fact that one has rejected the underlying premise of this law or statute.

At times, there may even be a practical difference between a rejection of a talmudic pronouncement, such as the existence of seven heavens, and an outright rejection of the truth of Torah. Suppose a Jewish astronomer, who has never studied the Talmud and thus is unaware of its opinion regarding the number of heavens, decides to research the number of heavens in existence. His research leads him to the conclusion that there are only six heavens. Would this individual be considered a heretic? Of course not. His belief in six heavens does not constitute a rejection of Jewish faith because the belief in the existence of seven heavens does not constitute a cardinal rule of Judaism. But someone who has studied the Talmud, and knows the talmudic doctrine of seven heavens, is considered a heretic if he rejects the Talmud in favor of an alternative theory, simply because he disputes the words of the eternal Torah.

On the other hand, he who is unfamiliar with the belief in the coming of the Messiah, or in the belief in the resurrection of the dead, or any other article included within the Thirteen Principles, is considered to have rejected Judaism in its entirety. And while the title "heretic" may be a harsh word for someone who is merely ignorant, there can be no question that this person's faith in Judaism and in the God of Israel is lacking in such centrality as to render it void. There simply can be no Judaism without a knowledge and acceptance of all of the Thirteen Articles.

The Thirteen Articles of Faith form the very constitution and fabric of Judaism. Not to know them is not to know Judaism, and not to believe in them is to reject Judaism.

Because of the overwhelming importance of these Thirteen Principles, it is essential that one understand them fully and deeply. A superficial glance, even a familiarity with all of their details, is insufficient. After Maimonides enumerates the Thirteen Principles, he writes: "One should return to them many, many times and meditate upon them with great insight."

What this study will attempt to establish is the absolute centrality of the last two principles in particular, namely, the belief in the coming of the Messiah and the belief in the resurrection of the dead. Because they appear last, one might assume that they are lower on the ladder of importance. In fact, the opposite is true. They are the consummation of the first eleven principles—the culmination of the entire historical process, the actualization of three-and-a-half millennia of Jewish existence, religious observance, and belief. The *mitzvot* we are commanded to keep and the Torah we are instructed to study are all leading to a single destination—the epoch of the Messiah.

We shall elucidate this centrality of messianism in Jewish faith by utilizing one of the deepest, most insightful, and most profound systems of Jewish thought in existence—Habad Hasidism. What we shall uncover will be novel and exciting.

Establishing this pivotal importance of messianism in Judaism is essential, especially in today's age, where many Jews treat the subject of the Messiah as an irrational, antiquated subject at best, and as a purely Christian concept at worst. To be sure, the pining for the Messiah is not something foreign to Judaism. Since the destruction of the Temple, it has been the Jewish people's most urgent cry. Throughout the generations our greatest sages have served as a bulwark against despair lest we lessen our cry for the arrival of the Messiah.

On the verse, "And he said to me, 'Until two thousand and three hundred evenings and mornings'" (Daniel 26:2), Rashi cites certain calculations of great sages concerning various possible dates for the coming of the Messiah, which have already long since passed. Rashi observes, "We are confident that the word of our God will forever be fulfilled. It will not be nullified. . . . We will trust in the fulfillment of our King's promise, from one calculated date for the 'End' [i.e., the arrival of 'the Messiah'], to another. And when the calculation of one sage will pass unfulfilled, we realize that he was mistaken in his calculations.''

Rashi makes a similar observation on the following verse in Psalms: ''My soul [waiteth] for the Lord more than they that watch for the morning, watch for the morning'' (Psalm 130:6). Rashi comments, ''I am among those who look forward eagerly to redemption, looking forward anxiously again and again, [anticipated] 'end' after [anticipated] 'end.' ''

It is indicative of the far-reaching significance of the concept of the coming of the messianic age and the ingathering of the exiles to realize that the rabbis included this theme in the very first benediction of the *Shemoneh Esrei,* also known as the *Amidah,* the central portion of every Jewish prayer service, comprising eighteen benedictions and recited silently while standing—''And He will bring the redeemer to their children's children, for His Name's sake, with love.'' Six of the nineteen benedictions are devoted exclusively to various aspects of this:

1. ''Please regard our affliction. . . . Blessed art Thou, O Lord, Redeemer of Israel'' (the seventh benediction).

2. ''Sound a great *shofar* for our freedom'' (the tenth benediction).

3. ''Restore our judges as at first'' (the eleventh benediction).

4. ''Return in mercy to Thy city, Jerusalem'' (the fourteenth benediction).

5. ''Cause the offspring of Thy servant, David, to flourish, speedily'' (the fifteenth benediction).

6. ''May our eyes behold Thy return in mercy to Zion'' (the seventeenth benediction).

The fact that this aspect of the messianic era was a primary factor in the creation process itself is alluded to in the *Midrash.* On the verse ''And the spirit of God hovered over the surface of the waters'' (Genesis 1:2), the *Midrash* remarks enigmatically, ''This refers to the spirit of the messianic King, [concerning whom] it is written (Isaiah 11:2), 'And the spirit of the Lord shall rest upon him' " (*Genesis Rabbah* 2:5). The *Etz Yosef* commentary observes, "For in his days shall [the following verse] be fulfilled (Isaiah 11:9)—'And the world shall be filled with knowledge of the Lord.' Therefore, even though God foresaw the wickedness of some of the upcoming generations, He did not refrain from creating the world." Thus, the purpose for the creation of the world was that it ultimately culminate in the epoch of the Messiah. Without the messianic age, there would have been no reason for creation. The epoch of the Messiah is the goal and destination to which we are all headed and toward which all of our efforts must be directed.

Throughout the generations, emphasis has been put on positive action as the primary means by which the Messiah will come. As the sages point out, "Action is what counts." To be sure, conscientious and scrupulous observance of the commandments and constant Torah study are indispensable in hastening the coming of the Messiah. However, this is only one facet in bringing the redemption.

The Messiah will comprise two unique dimensions in his role among the Jewish people. The first is that he will be a king. Simultaneous with this, he will also be a teacher. Therefore, to hasten his coming, one's activities must anticipate each of these two functions.

Rabbi Menachem Schneerson explains: A king relates to his subjects by issuing commands. Because of the distance that separates a king from the people he rules, he cannot altogether condescend and communicate his thoughts and feelings to his people. Thus, his primary form of relating with his people is by specifying activities they can perform on his behalf, and vice versa. Thus, the people have responsibilities to the king, and the king has responsibilities to the people. To prepare for a relationship with the Messiah, the most exalted of kings, one must enhance one's observance of the commandments, the reinstatement of which will be one of the Messiah's basic tasks. In this respect, it is particularly the giving of charity that brings the redemption near (see the *Tanya*, chap. 37).

A relationship based on mutual action on the other's behalf is incomplete and lacks an inner dimension. To foster a more

personal kinship with his subjects, so that the sublimity of the
Messiah will not be beyond the people and so that the Messiah
will be able to uplift them, the Messiah will also be a teacher.
Just as a parent invests within a child something of his essence,
a teacher similarly has the capacity to impart to his pupil
something internal and deep. Just as a parent brings a child into
the world, a teacher, too, can offer an entirely new view of the
world to his pupil. "Whosoever teaches another person Torah
is considered as if he had brought him into the world" (*Sanhedrin* 19b). Similarly, the Messiah will teach all of Israel the
secrets of the Torah and create an inner bond with all his flock.

To hasten the revelation of this latter facet of the Messiah, it
is of pivotal importance that one make an effort to study the
esoteric and mystical dimension of the Torah, particularly
those areas that illuminate the nature of the messianic era itself.

Rabbi Israel Baal Shem Tov, founder of Hasidism, relates in a
letter to a colleague that he had a clairvoyant vision of the
Messiah. He asked him, "When will you come, Master?" to
which the Messiah replied, "When the wellsprings of your
hasidic teachings spread outward." It is my fervent hope that
this book will make its own small contribution among many
toward the spreading of hasidic wellsprings and thus expedite the messianic redemption. "May a Redeemer come unto
Zion" speedily in our days—NOW!

There is a wealth of information, both qualitative and quantitative, found within hasidic thought pertaining to the messianic era. The spreading of these teachings, by studying them
ourselves as well as with others, brings the messianic era closer.
It is to this end that this book is dedicated.

One of the most recurrent themes of the Lubavitcher rebbe
regarding the obligation to bring the Messiah is that it must be
shared. Instead of simply passing on the responsibility to
another individual, even one's rebbe, each individual should
regard himself as an active partner in it.

I

THE BELIEF IN THE COMING OF THE MESSIAH

1

AN OBLIGATION TO WAIT

In his *Shloshah-Asar Ikkarim,* Thirteen Articles of Jewish
Faith, Maimonides includes the belief in the coming of the
Messiah and the special age he will usher in. The principle
which Maimonides bequeaths to subsequent generations is as
follows:

> We shall believe and affirm that he will come, and we shall
> not think that he will be late. "If he should tarry, wait for him"
> (Habakkuk 2:3). Nor shall the individual set a date for his
> coming. Nor shall he attempt to derive deductively, from scrip-
> tural verses, a set date for his coming. The sages said, "May the
> souls expire of those who calculate the date of the coming of the
> Messiah" (*Sanhedrin* 97b).
>
> We shall believe that the Messiah will be superior and have
> greater eminence and prestige than any other king who ever
> reigned. We should exalt him, love him, and pray on his behalf.
> This belief in the Messiah is in accordance with the prophecies
> concerning him, by all the prophets, from our master Moses until
> Malachi, peace be unto them. And he who has doubts concerning
> his coming, or he who belittles his eminent stature, has denied the
> Torah that foretold this in the *parshah* of Balaam[1] (Numbers

---

[1]Balaam is the non-Jewish prophet who was hired by Balak, king of Moab,
to curse the Jewish people so that they might fall before him in battle. The
Almighty, however, frustrated Balaam's plans to curse the Jews and instead

24:17–19), and the *parshah* of *Nitzavim*[2] (Deuteronomy 30:1–10).

Included in this Twelfth Principle is the awareness that every king of Israel must be a descendant of the House of David and a descendant of Solomon. Whoever disputes this family's right to the throne, denies [the words of] the Almighty and the words of His prophets.

This formulation by Maimonides has since been immortalized in most standard Jewish prayer books, in the *Ani Maamin,* recited directly after the morning prayers: "I believe with a perfect faith in the coming of the Messiah. And although he may tarry, nevertheless I await daily for him to come."

Concerning the other twelve principles of Maimonides, it is sufficient to accept them as truth and believe in them. The coming of the Messiah is different—one is required not only to *believe* in the coming of the Messiah, but to actually *await* his arrival.

Maimonides elucidates this matter at greater length in his *Mishneh Torah:* "And all those who do not believe in the Messiah or do not await his coming, not only do they deny the truth of the words of the prophets, but they reject the truth of the entire Torah and our master Moses" (*Laws of Kings,* chap. 11). Here we see conclusively that the cardinal principle of Jewish faith to believe in the coming of the Messiah must be accompanied by a longing for his arrival.

The Thirteen Articles of Faith are the foundation (*yesod*) that holds up the entire foundation of Jewish belief. Why is it that the coming of the Messiah is part of that foundation? What is the relationship between it and the structure of Jewish law that lies above it?

---

had him bless them on every occasion. In his last prophecy regarding the Jews, Balaam makes repeated references to the "end of days," sections of which the rabbis have interpreted as pertaining to the Messiah and the age he will usher in.

[2]*Nitzavim* is the name of one of the sections into which the Book of Deuteronomy is divided. It begins with Moses' declaration to the Jews, "You are standing today all of you before the Lord your God; your heads, your tribes, your elders, and your officers . . . all the men of Israel."

Furthermore, why is it insufficient to only believe in the coming of the Messiah? Why must one also await his coming?

The question is not *whether or not* or *why* one must believe in the coming of the Messiah. The entire Torah testifies to the fact that one *must* believe in the Messiah. Rather, why is it that Maimonides chose the coming of the Messiah, from the plethora of laws and beliefs in Judaism, to be one of its cornerstones?

Maimonides' first principle is the belief in the existence of God, the Creator. If one does not believe this, the entire Torah and its commandments are absurd and worthless. The very notion of serving God and believing in His Torah would constitute a profound absurdity without the existence of the Creator. So, too, it is clear that the eighth principle—the belief that the Torah in its entirety is divine—is essential to Jewish belief. Only if the Torah is given by an eternal and omniscient Creator can we be confident that it is just as relevant to modern man as it was to the ancients.

However, it is not readily apparent what would be lacking in the faith of the believer if he were to reject the notion of a messianic era. Why would this constitute a rejection, not only of a single tenet of Judaism, but of the entire Jewish religion?

Another critical question pertaining so centrally to the entire subject of Jewish messianism is why the perfection of society and civilization, which is the most fundamental tenet of messianism, necessitates a messianic redeemer? Why can't man do it alone? Surely, through the quantum technical, medicinal, and anthropological leaps that have characterized man's recent development, he will no doubt stumble upon the answers and cures to all of society's ills. Why wait for a Messiah when man seems perfectly capable of looking after himself and his world?

2

MAN CANNOT CREATE
A UTOPIA

Contemporary Jewish society treats the concept of the Messiah with much apprehension. Mainstream Jewish life, it seems, has progressed beyond the belief in a Messiah and it appears that only "fringe" Jewish religious groups still take it seriously. What most fail to realize, however, is that the belief in the coming of the Messiah is more central to Judaism than even the observance of the Sabbath or Yom Kippur. The apprehension that mainstream Jewish society feels toward messianism may be attributed to a number of factors, among which are its strong christological overtones, the abuse the concept has suffered through the ages because of pretenders, and the great fear of the unknown.

It is difficult as a Jew to be immersed in a Christian world— a world that has been pervaded by Christian thoughts and ideas for nearly two millennia—and still retain a wholesome kernel of Jewish truth. While Jews must learn to approach every area of life from a uniquely Jewish perspective, this is especially true of Jewish concepts with which one may be familiar not from Jewish but from Christian influence.

Amid the confusion caused by the penetration of Christian culture into Jewish life, that aspect of Judaism that has suffered the most is the concept of the Messiah and the messianic era. It appears that the more communally active a Jew is in Jewish communal affairs, the more he shuns the concept of the

Messiah. But this in itself is not surprising. On the contrary, it seems only proper that those people who work hard for the social, financial, or educational benefit of the Jewish people should feel alienated by messianism and its promises of a better world to be miraculously brought about by a mythical, righteous redeemer. If this Messiah is the one who will bring about a positive transformation of the world, why should one work for the betterment of mankind today? The belief in the Messiah thus seems at odds with the belief that *man* is capable of making a better world. Thus, a fundamental understanding of why, indeed, the world requires the Messiah, amid all the great energy being exerted by sincere activists the world over, is necessary.

This is why, ironically, the concept of the Messiah superficially appears most un-Jewish. If someone who was vaguely acquainted with Judaism were to be asked what, to him, was the very essence of Judaism, there are many things that he might answer. He might answer that Judaism believes in charity, and he would be right. Or, he might respond that Judaism believes in the family, and here, too, he would be right. Or, he might respond that Judaism is communally based, and again he would be right. But all of these answers scratch the surface of what Judaism really is about. They are mere components, and not the essence. Nor do they truly sum up Judaism, for they do not readily distinguish between Judaism and the other religions of the world.

In truth, Judaism is quite radical in its orientation, radical enough to noticeably set it aside from every other world religion. The reason is this: more than any other religious tenet, Judaism puts its emphasis on action. The single most fundamental and central statement that can be made about Judaism, and indeed the most beautiful and the most appealing to everyday people, is that it is an action- and goal-oriented religion. It believes in doing, accomplishing. It believes in conquering and mastering. It believes in perfecting, talking, arguing, whatever it takes. Whatever is needed to make a better world—that is where Judaism lies. Judaism is about changing the world in which we live. This should come as no surprise, since Jews recite this three times a day, in the very final prayer of the service, known as *Aleinu:* "to perfect the world in God's kingdom." That is what Judaism is about—it is about transforming and bettering the world. It is not a religion that meditates on faith, or puts emphasis on the goodness of the heart, or concerns itself with where one's thoughts and lusts lie. It is interested only marginally in those topics. The Jewish God is concerned with performance. Thus, Judaism is a religion replete with myriads of *mitzvot,* religious activity where man is dragged from the heights of theological discovery and enjoined to get his hands dirty in improving his fellow man's lot and simultaneously bridging the gap between the world and its Creator.

One of the most important ways in which this is demonstrated is in the difference between the Christian and Jewish concepts of charity. Charity is a Christian word, and it comes from the latin word *charitos,* which means "heart." In Christianity one gives from the heart—what one feels is important. It is not sufficient to give. One's giving must be prompted by heartfelt compassion. But in Judaism one gives from the pocket. What's important is that one gives, not that one feels for the poor person standing in front of him. Of course it is far better to feel compassion and not spite as one gives. But the intention carries none of the weight of the action. Man is under an obligation to give ten percent, and up to twenty percent, of his income. And this is something very beautiful, because what it says to the individual is "We don't care where your personal righteousness is standing right now, and you will not be judged by what is going through your heart. You will judged by whether you leave a favorable and positive impact on this world or not." In this respect Judaism has a wonderfully pragmatic and down-to-earth philosophy. All the sympathy in the world will not serve to alleviate the hunger pangs felt by this poor soul standing at one's door. But what will help is the money and food one gives him. Thus, one is obligated to *end* his suffering, not to *feel* it.

Having demonstrated that Judaism is concerned with perfecting the world through positive steps on the part of man, the question becomes, how could Judaism relegate the ultimate perfection of the world to a Messiah? Here stands Judaism, the most goal- and action-oriented religion ever to appear on the face of the earth, and its ultimate message to man is this: "By the way, we want you to work as hard as you can, but ultimately there are things that you cannot do. You will have to wait for a messianic epoch, for some mythical legendary figure who will come onto the world stage. He is the one that will ultimately perfect the world." It sounds downright anti-Jewish. The Christian religions await a "second coming" of its redeemer. If asked, "If your Messiah came, why is there still war and famine and hatred and contention?" a Christian's response is: "There will be a second coming. And at that time all of the world's ills will be cured." And this response is sufficient, at least temporarily, within the Christian tradition. But Judaism is very different. It demands that one confront the world's ills today, of one's own accord.

All of Judaism is a steady progression toward higher and higher states of perfection, both on a macrocosmic and microcosmic level. Man is instructed to better himself, to rid himself of animal tendencies and deprecating impulses. And yet, amid all this effort, mankind waits for a Messiah, a world savior. How can one reconcile relegating the perfection of world society to a Messiah with the Jewish religions's demands of man to better his world? Why is man incapable of adding the final touches himself, without any messianic redeemer?

This question is particularly pertinent in modern-day society, where one sees unmistakably how Judaism, with its vision of a better world, has influenced, even brought into being, many movements and "ism's" that can be referred to as secular messianic utopias. Judaism has influenced and had its impact even on Jewish visionaries who have not led Jewish lives. It is more than sheer coincidence that so many of the world's political idealogies have come about through Jews. On the contrary, the desire of secular Jews to perfect the world through every means is a direct outgrowth of their exposure to the teachings of the Jewish prophets and their promises of a perfect world. Those Jews who have even abandoned Judaism are still driven by its vision. But they substitute a divinely ordained messianic epoch with the concept of a secular utopia. The early fathers of Communism spoke of a time, almost directly out of the Bible, when all of the earth's inhabitants would have according to their needs, when no one would go hungry, when there would be peace and harmony among all of mankind. When one human being would not exploit the other because of an economic gap that separated them, a time when the hated bourgeoisie would stop manipulating the poor working proletariat. In fact, the only real difference between what Communism promised and the Jewish messianic ideal was that instead of a Jewish Messiah, they had a Bolshevik messiah, a Marx or a Lenin, but what was promised was still a utopia. Jews, even secular Jews such as Karl Marx, have had this overbearing drive to perfect the world. This is an outgrowth of their Jewishness.

But, what happened to secular Jewish intellectuals like Marx was that they said, "Why should we wait for this Messiah? Let's do it today! By joining together we are wholly capable of creating a utopia ourselves." And why was he wrong? Why was Karl Marx, or any other secular messiah, wrong? Why was the vision of John F. Kennedy inadequate when he started the Peace Corps in the 1960s, promising to cure the world's ills by focusing the world's attentions and the effort of the younger generation on a solution to the problem. So many people have been influenced by a Jewish concept of a utopia, of a messiah. Yet, Judaism itself rejects their notion of transforming the world into a perfect place, without the aid of a heavenly redeemer who has been awaited for three millennia.

The same question can be asked in relation to secular Zionism. It was the secular Zionists, many of whom were brought up in strictly Orthodox, even hasidic, eastern European homes, who rejected the Jewish concept of waiting around for a Messiah, and seized the initiative to go up and re-create a Jewish homeland. And they didn't just talk about it. They achieved their objective and created a remarkably successful and impressive country in the process, which in turn became the pride of the entire world Jewish population. Israel became the object of adoration that Jews had lacked since the destruction of the Second Temple. And there is hardly a Jew alive who does not swell with pride at the achievements of the Jewish state and pray for its survival. So who is right and who is wrong? Is

Judaism, the one religion that always told man to go out, conquer, and fix, now saying wait?

We live in an imperfect world. No one would say the world is perfect; and no one would claim personal perfection. But what is the world's primary imperfection? What is it about the world, and its inhabitants, for that matter, that makes one so willing to immediately pronounce it imperfect?

According to hasidic thought it is this: The first man, Adam, was born into a perfect world. God is perfect and what He creates is perfect. And Adam was put into the Garden of Eden, which was also perfect. But what constituted its perfection? The Torah, in the Book of Genesis, attests to the fact that there was evil in the Garden of Eden—there were trees from which Adam and Eden were not permitted to eat. They were not good for them; they were not conducive to their health. In fact, they were harmful. God warned Adam that if he did indeed eat from the Tree of Knowledge of Good and Evil, he would die. Surely this is proof that not everything in the Garden of Eden was good. Some things were so bad that they could kill. So how was the Garden perfect?

The perfection of the Garden lay in the fact that although there were good and bad trees, the evil was completely separate from the good. God was able to "point His finger" and indicate conclusively, "This is a bad tree. But this one over here is a good tree." God Himself discerned to Adam, "This is a good tree. This is a bad tree. This tree has good fruit. This one has bad, diseased fruit. Therefore, distance yourself, absolutely, from the bad tree. There is nothing good that can be gained from it." The perfection of the Garden of Eden was not that there was no evil, but rather that the good and evil were completely distinct entities. There was no mixture of the two. Good was good and bad was bad. And in the Garden of Eden, when someone did something good, there were no bad side consequences. When one took medicine that was supposed to cure, it didn't have any bad side-effects. In the Garden of Eden, Adam was very clear about what to pursue and what to stay away from, who the good people were and who the bad people were. That was what the Garden was all about.

Stated in other words, the evil forces that operate today

within creation existed even in the Garden of Eden prior to Adam's first sin. Yet, the difference between then and today was that evil was easily recognizable then, and thus easily avoided. All Adam had to do to avoid the evil was to obey God's commandment and refrain from consuming it.

But Adam did not listen, and he mixed the two fruit, the two trees. He decided to commit the ultimate sin, for which we all suffer to this very day. He interwove good with evil. He took all the blessings that God gave him as a human being—intelligence, insight, a wife, a residence in the beautiful Garden, sustenance—and he abused them. He used God's goodness to defy God's will and commit evil. Thus, for the first time in history, there was a mixture of good with evil. And this was the beginning of the confusion between good and evil that reigns till this very day.

This, according to Rabbi Yosef Yitzchak Schneersohn of Lubavitch (*Sefer Mamorim Kuntreisim* II, *"Ani Homa"*), was the sin of Adam in the Garden of Eden, and this is what we suffer from till this very day. This is what is so sad about life— that we all go through life knowing ahead of time about the confusion. Life is hard because everything is chaotic, and there is no lucidity. One enters life being taught that there will never be a beautiful moment that won't be accompanied by a hardship, and there will never be a tragedy from which something good cannot be derived.

One goes through life making decisions, making choices, feeling confident that what one has done is the right thing, only later to discover that what one thought was good was disastrous, and vice versa. No one is ever really sure if the path and the courses one embarks on will yield the desired result. If one invests in a business, will one become rich, or lose even one's home? Life is frought with uncertainty.

Furthermore, every newlywed is told, "Don't worry if you fight. Expect to fight!" That is the imperfection of this world. That is what is so sad. Even amid the most beautiful occasions, one knows to expect a harmful consequence. Even while the marriage is being drawn up, so is the prenuptial agreement, "in case the marriage breaks up." There is nothing in life that is only a blessing. When one has a child, there will be times when one will be swearing, "Why do I want another one!?" Similarly, the fact that one can learn from even gross errors, the fact that one cannot just dismiss them as unfortunate and forget them, is one's pain and one's curse.

This is the imperfection of life. This is the curse of Adam. When Adam sinned, all good and bad became mixed. Had Adam heeded God's prohibition and not eaten from the tree, life today would be black and white. One would know what is good and what is bad, and there would be no confusion and no pain caused by the inability to decide or the frustration at not knowing the outcome of one's choices. As a result of Adam's sin, there is no black and white, only shades of grey.

In his celebrated philosophical treatise, *Guide to the Perplexed,* Maimonides writes that a man once came to him and posed a powerful question: "Why is it that your God rewarded Adam in the Garden of Eden for eating from the tree of knowledge?"

Maimonides responded, "What do you mean *rewarded.* He was punished. Banished from the Garden." The man retorted, "No! If you look closely at the story, you will see that he was rewarded. Before Adam and Eve sinned with the tree of knowledge, the Torah says that they frolicked in the Garden totally naked; they were not aware of their nakedness. And yet immediately after their sin, the Torah says they became aware of the fact that they were unclothed. In other words, they were awarded with knowledge! What was unknown to them suddenly became known. Directly after the sin. Why was it that God gave them increased knowledge as a result of their sin?"

Maimonides then responded to the inquirer along these lines: "Truth in this world is 'Yes' or 'No'; 'true' or 'false.' That is truth. The kind of knowledge that Adam and Eve received after eating from the tree was not the 'Good/Bad' 'True/False'; it was the 'I like this, I don't like this,' kind of knowledge. They came to know their nakedness, and they were embarrassed, so they clothed themselves. No longer was it a question of whether it was right or wrong, good or bad, to walk naked; rather they clothed themselves because they *emotionally* felt uncomfortable. Their emotions would now forever help dictate their judgment, so that they had lost the ability to discern an objective truth. In other words, far from being rewarded, they were denigrated from being the possessors of objective knowledge to the possessors of subjective knowledge. They were punished. They were degraded."

Objective knowledge means identifying an objective truth. If one can distance oneself from a given situation and judge it fairly and honestly and say, "Yes, I know this is true," even if it hurts to do so, then one is being objectively honest. But just to say, "I like this, I don't like this," "I like this person, I don't like this person" is a far cry from something being a "yes" or a "no." "Like" or "dislike" was a curse, because suddenly there was no more truth. All at once truth was not absolute: it was relative to human whim and disposition. After Adam sinned he became aware of his own frailties, his own inconsistencies. He looked at himself and he saw that he was naked. He wanted to clothe himself, to cover himself. He didn't want anyone to see the true "him," the real "him." He wanted to put on a facade. And so did Eve.

From that time on, Adam and Eve, and all humans as their offspring, suffer from the chaos of not being able to see things objectively. Mankind agonizes from the mixture of good and evil created by Adam.

The one area of life that is the most beautiful, but also the most painful, is human relationships, and especially between the sexes. "He says he loves me, but I don't know if he means it. Is he showing me his true self?" "Is she showing me her true self?" People suffer from that curse of Adam until this very day—the inability to show ourselves completely and the inability to just accept truth, regardless of its source and regardless of its implications to our personal lives.

So great was Adam's amalgamation of good and evil that God gave man a Torah, His infinite Wisdom, whose very purpose is to undo Adam's evil. The purpose of the Torah is to teach man once again to be discerning and to extract good from evil. That is what the Torah is. In its most basic essence, the Torah is a way of identifying what is good and what is evil. The Torah says, "There are seven days in a week. Working on six of them is good for you, but working on the seventh is a mistake." "There are all kinds of animals in the world, but the kosher ones are good for you. The others are not.'' ''There are all kinds of peoples on this earth—this one you can marry, this you cannot.'' ''There are different ways of doing business. You can behave this way, but you cannot do deals in this manner.'' The Torah is the means by which to discern and teach what is harmful and what is beneficial. The Torah is the way one undoes the sin of Adam.

But this really is the sorrow of life—that in tragedy there can be happiness, that even when the worst possible things transpire, there will always be some light at the end of the tunnel. And that is sad. It is sad that in something so ugly there can be something so beautiful.

Steven was a childhood friend. His parents had a tormented marriage. The neighbors were constantly calling the police to get them to be quiet. One day in Israel, when Steven was seventeen, the car he was driving collided into a bus and he was killed. And yet from this terrible story, his parents found comfort from their grief in each other and became the most loving of couples.

This is the agony of life, that sometimes in order to achieve the most beautiful things one must endure the most painful suffering. The reverse is also true.

In talmudic law, if there already exists in a city one *heder* teacher, it is permitted for a new one to move into his territory and teach children Torah, even if it will encroach upon the business activity of the first. The reason the Talmud gives is simple. What the Jewish people need is the best possible Torah teachers and ''jealousy between scholars increases wisdom.''

Man will never be able to perfect the world on his own. The moment man says, ''Let us vanquish our evil traits. Let us rid ourselves of them. Let us declare war on jealousy, contention, ambition, discord, arrogance, strife, intuition. Let us cease from all those causes that make us hate each other and act indecently toward one another,'' he will simultaneously be killing part of himself. He will be annihilating a part of himself that makes him tick, that makes him human, that makes him successful, that makes him a winner. If one were to succeed at ridding oneself of all conceit, desire, vanity, arrogance, aspiration, pretension, and if one were to supplant it with contentment, satisfaction, lethargy, and indolence, what one would be left with is a very nice but a very pathetic human being. That is the curse of Adam. And that is why one needs a messianic redeemer.

This is also why Judaism contends that, strive as one might—and one must do everything one can—one must serve as a catalyst to usher in a messianic era, but ultimately that is not going to solve the problem. The problem is not out there in the world so that one could find it and kill it. The problem is within oneself. The problem is not just that the world has some evil bits and one must eradicate them. The problem is not just that there is famine, hunger, disease, murder, and insensitivity in the world and one must simply cure it and create a utopia. The problem is that the only way to rid the world of these ills is by calling upon some of one's own inner ills. For instance, it is specifically the scientist who competes to win the Nobel Prize for medicine or some similar international recognition that eventually cures the terrible disease. And it is the competitive, ambitious, young entrepreneur who sometimes must behave quite ruthlessly in business, who succeeds financially and is able to donate the money that will alleviate someone else's hunger. And it is the aspiring politician who wishes to be remembered as a great and humane statesman who sends his army into battle to combat the dark forces of the world (as in the case of George Bush and the Persian Gulf War of 1991).

But if one kills that part of oneself that aspires to these heights, the world will disintegrate because parts of the machinery that makes one what he is, that makes one successful, are not the greatest or most pleasant things that exist within us. Thus arises the need for the Messiah. One needs, ultimately, God Himself to come, after one has made a gallant effort to show Him one really wants to be better, to help bring about a transformation *in the human condition itself,* whereby it could actually be successful and compete alongside other human beings without wanting to outdo them. This is one area where as of yet no man has had true success.

Being a good person does not entail being pathetic or having no great achievements. Rather, it means that while one may be fantastic and successful, the world is large enough to contain a

great many successful people and a great many egos. Being
ambitious would be seen in Judaism as desirable, so long as it
does not intrude upon someone else's ambition. The problem is
that self-development usually entails outdoing one's fellow and
agonizing over other people's surpassing one's own victories.

There is a story of the Tzemach Tzedek, Rabbi Menachem
Mendel of Lubavitch. A young student from the *yeshivah* came
to him and said, "My life is miserable. I am leaving the
yeshivah." He was a new student, not from a Lubavitch family,
and he was sure the rebbe would encourage him to stay. "I
can't take it any longer," he complained. "Everyone steps on
me. Everyone abuses me."

The Tzemach Tzedek said to him, "Before you leave the
yeshivah, I want to ask you one question. Who asked you to
spread yourself out over the entire *yeshivah* so that every place
someone steps, they step on you?"

This is the secret to getting along with other human beings—
the ability not to spread oneself everywhere, to think that one
has to be it, the one and only. One must be "large enough,"
transcend one's natural paranoia and sense of threat, to leave
room for the expansion of others. Ultimately, it is specifically
through that kind of attitude and that kind of approach that
people have achieved success.

And this is why one needs the messiah. One needs God to
give just that little ingredient that will bring about a human
transformation so that one can bring all of mankind into a
better time, so that one won't have to leave part of oneself
behind. No one wants to do that. No one hates himself so much
to believe that one really has to kill off part of oneself in order
to be a better and more caring human being.

This is why, for instance, people do not like days like Rosh
Hashanah and Yom Kippur. One may look forward to Purim
and Chanukah. But Rosh Hashanah and Yom Kippur are those
days one would like to avoid. One hears those terrible words:
"teshuvah," "repent," "return." One reason people distrust
this concept of repentance so much is because they feel that
what it is saying to them is, "Leave part of yourself behind.
There is a part of you inside that is undesirable. Get rid of it."
No one likes knowing that there is a little beast inside him that

he must squash and be brought on the altar of God in order to get closer to God.

The messianic era is one that involves transformation, not eradication. It is not about exterminating the undesirable elements in the world. It is not about leading a crusade and saying, "Capitalism is bad. We will adopt a different way." Rather, it is about bringing all of oneself into a better time. It is about recognizing that it is the human in his totality who can bring about a better world, and that one just needs to redirect some of one's human drives so that they can be utilized for goodness as well.

The same applies to Israel. Israel is an extraordinary achievement. It is incredible that finally there is a place that can be defended by Jews. But it is not yet a messianic era. Brave young men and women must serve in the army from eighteen- to twenty-one years of age, and mothers have to cry over their young sons who die in battle. We are looking for a better, more prosperous world, where Jews will actually be Jewish and not have to fight for it; where people can be good without having to defend goodness; where decency, honesty, and morality will ultimately triumph and not only prevail over the forces that oppose it, but win over those forces and bring them into the camp of Godliness.

3

A HOME: THE REASON FOR CREATION

Why did God create the world? Why we exist and what purpose we serve are questions that perplex every individual, not just philosophers. Only the Creator Himself could identify why He called the world into existence.

In the *Tanya*—the central text of Habad Hasidism—Rabbi Shneur Zalman quotes the midrash that gives as the reason for the creation of the world: "The Almighty desired to have a dwelling place in the lowest of worlds." Although God created a great multitude of worlds, most being spiritual and one physical, it was His profound desire to reside specifically in the lowest of worlds, our physical domain. And He desired that this world be transformed from a mundane, and often profane, physical abode into a dwelling that would fit the residence of the supreme King of kings and Creator of the universe.

What is a residence? Consider an earthly king. A king always has a beautiful palace, and in the palace itself he has a great number of rooms and halls. But these rooms and halls are not set aside primarily for the king's use. Rather, they are used for the king to appear *in public* and entertain guests, visitors, and dignitaries. While technically these rooms constitute the king's *home*, for all practical purposes the king is never *at home* in them. But there is a section of the palace set aside for the monarch's private residence, his private apartment. No public meetings ever take place in this section of the palace. It is cordoned off for the exclusive use of the king and his immediate family.

The difference between the private section of the palace and the public ballrooms is this: when the king appears in the public section of the palace, he cannot appear the way he would like or the way in which he is most comfortable, but rather in the manner befitting a king. He must appear in royal garb, in the dress of the head of state. And garb refers not only to physical garments, but also to spiritual garments. Not only must the king dress in the proper way, but he must also behave in a desirable fashion. All his actions and speech must bring about the desired effect of impressing upon his subjects the grandeur and majesty of the king. Thus the king is virtually a prisoner of protocol—and this in his own house!

The only location where the king can be his own person, and not a sovereign, is in his own private residence. In his private apartment the king dresses as he pleases, not as the public expects him to appear. To be sure, there are times in the king's private apartment when he does not wear anything at all! Of course, in public this could never be. The guidelines for the king's behavior are seen as so significant in Judaism that there is a whole body of laws outlining how the king must behave, for example, "It is forbidden to see a king of Israel when he is naked" (Maimonides, *Laws of Kings,* chap. 2). Again the reference to "naked" here means not only being void of physical garb, but spiritual garb as well. A king dare not behave as an ordinary person naked of royalty. Therefore, the implication of a residence is the ability for one's inner self to be revealed unhindered. A private dwelling gives one the ability to express one's true nature without it being measured and tempered to suit a specific receptor.

This point is born out most aptly by the Talmud: "Every person who does not have a home is not a person" (*Yevamot* 63a). What makes having a home so central to the definition of one's humanity? When one lacks a home, one can never "be oneself." One is constantly acting, speaking, and behaving in a tailored fashion. Without a home, one is always *somebody else's person.* But in the privacy of one's home, one becomes a person, his own person, not a robot or servant of society, but a self-expressive and creative individual.

This is the desire of the Almighty in His creation of our physical world. God desires a residence. Even in the higher, more spiritual worlds, God cannot be Himself, as it were. He cannot radiate His true light or reveal His true essence. Even the lofty spiritual worlds are shallow and minuscule in comparison to God's infinite Being. He's simply too large for those worlds to contain Him. Thus, He must contract and condense his infinite Self when He radiates His light in the higher worlds so as to suit their consumption. God must be careful to "tailor" and limit Himself to suit the capacity of receptacles much lower than He. Thus the worlds cannot serve as a home or residence to the Almighty. He cannot reveal His true self within them. It is impossible for the infinite God to radiate his full intensity in a finite domain. It would overwhelm the worlds. Although the spiritual worlds are indeed lofty and transcendental in nature compared to the physical world, and they enjoy a far higher and greater manifestation of Godliness than the physical world, they are nonetheless limited and of finite character.

The severe limitation of the spiritual worlds can be compared to the king when he is in the company of his inner circle of advisers and friends. While it is true that the king may dress in more ordinary clothing and act more like himself around his advisers than he does in public, since they are much closer to him, nevertheless, even amidst his confidants he is still a king and must dress and behave somewhat accordingly. For instance, even in the company of his closest confidants, the king would never appear without clothing. So long as he is in the company of even one subject, he is still a ruler. When in the company of anyone besides himself, the king is doomed to be somewhat of a hostage to another party.

The more glorified and famous the individual, the more is expected of him in terms of morality and behavior and the more he is required to comply with the constraints of greatness. If this be true of a mortal king of flesh and blood, who must conform to the expectations of his subjects, how much more so when we speak of the King of kings, the Creator of the universe. As can be readily appreciated, God, Who is infinite, bears no relationship whatsoever to even the highest spiritual worlds, which are finite. Thus it is clear that the Almighty cannot reveal Himself even in the spiritual worlds the way He is in His essence, but rather He must contract and limit Himself. Jewish mysticism teaches that God must "adorn himself in a garb that conceals his true nature." What is truly amazing is that God desires, somehow, to have the full intensity of His infinite essence manifest in our physical world. God wishes to dwell in our world without any garb or attire that would alter His infinite presence.

This desire of the Almighty will come to fruition only in the messianic age, when God will reveal Himself and radiate His true essence without any curtain or obstruction. Commenting on the verse "And your teacher will hide no more" (Isaiah 30:20), the Tanya explains, "This means that God will no longer conceal Himself in any garment or veil. For in that time God will reveal himself the way He existed even before the Creation of the world" (*Tanya,* chap. 36).

This dramatic event cannot transpire on its own. It is through service to the Creator and the fulfillment of His commandments that this desire of the Almighty will be brought to fruition. This is why the Torah and its commandments were given to earthly inhabitants rather than to the ministering angels (the Talmud relates that the angels requested the Torah but were not granted it). The purpose of our study of Torah and fulfillment of commandments is to bring this world to a state where it is conducive to the full revelation of God in all His glory. This can be accomplished only through human beings here in this physical realm. Through every moment of Torah study and every commandment we fulfill, we bring more of God's Essence into our world and hasten the time when God will be revealed in the messianic epoch.

When the Messiah comes, no new dimension will be incorporated into the creation; the true, fundamental character of the world will not change. The time for changing and enhancing the world is not in the messianic era, but now. The Torah states, concerning the performance of *mitzvot* (commandments), "*Ha-yom Laasotam*—they must be done today [and not in the world to come]" (Deuteronomy 7:11). The change that the Messiah will bring about is the revelation of all the Godliness that man has brought into the world from the time the Torah was given over three thousand years ago. The transformation accomplished through the fulfillment of Torah and *mitzvot* cannot be seen; man lacks the instruments to observe this radical, spiritual upheaval. However, when the Jew fulfills a *mitzvah* today, he draws into this physical world God's essence, even though he cannot see the effects of his action. In the time of the Messiah, this obstruction, which blocks our eyes from seeing the true effects of our actions, will be removed, and God will be seen by all of the world's inhabitants. It will be then that God will be seen to take up His residence in His private chambers, which is our world.

4

WHY WE CAN'T SEE MIRACLES

A story is told regarding Rabbi Shneur Zalman, the Alter Rebbe. Two days before his passing he called his grandson—later known as the Tzemach Tzedek—to his bedside. The Alter Rebbe asked his grandson whether he was able to see the rafters in the room's ceiling? Perplexed by the unusual question, the Tzemach Tzedek stood quietly, gazing into the bright eyes of his grandfather.

The Alter Rebbe broke the silence as he continued: "I do not see them anymore. Here, in the last few moments of my earthly existence, I see nothing but the spiritual life-force that forms the true makeup of the universe, the Godly power that constantly re-creates and vivifies the physical existence of the world."

There are always two possibilities why something cannot be seen. Either there is some obstruction hindering the eyes of the *observer,* or there exists an obstruction on the *object* itself—either the eyes cannot see, or the object cannot be seen. What had changed with the Alter Rebbe? What was he now seeing and why had he not seen it previously? Was it that in the last moments of material existence he had been found so meritorious by the Almighty that the spirituality of the creation was *revealed* to him, or was it that he had elevated himself to such a state of consciousness that he was now seeing that which he previously could not? In other words, was the spirituality of

27

the world previously concealed and now the obstruction had been removed, or was it that his eyes had been blind to something that was always visible? Had the world changed, or had the Alter Rebbe changed?

In answering this question, it will be necessary to briefly explore the true substance of the world. The world functions with a natural order, a phenomenon called "Mother Nature."

But what is nature? *Tevah,* the Hebrew word for "nature," also has a second meaning, "sunken, submerged." The etymological relationship of the two words is not merely coincidental. The fact that *tevah* translates as "submerged" is an important clue as to the true substance of nature. When one gazes upon the ocean's surface, one sees only water. One perceives only water. But would it be accurate to state that there is nothing to the ocean but water?

Of course not. Even the Talmud proclaims that "everything that exists upon the dry land has an equivalent within the sea" (*Hullin* 127a). Deep below the ocean's surface lies an underwater world with billions of species of plant and sea life. Yet, to the observer this is not seen or perceived, at least not until one gets hold of the proper equipment that allows the ocean surface to be penetrated. Otherwise, all is sunken beneath the ocean's waves, drowned within the all-encompassing water. Even though we see only water, is this all that exists in the ocean? If something is not readily visible, does this negate the possibility of its existence?

We live in a physical world, but is this its only reality? Perhaps the word *tevah* itself signifies that the true reality of the empirical world is sunken and drowned somewhere within the material structure of the world.

Before creation there was nothing except the existence of God. Yet, this infinite God desired the creation and existence of a finite world. To accomplish this feat, He would have to undergo a transition from the infinite to the finite. Only then could He exist within the confines of that world. This may be compared to a professor who wishes to teach his students some very difficult and sublime theory whereby he is forced to contract his own intelligence in order to condescend to the level of his students. If he teaches his pupils the theory on the level at which he understands it, he will not develop his students' thought processes, but rather will overwhelm them. He will not only gain nothing, but his approach will be counterproductive. He must therefore contract and condense his understanding until he reaches the level of his students. On the other hand, if he lowers the theory totally to the pupils' levels, he accomplishes nothing since he has not challenged their thought in any way. What then is his solution?

A contraction doesn't necessarily imply a reduction or degradation from one level to the other. Rather, a contraction can mean a concealment or condensation. In other words, the professor must display the theory in a different light. While externally concealing the intricacies and difficulties of the theory, he must internally retain its depth, even if that depth is not immediately tangible to the students. In other words, the professor's concealment must be of the sort that does not truly downgrade the level of the theory, so that later, with the intellectual maturity of the students, they will be able to rethink the theory and uncover its pregnant meaning. One way of doing this, by way of example, is to enclothe the theory in a story or parable. For example, a professor teaching Einstein's theory of relativity may tell a simple story of two men, one on the sun, the other on earth, each one with a different but equally acceptable theory as to which celestial body is revolving around the other. This analogy, of course, is only an external vestige of an amazingly deep theory, which, had it been taught in its fullest way with mathematical equations and scientific statements, would go over the heads of uninitiated students. But within the analogy lies the same depth of insight and intellect, now concealed by its outer garment.

We all wear clothing regularly, and we change our clothing regularly. But we remain the same. External garb has no effect on its wearer. The shell may change, but the contents inside do not. So, too, the professor teaches by way of analogies and parables, which externally simplify and decrease the depth of understanding. But lying within is the complete intensity of the professor's understanding, the students discovering this only later.

The same applies in the creation of the world. The infinite, one God must contract His infinite light and emanation down to a level of individual divine sparks, which will be enclothed and will form the material makeup of every physical entity of the empirical world. For, while God is One and unified, the physical world is diversified and pluralistic. Thus God must contract Himself and bring into being a network of divine sparks of contracted light, which are the source of and give birth to all physical existence. The physical aspect is the external shell, and the divine spark is the internal "soul." This contraction of the divine light is merely a concealment—the inner Godliness lies latent with its former intensity still intact, but it is concealed by its outer shell.

It is this divine spark that forms the true existence of every physical object. The physical object exists, but only because of its internal component, the divine spark embellished within it.

If this is nature's true existence, why doesn't one see it?

The story is told of Rabbi Dov Ber (son of Rabbi Shneur Zalman and father-in-law to the Tzemach Tzedek), that he once remarked that he no longer possessed any corporeal flesh. When one of the students touched his hand and exclaimed, "But Rebbe, I feel your hand!" the rebbe answered, "Ah—but this is because you are touching me with a hand." What did he mean by this?

The definition of a physical world is that everything contained therein conceals Godliness. A physical object is limited within itself. It possesses borders, limitations, and boundaries. The fact that it exists as a physical object means that it exists within constraints intrinsic to it.

Godliness is the opposite—unlimited, undefined, totally infinite. The limitations of the finite physical world conceal the underlying infinite radiation of the omnipresent God. The question, though, is this: Can one reveal it? Why can't one see and experience miracles and other forms of open spirituality that were so commonplace in biblical times?

The Talmud relates a story concerning this very question: "Rav Papa asked of Abaye, 'What is the difference between the previous generations who experienced open miracles, and we who do not merit the occurrence of any miracles whatsoever?' He answered him, 'The previous generations had *messirat nefesh;* they sacrificed their lives for the sanctification on God's Name. But we have no *messirat nefesh (Berakhot* 20a).''

A miracle is the revelation of the unlimited spiritual energy that, by its very nature, defies and overwhelms all physical limitations of the natural world. A miracle is outside physical reality. But we are physically limited. When one asks for miracles, by way of implication, one is actually asking why one cannot defy and go outside of one's own limitations.

One can. A miracle is the nullification of nature. It is the revelation of underlying spirituality. Infinity cannot be openly contained within the physical, for it is limited. Its revelation automatically overwhelms the laws and constraints of nature. The antithesis of finite is infinite. The antithesis of physical is spiritual. The antithesis of nature is miracle. They cannot openly exist together. They are inversely proportional.

The exception to this rule of opposites, however, is the fact that every human being possesses a body and a soul. The spiritual and the physical are welded together. While one's physical being is intrinsically limited—by the intellect, emotion, energy, and so on—when one undertakes an act of *messirat nefesh,* self-sacrifice, one brings about a denial and nullification of self. This allows for the outpouring and manifestation of the infinite soul. This revelation itself overwhelms and nullifies the limitations of the body. As the spiritual increases, the physical decreases.

And this is the intention behind Abaye's elusive statement in the Talmud. Because the generations of old had self-sacrifice, they saw miracles. Their soul had constant dominion over their bodies, and they constantly saw the Godly revelation, the spiritual character of the world. What they saw was not a world that God ruled or controlled from above, but a world in which God could be found in every stone, plant, animal, and human being.

Stated in other words, these generations did not make the mistake of touching with their hands. When they gazed upon the world, they weren't looking with fleshy eyes. Through constant self-nullification and sublimation, they had refined their bodies. Their physical bodies were no longer opaque, concealing Godliness; rather, they were transparent. They were no longer an obstacle to the revelation of the soul, but a lucid window—a vehicle serving the revelation of the soul.

This, then, is modern man's deficiency. It is as if one walked into the street with dark sunglasses and exclaimed, "Alas, the world has become dark." No! The sun has not burned out, and the world has not become dark. By merely taking off the sunglasses, one can once again experience a bright and sunny world. The fault is in the observer, not in the world.

Thus, although one cannot see the Divinity inherent in creation, this does not contradict the true reality. One cannot expect to see an internal spiritual truth while gazing with mundane eyes and utilizing sensory perception. Rather, one must first reveal the spirituality that exists within oneself. Only then will one be able to experience miracles, or rather, the revelation of the world's rudimentary spiritual fabric.

This is what transpired with the Alta Rebbe just before he expired. In his last moments of life, he had tapped the well-spring. He had refined his physical body to such an extent, through life-long and devoted service of God, that he had removed the physical property of his eyes and was able to see the underlying spirituality that permeates all of creation. He had become one with it. He had overcome the external concealment. He no longer saw the rafters in the ceiling, but rather the divine life-giving force that existed within it.

With this, one may appreciate the full extent of "God's concealment" in this world. Whereas in truth the entire world is just an extension of Godly light and every single creature and every single object that exists in the world is completely dependent on God's sustenance, nevertheless what one sees is an independent entity with no strings attached. Nature does not even do one the justice of pointing in the right direction when one seeks clues as to its origin. Thus, Godly light in the world is hidden completely, and what one sees is the very opposite of the true character of the world. Instead of seeing how the material world is totally dependent and therefore nullified and insignificant in the face of God's light, one's subjective observations notice only the visible and deceptive material world.

But how could such a state of affairs have come about? After all, is it not difficult to conceal the true character of the world? Surely, it is difficult, almost impossible, for God to hide!

The answer is that in reality God's concealment is also a product of His infinite power. God has the incomparable ability, completely unintelligible to the human mind, to create a world and yet conceal His active involvement with it. And thus one arrives at the state of affairs that exists today when Godly light is hidden and the reality one perceives is one that is completely contrary to Godliness and at times even to morality and holiness. An immense exertion of effort and much purification and elevation are necessary before one is able to uncover the true nature of the world.

But notwithstanding the inability to *see* the truth, when one *understands* fully the concepts outlined above, and accepts, not just superficially but deeply, the truth of creation, then the light of truth will always illuminate one's darkness.

One will also be able to believe and accept that it was not God's intention for the world to remain dark forever. God desired that one manifest to all, by way of Torah and *mitzvot* or through using every physical object for the service of God, the truth that it can be used for the service of God, because underneath all of its coarse materialism, it is really Godliness. Witness the power of performing a *mitzvah*. It is a public statement that the physical world has an underlying layer of holiness.

One's mission in life is to reveal the latent Godliness of the world. The first individual to undertake this primary duty was Abraham. What was Abraham's principal preoccupation throughout life? "And he [Abraham] called the place in the name of God, Master of the world" (Genesis 21:33). Abraham brought God's proprietorship to all corners of the earth.

A similar thought is echoed in the *Midrash,* which relates a dialogue that took place between the Almighty and His ministering angels. "Why," the angels demand to know, "have You forsaken us and shone your countenance upon Abraham, being utterly preoccupied with Him, to our exclusion. What is our sin?" "You," the Almighty turns to the angels, "have crowned me King only in the heavens. But thanks to Abraham,'' the Almighty responds, "I am now King over the heavens *and* the earth.''

But the accomplishment of Abraham went even further. The words used in the verse are not "God of the world" *(El Ha-Olam)* but "God world" *(El Olam)*. The difference between the two expressions is immense. "God of the world" implies that there is a God and there is a world, and God is Master over that world. The words "God world" teaches that there is in no way an independent, albeit inferior entity outside of the Almighty's unity. Rather, the world is completely united and one with God. That this became known was the everlasting achievement of Abraham.

This idea that the fundamental substance of our world even now is holy and Godly also brings us to a much deeper understanding of the "reward" that is promised as a result of the study of Torah and the fulfillment of its commandments. Rabbi Shneur Zalman explains in *Tanya* (chap. 37) that "that which causes the reward of a *mitzvah* is the *mitzvah* itself." The meaning of this somewhat puzzling statement is that the reward of a *mitzvah* is the desirable state of existence that it brings about. Since *mitzvot,* which basically consist of the usage of material objects for divine worship, cause a translucence in the physical world that enables us to see exactly what our *mitzvot* have been accomplishing over the last three millennia, the reward thus is a product of the *mitzvah* itself.

In this respect the reward for a *mitzvah* is different from every other reward that can be earned in the empirical world. When a laborer, for instance, works and receives payment for his labor, the reward is not only unconnected but entirely different from the work he has done. For instance, if one ploughs and sows a field, one sows the produce of the field for money; of course one did not mint the coins oneself, nor print the paper with which one is paid. The reward thus has no intrinsic relationship with the work performed; rather, it is something that is given *in exchange* for or in compensation for services rendered.

On the other hand, when one labors in Torah and *mitzvot,* one is not performing a deed and receiving an unconnected reward. Rather, the reward one receives is merely the revelation of that which has been caused and brought about through one's divine service. When a Jew studies Torah and fulfills *mitzvot,* he is bringing into this world the quintessence of God, which is enclothed in the Torah. In the words of the Talmud (*Shabbat* 105a), the word used to refer to God in the ten commandments, *"Anochi,"* is an acrostic for *Ana Nafshi Ketovit Yehovit*—I, Myself, wrote and gave [the Torah]—which means to say that God put Himself into Torah, and His essence is enclothed and imbued within the Torah. All of our own actions with anything to do with Torah and *mitzvot* thus draws God's presence into our world more and more.

Needless to say, if a human being had the ability to observe this phenomenon alongside his work, he would not consider his religious worship cumbersome at all. His worship of God would be a source of the greatest pleasure and comfort. But since the effect of our actions is invisible to us, religious duties can often become bothersome and, in our own terms, nonprofitable. But in the messianic epoch, when the concealing garb of God's essence is removed and all of us see clearly what our religious practices have wrought, this will be our just and deserved reward. Thus, one may appreciate how the reward for a *mitzvah* is actually the *mitzvah* itself.

The coming of the Messiah is the climax and culmination of the whole creative process; so long as the Messiah has not yet come, the true purpose for the creation of the world cannot be enjoyed and cannot be seen. So long as God has not taken up His residence in this private apartment, in the revealed sense, the world has not yet fulfilled its true function and purpose. But when the Messiah comes, and God dwells openly and comfortably in this lowest of worlds, then not only will our actions not have been pointless, but we will see how they have brought about the world's perfection.

The belief in the coming of the Messiah is not a side concern of Torah and its commandments but rather the pinnacle and crowning achievement of three thousand years of Jewish living. If there is no messianic era, then there is no such thing as God openly dwelling among us in our world. Without a messianic era the God–man relationship will always be lacking since man is not fully aware of the extent of the relationship and how far it has developed.

It is thus imperative that a Jew know the effect his Torah-study and fulfillment of *mitzvot* has. With every act of self-sacrifice, self-negation, and putting God first, one is adding another brick and another layer of mortar to God's domicile. One must be made aware of the overall design and scheme of things of which he and his activities are a part. The messianic era is God's overall plan for creation—that it be seen how His essence resides and is revealed in the lowest of worlds.

5

TORAH STUDY AND SPIRITUAL GAIN

The *Mishnah* in *Ethics of the Fathers* (6:2) reads: "Rabbi Yehoshua ben Levi said: Each and every day a Heavenly Voice goes forth from Mount Choreb proclaiming and saying, 'Woe to the people because of their affront to the Torah, for whoever does not occupy himself with the Torah is called "censured," as it is stated: Like a golden ring in a swine's snout is a beautiful woman who lacks discretion.' " What is the meaning of this obscure, yet often quoted, *mishnah?* At a cursory glance, it seems as though the *Mishnah* is rebuking those who completely forsake the study of Torah, having no time for it at all. Such a person, the *Mishnah* proclaims, is "censured."

The difficulty with this interpretation of the words of Rabbi Yehoshua Ben Levi is another statement in the Torah directed at those who do not study Torah at all, from which it is clear that such individuals are punished far more severely than mere censorship. On the biblical verse, "For he has disgraced the word of God, he shall surely be cut off," the Talmud (*Sanhedrin* 99a) comments, "Ben Nehorai says that this text refers to 'all those who are able to engage Torah study yet do not.' " Clearly, the punishment for complete neglect of Torah study is excision, i.e., being cut off from one's God and people, and not mere censorship.

Rabbi Yehoshua ben Levi's statement, "Whoever does not occupy himself with Torah," is not directed at those who are able to study Torah but do not, but to those who do study Torah, yet are not "occupied" with its study. This may even include someone who studies Torah as long as eighteen hours a day and never misses a moment from possible Torah study. The deficiency thus is not that one does not study the Torah, but that one is not *occupied* with it.

What distinguishes *studying* Torah from being *occupied* with Torah? The main difference is that occupation with Torah constitutes the desire to make profit from the Torah. Here, of course, it is not financial gain, but spiritual gain being discussed. The Talmud states: "If a merchant buys and sells at the same price, is he indeed considered a merchant?" to which Rashi explains: "This is a question. It is a talmudic parable whereupon one says to an imbecile, 'You sold the item for the same amount that you purchased it without any profit whatsoever, and we should call you a merchant?' (*Bava Metzia* 40b)." Stated in other words, there exists the possibility for an individual to rush through the marketplace throughout the day, buying, selling, and working very strenuously, yet not being considered a merchant or a businessman at all. The definition of a merchant is someone who earns a livelihood from his trade, who makes profit from his occupation of buying and selling merchandise. But this individual, although exerting himself to the maximum, derives no gain from his occupation. Thus, while he is a laborer, he cannot be considered a merchant or a businessman.

This same principle may be applied to the study of Torah. There exists the possibility for a Jew to sit and study Torah the entire day, without pausing for an interruption, and he may nevertheless be considered "one who does not occupy himself with the Torah," since he is not thinking at all on the gain that the study of Torah is meant to produce. This person is punished with censorship from the heavens.

What is this profit from Torah to which we refer? The study of Torah and fulfillment of its commandments are meant to bring about a desired result, namely, the fulfillment of the purpose of creation. As the *Midrash* quoted earlier declares, "The Almighty desired a dwelling place in the lowest of worlds." One who studies the Torah must be cognizant of the fact that the study of Torah and fulfillment of *mitzvot* are not mere commandments of the Almighty that should be performed in the same manner as a slave who fulfills the bidding of his master, without ever pondering the significance of his master's request. Rather, it is incumbent upon the individual to ensure that Torah and *mitzvot* are used as a tool to bring about a desired result and profit, namely, the transformation of the mundane physical world into a dwelling place for Almighty God, as discussed in the foregoing chapter.

Rabbi Shneur Zalman clarifies this point at length in *Tanya* (chap. 36). The purpose of creation was not the existence of the highest spiritual worlds, but the earth, the lowest of all worlds. God desired that in this physical domain where "darkness covers the earth" and Godliness is concealed, a transformation should be wrought whereby God's light can rest peacefully, comfortably, and without any restrictions in our world. It is for this reason that our world, in contrast to the higher spiritual worlds, was created with a complete void of Godly light; one can mistake this world as an entity unto itself without any origin in the form of a creator.

Why was all this necessary? Because it was the desire of the Almighty that this "dwelling," which He desired, be brought about by the world's earthly inhabitants. Through Torah and *mitzvot,* which have the effect of drawing God's infinite essence into our world, one can slowly illuminate the dwelling and make it a fit abode for the King of kings. Stated in other words, the purpose of man in his fulfillment of Torah and *mitzvot* is to reveal the true nature of the world, that "there exists nothing besides Him" (daily prayer liturgy). The purpose of service and Godly devotion is to reveal how "there is no other beside Him," which means that not only is there, of course, no *God* beside Him, but there is no *existence* whatsoever aside from His being. The false impression conveyed by the world that it is indeed a separate and independent entity is a distortion of the true face of creation. In truth, the world is but a mere extension of God's omnipotence and radiance. But the concealment, the veil, that the world wears refuses to disclose the truth. Hence the need for the Torah and *mitzvot* to remove the veil and manifest to all the latent truth.

Hasidism spends much time and effort emphasizing how the world's entire existence is dependent upon the divine utterance that vivifies and sustains it. The letters of the "Ten Utterances" with which God created the world ("Let there be light. . . . Let there be a firmament. . . .") are said to be invested into every created body, serving as its sustaining life force (*Tanya, Shaar Hayihud Ve ha'emunah,* chap. 1). If the Almighty were to withhold His utterance or His divine creative power for even a moment, the world would cease to exist. The entire existence of the world is dependent on God's constantly re-creating it. Many people entertain the absurd folly that before creation the world was a huge glob of shapeless matter. What God did was to come along and give it shape, order, and structure. This is absurd because before God created the world, there was nothing. And from this lack of existence and utter emptiness He called forth the existence of the world. Thus, in order for this "nothing" to be sustained as an existing entity and not revert back to its original form, God must re-create it constantly.

A famous hasidic story is told of a naive young child who was asked, "If God desired to destroy the world, what would He have to do?" The child responded innocently, "Well, burn it, I suppose."

But the questioner returned, "And what would He do with the ashes?"

"Why, wash them away with an ocean of water," responded the child.

"But what would He do with the water?" returned the questioner.

"Vaporize it with an intense inferno."

"What will He do with the water vapor, clouds, and rain that result from the evaporation of the water?" came the question, and on and on. The questions kept on returning regarding the refuse and debris of the destroyed world. If God decided to end the world, would He indeed have a pollution problem?

Of course not. The truth of the situation is this: if God desired to destroy the world, it would not necessitate a new action on His part—He would simply stop creating it.

This is analogous to a stone thrown into the air. Superficially, one would be led to believe that as the stone is observed flying through the air, its intrinsic nature has been transformed. Whereas all other ordinary stones are heavy and gravitate toward the earth, this stone transcends and defies the earth's gravity. It thus possesses the ability to fly. Needless to say, this is an absurd description of what has taken place. The stone has not changed its essence in any way. It remains a lifeless, dead, inanimate object, as it was previously. The fact that it is observed flying through the air is not a statement about the stone as much as it is about the person who threw the stone. When one throws a stone, one transfers potential energy from one's muscles onto a lifeless stone; so long as the energy is not counterbalanced by friction and other forces acting upon it, the stone will fly. This phenomenon is not due to any intrinsic property of the stone, but rather to the energy that is constantly acting upon it, pushing it to defy gravity. When this energy is consumed by the counterforces, the stone will once again return to its natural state of lying motionless on the ground, until, of course, someone else comes along and throws it into the air and causes it to fly once again.

This analogy accurately describes the continued existence of our world. Before God created the world in six days, the world was nonexistent. What reigned in its absence was absolute nothingness. So where did this world spring to life? The Almighty drew upon His infinite power and brought about a completely new concept: the emergence of something from nothing. Amid an absolute vacuum of existence and empty space, God brought into existence a pluralistic, diverse, and complex creation. When God said, "Let there be light," light was called into existence from nothingness. When God said, "Let there be a firmament," that was also called into existence from an utter void.

Can we properly refer to our world as an independent entity? Can we say that it's true nature has now been formulated and exists on its own? Can we say that the creation that was called from nothingness has become an independent existence and now is a "something"? Obviously not. Our creation, which began as nothingness, is being retained as something not through its own intrinsic nature but through God's constant creative energy acting upon it, just as the stone flies through the air as a result of the transference onto it of human force.

Thus the creation differs greatly from the average physical product of human labor and creativity. For example, when a carpenter takes a rough and coarse block of wood and, through his craftsmanship and skill, cuts, sands, and polishes it into a beautiful table, he actually starts with an independent existence, a block of wood. In essence, he has brought nothing new into existence but rather has refashioned, re-formed, enhanced, and beautified an existent block of matter. In fact, the carpenter introduces no qualitative property into the block of wood that did not exist previously; rather he enhances its value and its use. Had the carpenter never come along and never redesigned the block of wood, it would have remained peacefully unmoved in its natural environment. Thus we say, "Our human action bears no resemblance to yours, O Lord" (Yom Kippur prayer liturgy).

Since it is not the nature of nothingness to become something, and it was God who brought nothingness into existence, therefore God must do so constantly. Were He to uphold His creative effort for even a single instant, the world would revert to what it was previously and what it is now without God—absolute nothingness. Therefore it cannot be argued that the world in any way is an independent existence. It is wholly dependant on God's sustaining utterance.

The unity of God, the absolute oneness of God, and the indivisibility of God are not statements meant to negate the possibility of a deity other than God or to contradict the potential for a being of God's awesome might and power. Man would not naturally have been led to make such a gross misjudgment in the first place. Rather, these concepts reinforce and reemphasize that the entire creation, which to the naked and untrained eye appears to be an existence independent and outside of God's presence, is totally within God's all-encompassing unity.

This explanation refutes even those who would concede that indeed God created the world, but has since abandoned it to its own indigenous processes. There are those who would argue that now that the world is in existence, it no longer needs

God's constant interaction and providence. But the concept of the unity of God safeguards us from even that type of *idolatry*.

Idolatry is not the belief that there are any gods aside from the one God. Rather, idolatry is the belief that there is any independent object that is not directly dependent on God for its existence. This includes even those things that were once created by God and are now believed to exist outside His unity, independent of His being. The fact that everything is dependent on God means that there are not *two* entities, a God and also a world. Rather, there is only God, and then there is the world, which, if not for God constantly holding in the air, would not be.

[It is also important not to argue that the world doesn't even exist and is merely an illusion. The Torah, which is a Torah of truth, makes positive and definite statements about the world's existence and makes irrevocable demands on man to work the land and enhance the goodness of the earth. The purpose here is not to negate the world's existence as such but to affirm its dependency on God and its incorporation within God's indivisible unity.]

6

NOT A BOOK OF
INSTRUCTION BUT A BOOK
OF LIGHT

That everything is wholly dependent on the Almighty for
its existence is not easily discernible to the observer. It is
possible to imagine that the world created itself or came
into existence by mere chance and coincidence. And if not for
some divine teaching that argues otherwise, one might well
have remained at that conclusion forever. It is this magnitude
of darkness and lack of revealed Godliness that one must
contest and battle with in the physical world, a world that the
Kabbalah describes as being darker than all other worlds. The
poverty of Godly illumination in our world is alluded to
constantly in kabbalistic and hasidic literature in the form of
the alias used to describe the physical earth, ''the lowest of all
worlds.'' This expression serves as Jewish mysticism's constant
reminder of the state of lowly earth in relation to the higher
spiritual spheres where God's light shines openly, albeit in
varying degree. Whereas all the spiritual worlds readily ac-
knowledge their attachment to their source and the fact that
they emanate from God's creative ability, the physical world
conceals the truth. It was the rule of the creator that specifically
in the lowest of worlds there be a veil to conceal the world's
umbilical cord to its origin. It would be left to humans, who are
part of the created world, to uncover the truth and reveal the
subliminal layer of creation, the God who is submerged beneath nature.

This reflects the difference between that which is spiritual and that which is physical. In the minds of most, a "spiritual thing" is something that cannot be seen, occupies no space, cannot be apprehended with human sensory perception, and so on—basically, an angel. When one thinks of an angel, one conjures up an ethereal being in the eye of the mind cannot be seen or sensed. One contrasts an angel's existence with one's own because it seems so utterly antithetical to one's own. One is course, palpable, and driven to materialistic ends. An angel, in one's mind, is made of higher, intangible things and pursues higher things. A person, on the other hand, being a physical organism, can be touched, heard, and seen.

But why? What *defines* the spiritual and the physical? What makes them what they are? What is it about a spiritual object that makes it intangible and "propertyless," and what is it about a physical object that makes it assume the confines of spatial-temporal reality.

Both have to do with either being aware and attached, or unaware and disattached, from their source. A spiritual being is one that is constantly cognizant of and in close proximity with its source. It thus cannot become an independent identity since it knows the truth and *is always conscious of its source.* How could an angel become detached and physical if at every moment it feels God looming over it. A spiritual being is one that is naturally subordinate to and nullified by the origin of its existence, which it constantly senses. On the other hand, a physical being becomes physical precisely because God, its Creator, is hidden from it. Once dependency on God is no longer acknowledged, automatically the being assumes the confines of spatial-temporal existence. It convinces itself of its own independence, accepting the illusion of freedom.

By way of analogy, imagine a king who has two very important ministers: the minister of war and the minister of foreign affairs. The source of their immense power is obviously the king. Without the monarch having conferred upon them these positions of power, they would be like every commoner. Now, when they sit in their own respective ministries, receiving illustrious visitors from home and abroad, accepting gifts from heads of state, and hearing the pleas of common folk who seek their help, in their own minds they are the most important people in the world. They are their own little kings, so much so that at state receptions, when the king is not present, each of them sees himself as the ruler of the kingdom. The two ministers may even begin to quarrel or harbor nasty feelings toward each other because they see each other as the nemesis. Sitting together at this state reception, they may refuse to speak to each another, or may even quarrel. After all, each one is a very powerful man and thinks to himself that he is far more important than the other. Thus, it is difficult for them to tolerate a rival. However, whenever they are summoned to the king's palace, something strange occurs. There, in the presence of the true absolute ruler of the land, a man so powerful that he is not only the one who has conferred their high offices upon them, but can with a flick of the wrist have the two of them beheaded with no questions asked—they suddenly fall silent. They feel no animosity toward their ministerial counterpart. In fact, even if the war minister were to insult or slap the foreign minister in the presence of the king, in all likelihood the latter would have no response. He would not even feel the insult. For, in the presence of the king, the source of his power, he is absolutely nullified and, figuratively, nonexistent.

The same is true with the objects within creation. Because the spiritual realm is one where there is no veil that conceals God's light from its inhabitants, the inhabitants—angels and the like—never become physical. How could they? Their existence is so totally nullified by the intensity and power of God's presence that they never assume the confines of physical, and seemingly independent, reality.

On the other hand, the physical is separated from the spiritual by a major contraction of God's light, known in the Kabbalah as a *masakh uparsa,* a curtain and a veil. God is hidden in our world. Because of that fact, automatically the world assumes the dimensions of spatial-temporal existence. Objects and things feel themselves to be independent, and thus they express that independence through becoming corporal and physical. A physical object is something that conceals its source and shouts to the observer, "I am not nullified and dependent. I am a something."

The purpose is to try and manifest to the earth's inhabitants the true subservience and ultimate dependency of the world on its creator. One is commanded to illuminate the dark world created by God. When one studies Torah and fulfills its commandments, whose very essence is Godly light, as it is written, "The flame of the *mitzvot* and the light of the Torah" (Proverbs 6:23), one illuminates the earth and reveals the truth, that veil or no veil, everything emanates and is not detached from God. And in this way the world is transformed into God's dwelling place, a world inhabited by the Almighty.

It is with this explanation that one can make sense of one of the greatest theological riddles of all: Why would the Almighty God take something as holy as a *neshamah,* a soul, which "is carved from underneath God's throne of glory" (see Isaiah 51:1) and cause it to descend to such a fraudulent and treacherous world? What advantage could such a holy and sublime entity possibly have in descending to the "the lowest of all worlds"?

In reality, though, this degradation is well worth the effort, since it is only via this means that God's dwelling place in the lowest of worlds can be forged. Had it been true that our physical realm was actually, as it appears, unholy and coarse, then the *neshamah* would have no place here. But this is not the case. The *neshamah* can feel just as at home in the material world as it does in Heaven, by making Heaven on earth. With every extra Godly deed and with every extra Godly thought and with every extra Godly word, the human organism, keeper of the soul, causes the radiation of another point of light, another of the divine sparks submerged within physical existence, until these "thousand points of light" can be gathered together as the many seemingly unrelated pieces of a jigsaw puzzle, so that the true picture of our world can be seen.

This will happen only in the time of the Messiah. Today, the effects of performing one's religious duties cannot be seen because of the veil mentioned earlier. This does not mean, of course, that the light one brings into the world today is lost or ineffective. On the contrary, it remains intact and will be seen when the Messiah comes and the cloak is lifted. What is important is that one feels and recognizes the need to conquer every veiled aspect of the material world and draw it nearer to the realm of holiness and Godliness. One should always see his religious observance as part of an overall plan: the transformation and reclaiming of the world into the camp of divinity. The more one does, the closer one brings the redemption.

Judaism is a statement of God to man to continue His work. God's message is, I created a world that is not readily recognizable as Godly and holy. My intention, though, is for Godliness and holiness to permeate the entire world. To this effect I have begun a process. I have taken a slight portion of the two fundamental components that comprise the physical world— time and space—and made them holy. I have made one day of the week, *Shabbat,* holy; and I have made one place on earth holy: the land of Israel. Now, your job as human beings is to continue this process. You must make more times and more places holy. You must extend the borders of Israel and cause the holiness of *Shabbat* to permeate the remainder of the week. You must extend the perimeter of the Godly camp until it envelops the entire earth—"as the waters cover the ocean floor" (Isaiah 11:9).

No wonder, then, that the Talmud promises that "in the world to come the land of Israel will extend beyond its borders and encompass the entire earth" (*Yalkut Shimoni* on Isaiah 66:23, *Remez* 503). The entire world will be shown to be just as holy as Israel. Today this fact is concealed; in the future it will be revealed.

One of the primary followers of the Baal Shem Tov wished to emigrate from Russia to the land of Israel. He wished to leave all of his many communal responsibilities behind him—he was a great rabbi—and all the important charitable work in which he was engaged, and move to the holy land. The Baal Shem's response to him was short and to the point. "Don't run to Israel. Rather, *mach da Eretz Yisroel,* change Russia into the land of Israel."

This perspective on Judaism's principal goal also lends commentary to a question that has vexed generations of scholars. God's first commandment to the *Jews,* given on the eve of their departure from Egypt, the very first *mitzvah* in the Torah, was the obligation to identify and consecrate the New Moon with witnesses, thus establishing Rosh Hodesh, the beginning of a new month. But why should this be the first *mitzvah?* What great message is inherent in this *mitzvah,* which serves as the forerunner of all the other *mitzvot?*

After examining and displaying the shortcomings of different explanations offered by various scholars throughout the ages, the Rebbe Menachem Schneerson offers a brilliant insight. The commandment to consecrate the New Moon was chosen as the first *mitzvah* because it forms the basis for what Torah and *mitzvot* are all about. Consecrating the New Moon is a process by which a Jewish court, and by extension the Jewish nation, takes an ordinary, mundane weekday and makes it a holy day, Rosh Hodesh, so holy that a special prayer of praise, *Hallel,* must be said along with an additional prayer service, *Musaf,* which is only said on holidays, a special sacrificial offering is brought, and so on. So the first *mitzvah* immediately spells out exactly what is required of the Jewish people: to make more times and more places holy, ultimately bringing in a messianic era—an age when the holiness of all things will be apparent.

The knowledge of this mission should lead to an abundance of joy when an individual realizes that it is within his ability to redeem and free all sparks of Godliness that hitherto were under the domain of *Klippah,* the concealing darkness. A Jew must feel that he can conquer whole areas of the earth and bring them under God's dominion and that he can play an integral part in the final conquest of the remainder of the earth that will take place in the messianic era. As Scripture states, "In that time the Lord shall be King over the entire earth; and on that day the Lord shall be one and his Name one" (Zechariah 14:9). There is no question that this knowledge will fill the individual soldier with boundless energy and joy, and his study of Torah and fulfillment of *mitzvot* will assume a new dimension.

Sadly, though, there are those to whom Torah and *mitzvot* are not part of an overall plan. Even among many Jews who study Torah and fulfill the *mitzvot* with heartfelt sincerity and devotion, it is difficult to accept that what they are doing is radically transforming the world and imbuing it with Godly light.

It is ironic that a Jew may go through an entire lifetime being absolutely meticulous in his observance of the Torah's commandments, and yet remain completely oblivious to the fact that all of these activities are part of a specific program designed to bring about an exceptional and revolutionary world, a world of illumination and Godly light. He may rise every morning and immediately recite the *"Modeh Ani,"* "I offer thanks to You, living and eternal King, for You have mercifully restored my soul within me; Your faithfulness is great." Immediately afterward he might wash his hands as prescribed by *halakhah* (Jewish law); go to *shul* for the morning prayers, and from the *shul* proceed to the *yeshivah* to study Torah. In short, he might do everything in accordance with Jewish law, but not know why.

Many observant Jews feel it futile to battle with the darkness of the world. Their reasoning takes the following argument: If all the previous generations who were of far greater stature and nobler, and moreover lived in generations when the world was not as boorish and crass as it is today, if they were unsuccessful in dispelling the darkness of the world and bringing the redemption, how much more so that today that we who are inferior to their piety and live in far less holy times cannot bring the Messiah. Can I, one asks oneself, through my Torah and *mitzvot,* surpass the achievements of all my great ancestors who were towering *tzaddikim* and saintly individuals?

Yet, it is precisely this attitude that Rabbi Yehoshua ben Levi warns against in his statement censuring he who studies the Torah, yet is not occupied with it, as discussed in the previous chapter. This individual studies the Torah but is not occupied with it. This is an individual who is not a merchant—he does not try to bring about the desired profit from the Torah. He doesn't see the Torah as the vessel through which the world is illuminated and redemption is found. And although he may be observant, pious, and righteous, his religious worship is directionless and ineffective. The ultimate irony is that there are those who are so preoccupied with studying the Torah that they can come to the point where they forget what the whole thing is all about.

We are faced with countless individuals whose primary

objective in studying the Torah is to enhance themselves: to become great scholars and great rabbis, even to become better and more refined people, to publish books and essays, to be a credit to the Torah nation, to be eternal through making a name for themselves. *But what about the Messiah? What about God? What about His desire that this world become His dwelling?* It is important not to lose sight of the ultimate objective. In the words of Maimonides, "The final goal is the attaining to the world to come, and it is to it that the effort must be directed."

Rabbi Yehoshua ben Levi says, "Woe to these people because of their affront to the Torah." There are those whose attitudes affront and denigrate the power and qualitative virtue of the Torah. They deny the Torah's ability to battle the evil and fend off the darkness found on earth. They completely miss what the Torah is and what it is meant to accomplish. Can there be any greater affront than this? To view the Torah as a book of instructions and commands rather than a book of light? No wonder, then, that these people, with all their good intentions, are "censured" from Heaven. For they have conquered the Torah and made it their own. God's intention in giving the Torah is ignored.

This explanation affords new insight into another aspect of the same *mishnah* quoted at the beginning of the previous chapter. Rabbi Yehoshua ben Levi discusses why the Torah was given at Mount Choreb, and not the traditional Sinai. He says, "Each and every day a Heavenly Voice goes forth from Mount Horeb." Mount Horeb, which is just another name given to Sinai, is meant to express a specific facet of the Torah. *Horev* is the word for war, as the *Mishnah* explains that Mount Sinai is referred to as Horev because the proper observance of Torah necessitates fighting a battle (*Shabbat* 89b). The main objective of the Torah is to battle the facade and mask of the earth and utterly eradicate them. One who studies Torah, but does not occupy himself with the ultimate battle and conquest that Torah is meant to achieve, ignores the power of the Torah to bring victory over the grayness and absence of Godly presence.

The messianic era expresses the culmination of thousands of

years of Godly service, its summit and purpose. A Jew is obligated to feel this purpose as he goes about his days executing the Torah's commandments. While the Torah advocates that one fulfill its commandments even if one cannot appreciate their importance and has little sensitivity as to their sublimity, nevertheless it behooves the individual not to be blind to one's ultimate objective and destination.

7

JUDAISM: A RADICAL RELIGION

In kabbalistic and hasidic literature, this world is referred to as *Olam Haklippot,* the world of husks or shells. This reference is meant to convey the essence of our world. *Klippah* is a skin or covering around a fruit. When one gazes at a fruit, one sees only the worthless shell and is oblivious to the fruit that exists beneath the shell. If one does not know that a fruit is contained within the skin, one is likely to discard it because the covering looks unappealing, thus missing out on its luscious contents. A shell conceals its more significant element, the fruit that lies within. In order to obtain the fruit, one must first remove the shell.

Our world is the same. The essence of our world, in truth, is Godliness. The true character of every single created body is the Godly energy contained within it that sustains it. The problem is that this truth is concealed by *klippah,* a casing that sheaths the world's Godly nature, leading the observer to the conclusion that there is only a skin and no Godliness submerged within it. In modern-day terms, this skin might be referred to as nature and the forces of nature. The world seems to operate with its own dynamics and seems to have a whole momentum of its own.

This world of *klippah* was not an accident of creation, but was part of God's divine plan. The plan was for the Jews to enter into a dark world and illuminate the earth, thus removing the shell that conceals the truth, revealing the underlying Godly character of the world. This is the mission and the special powers entrusted to the Jewish people: to radically alter man's perception of the physical world by utilizing all of the world's bounty in the performance of Godly deeds, thus returning and reclaiming everything to the domain of holiness.

It is for this reason that Judaism, unlike most other global religions, does not concentrate on "other-worldliness." In Judaism, the purpose of religious duties in this world is not to inherit life in the hereafter. Judaism does not concern itself with "spiritual salvation." Nor does it advocate that man's spiritual ascendance is directly dependent on his abstention from physical pleasure and material indulgence.

The philosophical ideas detailed in the foregoing chapters, namely, the belief that even the physical earth is Godly and man's mission is to expose that Godliness, serves as the basis for Judaism's exceeding preoccupation with the minutiae of human life and the sublimation of physical existence. Because Judaism believes that beneath all the darkness of the world there is an underlying Godly layer, it thus advocates that man, rather than abstain from the "evil" world and not get his hands dirty, engage the physical world and manifest its true character. The best possible way of displaying this uniqueness in Judaism is by contrasting it with religions having a fundamentally different philosophical perspective of physical reality and of life itself, religions that advocate abstention and withdrawal from it as a means to a higher spiritual end.

The religions that promote these values do so because they see this world as being subordinate and insignificant in comparison with "heaven" and the spiritual realm. Thus, there is a universal tendency by the world's leading religions to advocate abstinence, meditation, celibacy, physical denial, fasting, even self-flagellation. The whole purpose of these exercises is to deny the physical in the belief that the descendance of the physical will lead to the ascendance of the spiritual, that the soul can achieve supremacy over the body only by means of the body being denied. Of course, what follows from this is a fundamental rejection of the holiness of the body, the physical world at large, and a denigration of physical necessities. Everything from sleeping, eating, marital relations, even speaking can be looked upon as being unGodly. Riches are the road to spiritual disaster and only "the meek will inherit the earth."

Judaism, however, demands and even obligates man to take part in physical reality. Jewish life is not about abstention, but sublimation. Man must actively engage in commerce, feasting, marriage and procreation, laughter—but in all of these activities his purpose is to consecrate and uplift them from their mundanity. One must scrupulously adhere to the code of Jewish law so that these activities will not be base, but Godly. By going about physical concerns and needs in conformity with Jewish law, one brings God into all one's endeavors, thus revealing the Godliness inherent in material existence. This belief is epitomized in the immortal saying of our rabbis, "Know Him in *all* your ways" (Maimonides, *Shemoneh Perakim,* chap. 5). If man were to abstain from physical needs, it would be a statement of the belief that essentially God is not a part of our world and can only be found in what we refer to as the higher, spiritual sector.

Thus the difference between Judaism and Christianity and Islam is one of direction. The difference that distinguish these faiths and Judaism is not merely selected beliefs, such as the identity of the Messiah or the legitimacy of a specific prophet. Rather, Judaism has a completely different orientation to these systems of belief, which can be expressed in the following statement. *Whereas Christianity and Islam are about lifting man to the domain of God and heaven, Judaism is about bringing God down to man and the earth.* Whereas Christianity and Islam are *upward*-oriented, and the focus of their attention is about man's relinquishing his physical needs, which serve as shackles tying him down to the physical earth and away from God, thus preventing him from ascending to God, Judaism is about engaging physical activity and dragging God along with us so that He inhabits and is sovereign over the earth.

The renunciation of materialism in Christianity is found primarily in the debasement of money and sexual relations. Riches and marriage seem to have been shunned by the fathers of Christianity. This is epitomized in Paul's declaration: "So then, he who marries the virgin does right, but he who does not marry her does even better. A woman is bound to her husband as long as she lives. But if her husband dies, she is free to marry anyone she wishes. . . . In my judgment, she is happier if she stays as she is—and I think that I too have the Spirit of God'' (I Corinthians 7:37–40).

Furthermore, in a telling description of how the Jewish and Christian attitudes differ as the nature of the world-to-come, Jesus stated, ''At the resurrection people will neither marry nor be given in marriage; they will be like the angels in heaven'' (Matthew 22:30). Thus, the founder of Christianity envisioned a world that would be totally devoid of anything physical; man, after the final judgment, will be elevated the heights of the angels. Judaism foretells of a world in which the human body will be resurrected and will live forever.

Jesus also taught that the rich would have difficulty getting into heaven. ''I tell you the truth, it is hard for a rich man to enter the kingdom of heaven. Again I tell you, it is easier for a camel to go through the eye of a needle than for a rich man to enter the kingdom of God'' (Matthew 19:23–24). The rich would be driven away—''He has filled the hungry with good things, but has sent the rich away empty'' (Luke 1:53).

Paul echoes Jesus' disdain for the rich with various statements. ''Listen my brothers, has not God chosen those who are poor in the eyes of the world to be rich in faith and to inherit the kingdom he promised those who love him? . . . Is it not the rich . . . who are slandering the name of the him to whom you belong?'' But the one who is rich should take pride in his high position, because he will pass away life a wild flower. . . . The rich man will fade away even while he goes about his business'' (James 1:10–11).

Paul also speaks of the excessive evils to which love of money will lead. ''People who want to get rich fall into temptation and a trap and into many foolish and harmful desires that plunge men into ruin and destruction. For the love of money is the root of all kinds of evil. Some people, eager for money, have wandered from the faith and pierced themselves with many griefs'' (I Timothy 6:9–10).

Similar renunciations of materialism and this-worldliness are found in the Koran, where man's ultimate purpose is systematically described as earning a place in heaven alongside God. "The present life is naught but a sport and a diversion. Surely the Hereafter is best for those that are God-fearing" (Koran 6:32); "It was the life of this world that deceived them" (Koran 6:130).

Similarly the Koran asserts the supremacy of heaven over this world with its statement, "Oh! You who believe. What is the matter with you that, when you are asked to go forth in the Cause of God, you cling heavily to the earth? Do you prefer the life of this world to the hereafter?" (Koran 9:38).

And concerning material necessities the Koran states, "The material things that you are given are but the conveniences of this life and the glitter thereof; but that which is with God is better and more enduring. Will you not then be wise?" (Koran 28:60).

In like manner, in most Eastern religions we find great emphasis on meditation and withdrawal. It is the world of the spirit and mind that is longed for and desirable, while the mundaneity and suffocating strictures of our world are to be rejected.

Judaism is different. Man cannot remain celibate, even if he wishes to. The Talmud encourages man to marry and "experience life with the woman which you love" (Ecclesiastes 9:9). An abundance of children is also highly desirable. In fact, Judaism goes as far as declaring the marital act to be one of the holiest activities in which man can engage. It is the only means by which a Godly soul can be brought into the world.

Fasting in Judaism in done only on days that commemorate great misfortune befalling the Jewish people. Otherwise, not only is fasting deemed an inappropriate means of serving God, but the very way in which the Sabbath and the festivals are celebrated are "with wine, meat, and delicacies" (*Shulhan Arukh, Orah Hayyim, Laws of Shabbat* 242, *Laws of Yom Tov* 529). Man is encouraged to engage in commerce, thus enabling him to support the poor and ease suffering. Riches are to be pursued, so long as they do not become an end in and of themselves, but are also used to benefit the needy.

Aesthetic pleasure that teaches man to glorify the God who

created such a magnificent creation is strongly encouraged. In short, Judaism views all earthly activity as an avenue to finding God *since God dwells in and is part of our world.* And as long as man pursues these activities for the sake of heaven and in accordance with God's law, he has the great merit of consecrating material existence and thus reunifying God with His world. Through a Jew using all of physical existence to serve God, he demonstrates that the world is and was never detached from God.

There is perhaps no greater indication of how the orientation of Judaism runs counter to that of all the other religions of the world than in its attitude toward life and death. The Jewish attitude toward death is summed up well in these lines by Rabbi Adin Steinsaltz:

> It is one of the many paradoxes of Jewish history that although the Jewish people have known premature and unnatural death as a constant companion, probably more than any other nation, culturally and spiritually the Jews are remarkably unpreoccupied by death and the hereafter. . . .
>
> The Jews never equated death with holiness. Cadavers, far from being treated as objects of sanctity and adoration, are regarded as impurities from which one must keep a distance. Of all the many forms of defilement in Jewish law, the gravest is that caused by a corpse. . . .
>
> In Judaism, holiness is first and foremost the sanctity of life. Where life abounds, holiness is at hand. "Life" is a synonym for all that is most exalted in Creation. One of the names of God is "the God of life." The Torah is described as "the Torah of life." The Torah itself speaks of "life and goodness" as of one and the same thing. "Living waters" are seen as a source of purity. It is thus not surprising that the Jews rejected all forms of the myth of the Dead God. Death is the negation of the Divine reality in all its manifestations.
>
> The Jewish belief that "this world is the antechamber to the next" may well have inspired massive Gentile speculation on heaven and hell and purgatory, but, by contrast, Jewish literature and tradition engage in scant exploration of paradise. Judaism makes no attempt either to forget death or to smother it in false jubilation. "The dead praise not the Lord, nor do they who go down into the silence of the grave. But we will bless the

Lord from this time forth and for ever more, Hallelujah" proclaims the Psalmist.

The basic attitude of Judaism to death . . . is life diseased, distorted, perverted, diverted from the flow of holiness, which is identified with life. The remedy for death is faith in the resurrection.

In the combat of life against death, of being against nonbeing, Judaism manifests disbelief in the persistence of death, and maintains that it is a temporary obstacle that can and will be overcome. Our sages, prophesying a world in which there will be no more death, wrote: "We are getting closer and closer to a world in which we shall be able to vanquish death, in which we shall be above and beyond death." [*Strife of the Spirit,* pp. 192–193]

In contrast, Christianity devotes much spiritual energy to death and young Muslims are today promised that if they lose their life in a holy war, they will gain automatic entry to heaven. The reason is simple. Both of these religions see heaven as the apogee and culmination of the creative process. God dwells in heaven and man must reach God. Since death is, practically speaking, the only way to actually leave earth and enter heaven, death is seen as a holy and sometimes even desirable state. Judaism, however, which views the purpose of creation as being achieved in our physical world, where one has the ability to connect oneself with the Almighty via the fulfillment of His commandments, chooses life. Death is undesirable in every form and description.

But why indeed does the rejection of the body and the material world in favor of the soul, heaven, and the afterlife play so prominent a role in many of the world's major faiths? The answer lies in the natural and intuitive human understanding of divinity. One doesn't know much about God. And the little one does know has more to do with what He *isn't* rather than what He *is*. All of the most accurate statements about God are negative statements. What one does know suggests that, at the very least, God is superhuman—metaphysical and celestial. He doesn't eat or sleep, doesn't have a wife, and engages in strictly spiritual pursuits. Stated in other words, when the mind begins to ponder Godliness, the only conclusion that one can reach is that God is none of those things that we are. We have physical needs; He doesn't. By negative extrapolation away from ourselves, we somehow get a glimpse of God and His essence.

Thus, if it is true that God is none of the things that one is, if it be true that God is totally nonmaterial, it would then seem logical to suggest that the only way of growing in proximity to Him is to stop being what one is already. And thus religion, which at its most basic is an attempt to bridge the infinite gulf that divides God and man and bring the two closer together, argues that only way to approach God is to be more like Him, and, by extension, less human! So, by minimizing sleeping, eating, sexual relations, quest for material wealth, etc., man grows closer to God. For Godliness and human experience are mutually exclusive.

Of course, it is impossible for man to fully renounce materialism while still in this world, or he would surely die. The body has basic needs that cannot be ignored. So ultimately, these religions cannot accept that our world, where God is not seen and represents the antithesis of spirituality, cannot be an end in itself. Rather, it is adamant that man abstain from physical necessities and pleasures as much as possible, until such time that he will expire and merit to experience God face to face. Thus one arrives at a complete subordination of the world to the higher, spiritual realms.

All this seems fairly logical. So why does Judaism reject it? Because this type of thinking makes the mistake of creating God *in one's own image.* Everything stated thusfar, notwithstanding how logical it immediately appears, is based entirely on human points of reference. But one cannot use his own points of reference to describe a Being who utterly transcends them.

Numerous adjectives are employed by man to describe God. Man is accustomed to referring to God as omniscient, omnipresent, infinite, wise, to name but a few. But from a more lofty perspective, all of these descriptions, though stated with the intention of glorifying and elevating God, do not describe His true greatness. In fact, paradoxically, they serve to conceal, to mislead us from discovering His true nature. When referring to God with these adjectives, God is regarded within the human frame of reference. Human notions such as power, presence, and kindness are applied to God. Thus, a true definition of God on His *own* terms is not arrived at.

To be sure, according to Jewish teaching, God's true nature is totally inaccessible to man. By his very human nature man can never cross into the reality that is God's. The notion of God's transcendence implies not only that God is, as it were, at the highest rung of a ladder upon which both He and man stand, that God is at the most subtle end of a continuum that leads from mundane man to Him. Rather, it implies that an uncrossable chasm divides man and God.

Imagine a blind man trying to appreciate a beautiful painting. It makes no difference whether he can appreciate fine art or if he is a student of art. Sadly, this individual lacks the basic faculties necessary for apprehending light, color, and visual form. There is simply nothing that can be done to enable the blind man to conjure up, in any way, what this painting looks like. No doubt, he might gain an abstract sense of the painting's beauty by way of analogy. For example, he might be told that viewing this particular painting arouses sensations similar to those experienced when hearing a musical masterpiece. Nevertheless, even this brings him no closer to a true appreciation of the wondrous colors of the painting. The chasm is unnegotiable.

Similarly, God operates on a different plane to man. God exists in a different frame of reference, and hence an uncrossable gulf divides him from God. Consequently, all descriptions the human mind might employ to apprehend God are ultimately inefficient. They are merely descriptions of what man encounters of God in his own, very different, frame of reference.

Moreover, unlike the blind man, God and man's realities are not parallel. They are not two experiences that share some common ground, whereby reasonably accurate analogies can be drawn from one to the other, as from a melody to a painting. Vision and hearing ultimately can be compared since they both are part of human sensory perception; they employ the same space-time coordinates. But when it comes to God and man, a quantum gap separates the former from the latter. Consequently, no analogy within one system can be used to describe both simultaneously. They cannot even be said to exist and be contained in the same realm. No adjective or metaphor appropriate to man's world can be used as an approximation of God. Thus, all descriptions of God, all adjectives employed with the aim of circumscribing His greatness, describe only how God manifests Himself, how He relates to our world—what He represents when He, through an otherwise impregnable veil, filters into the world of men. Thus, these adjectives can best be described as approximating what God *does,* but not what he *is.*

A freshman student, for example, would attempt to display ought but his highest intellectual acumen and knowledge when speaking to a professor. An ordinary person would be on his best behavior in the presence of a holy man. So it is through much of our experience: the informed, not the ignorant, can consult meaningfully with the expert; the talented, rather than the mediocre, can collaborate with the truly gifted; the strong, not the feeble, can spar with the mighty; the bright, rather than the dull, can converse with the brilliant; the noble, rather than the ordinary, can approach the sublime.

It is superficially assumed that in communicating with transcendent God, only man's most sublime features, only his spiritual features, can be of use. His more mundane dimensions must be suppressed and hidden. One observes how the emphasis of many religions lies far more in articles of faith and the importance of belief, rather than in commandments and the realm of action. After all, if it believes that it is specifically rungs eight and nine of the spiritual ladder that are appropriate in communicating with rung ten, then it is certainly they that are appropriate in communicating with rung one hundred and beyond. Thus, if one communicates with a righteous sage and *tzaddik* by speaking about Torah rather than about business, then surely one is led to believe that one can get closer to God through business matters. Only in the synagogue wrapped in a *tallis* does God listen, not in the marketplace when one is engaged in the pursuit of material wealth.

The problem, though, with this pattern of thinking is that it presupposes that God and man are in fact on the same ladder, that God is at the highest end of the same continuum as man.

But in truth the greatest divide separates all of man's faculties, including his mind, from God. Man is so infinitely removed from God so as not to be fit for any mode of comparison. The idea then, that heaven, faith, or the human mind is any closer to God than the stomach or the physical earth, is illogical.

How, then, can man apprehend God at all? If man is indeed infinitely removed from God, what can he possibly do to reach the Almighty? The answer is that this can be achieved only through divine revelation. *God must tell man* what He requires. Though man's activities cannot relate to God along the terms of their own frame of reference, they can be of value to God along the lines plotted out by Him, on terms man can never truly apprehend.

This insight reinforces the notion that physical *mitzvot* are in no way inferior to prayer or meditation. For inherently, neither is of value. And since God's instructions are the only clue to meaningful communication with Him, if God declares that physical *mitzvot* carry weight with Him, one must acquiesce, as one has no faculties with which to make an alternative assessment. Indeed, if one insists upon emphasizing one's faith when the Almighty has requested wearing woolen strings, *(tzitzit),* one ends up serving the God that has been created in one's own image. Religion is about serving God, not about one serving the conceptions of God that one entertains.

Judaism thus completely and utterly rejects the notion that God is found only in the heavens. The very first verse of the entire Torah reads, "In the beginning the Lord created the heaven and the earth" (Genesis 1:1). Clearly, the heavens are just as much a part of the creation as the earth, and it is immature and fraudulent to accept the heavens as serving as any more of a receptacle to God than the earth.

God is infinite and the *Midrash* expresses how "there exists no space on earth that is void of the *Shekhinah,* the divine presence" (*Numbers Rabbah* 12:4). And the reality of the world's nature is that it is just as Godly as the spiritual realm. It is only that the Godliness of the world is concealed, and the task is to generate light and illuminate the earth.

This is the deeper, more intimate meaning of the messianic era. The messianic era will be a time when all of the good and

Godly deeds performed throughout the past millennia, since the creation of the world, will shine. All of the myriad points of light engendered by the multitude of *mitzvot* will be joined together, thus creating one great beam that will dispel the darkness of the *klippah* and manifest the world's true essence.

8

THE MARCH TO VICTORY

A Jew who works to bring the Messiah is not merely executing the duties of a loyal servant, but is setting the stage for the full revelation of his Master in this, the physical world. The heavens are holy and God resides in the heavens. The angels are also holy. The knowledge that God promises that there will be a time when He will make the earth His principal dwelling place, in a revealed fashion, in a home built by the sweat and labor of human beings, is utterly remarkable.

It is possible to be totally oblivious to the overall purpose of the Torah and *mitzvot*. Even a devout Jew thinking too narrowly can be led to believe that it is not within one's ability to radically transform the character of this world and reclaim it into the domain of holiness. It is possible not to think of the profit or yield that the Torah is meant to bring about, but of individual details of Godly service that don't seem to comprise an overall plan. *Mitzvot* performed with this attitude are like a whole stockpile of incongruent pieces of a jigsaw puzzle. Although each piece is an important and beautiful entity unto itself, it cannot be placed together with other pieces to form a more perfect whole.

Being aware of this overall plan while fulfilling Torah and *mitzvot* is of pivotal importance. Imagine a soldier drafted into an army. His first task is to go through basic training. In basic training he learns to run, fire accurately, wear fatigues, camouflage himself, use a bayonet, develop an expertise in explosives, and everything else that will enable him to be successful in battle when the time comes. Most of all, he learns to take orders. He learns to subordinate his own will and his own way of doing things to the army's way of doing things. He accustoms himself to the fact that, come what may, his commander's word comes first. And he does so happily, knowing full well that the officers who are training him are far more educated in the art of combat than he is.

When the battle does finally come, the soldier executes his training perfectly. He fires accurately at the enemy, he mines the enemies bridges and devastates them, disrupts their communications, parachutes from planes directly on the desired target—in short, he is everything a soldier should be. There is only one detail this particular soldier is lacking. Unfortunately for everyone involved, the detail he is lacking is the most central part of his entire training. The whole purpose of the shooting, parachuting, laying mines, and explosives is for the army and his country to be victorious in battle and to win the war. This soldier is so preoccupied with executing his training perfectly that he has completely forgotten that none of the activities in which he is presently engaged is an end in itself. So he runs, fights, and takes orders—but for what purpose? He has forgotten his objective. He remembers that a soldier must take orders, but he does not even concern himself with the reason for his orders.

Being unaware of the overall plan can severely hamper a soldier's enthusiasm. To him, the war is barely different from a regular training exercise. He doesn't get emotionally prepared for the battle, nor does he tap into the vast storehouse of hidden human potential and bravery necessary to overwhelm the enemy.

This lack of familiarization with the overall objective can be dangerous. Since this soldier is more preoccupied with taking orders than fulfilling the objective of the orders, he can arrive at a point where he truly believes that his army is incapable of defeating the enemy. He can believe that the enemy is far better trained, more experienced, and more courageous than his own army. To be sure, even these thoughts will not deter the soldier from being loyal to the orders given to him, and he will continue to fight. He will fight because a soldier takes orders, whatever the consequences. But in his heart he will believe that his actions have no overall purpose and cannot ultimately bring about a victory. The morale of a soldier who discharges his duties without any hope for success is understandably low. He will obey his orders rhythmatically and robotically, devoid of life and excitement. Worse, this void of enthusiasm or confidence of victory will spread among his colleagues, and the whole army may be rendered ineffective.

Clearly, in order for an army to be victorious, each individual soldier must be conscious of the overall plan: vanquishing the enemy. With this knowledge, a soldier has a completely different perspective on the battle. He understands that with every bullet shot he weakens his enemy, with every mortar fired he frightens his enemy, with every bridge destroyed he cuts off the advance of the opposing army, with every communication intercepted he foils his enemies plans. In short, he is aware that there is absolutely nothing he does that is insignificant. Even the most trivial of actions, such as having a wholesome meal or a good night's sleep, gives him added strength to bring about what he is certain will be the final outcome—the complete retreat of the opposing army. When a soldier with this attitude is instructed to conquer a certain strip of land, he feels that he is not merely executing an order but that he is bringing to fruition an overall objective. Every piece of territory he conquers forces his enemy to retreat, until at last the enemy will be pinned down and cornered, outflanked, leading to surrender. One can also imagine the great fervor, determination, and strength of will with which this soldier will execute his duties. This soldier's attitude transforms not only the way he views the orders given to him, but also how he performs them.

The same is true of adherence to Torah and *mitzvot.* One must feel that with every *mitzvah,* with every act of kindness, with every moment of Torah study, even with every meal and with every moment of required rest, one is bringing about the dispersal of *klippah* and the establishment of God's kingdom on earth. This awareness will transform the way in which one studies Torah and fulfills the commandments. Any robotic actions heretofore performed out of habit will henceforth be energized and electrified with passion, will, and life.

But if one lacks this awareness, one becomes like the soldier who in his mind has surrendered to the enemy before he has even fired his first bullet. Of course, this does not mean that one will cease performing Torah and *mitzvot;* neither will one necessarily cease to believe in the coming of the Messiah. After all, the belief in the Messiah is one of the thirteen cardinal principles of Jewish faith. The individual unaware of how his *mitzvot* contribute might feel that the messianic redemption will probably be a product of great compassion, whereby God's mercy on his people will force the Almighty into sending the Messiah.

How sad it is that this Jew is oblivious to the relationship between these two quintessentially connected items: the observance of the Torah and *mitzvot* and the coming of the Messiah. He fulfills the Torah and *mitzvot* because he is a soldier. He is obliged to take orders. The Almighty created him to execute His will, and he does so. When he is questioned regarding the arrival of the messianic redemption, he replies that this is none of his business. It is God's business. And whenever God feels it appropriate, he will send the Messiah.

Furthermore, this Jew can even find ample rational ground for his and his generation's inability to bring the Messiah. He argues that if the previous generations of saints and scholars, who were far greater than now, could not bring him, then how can our time—a generation stripped of the piety of the previous generations, their scholarship, devotion, and self-sacrifice— bring him? Thus, he abandons control of the messianic redemption and relegates it to the domain of the Creator.

To be sure, in an actual battle it is not a single bullet that brings about final victory, but a whole series of offensives and battles, comprised in turn of individual bullets and artillery shells. Only when individual soldiers team up together as a force and fire together in conformity with the battle plan, and take orders from those who are overseeing their individual performance with the responsibility of orchestrating their individual efforts, together not only with each other but with those with more powerful armaments, such as tanks, jets, and artillery, that final victory is achieved. It is only then, through a combined effort of all the resources at the army's disposal, that they can encircle the enemy and subdue him. Every bullet fired does not hasten victory, but is an actual part of the victory. And so it is with the fulfillment of Torah and its commandments. Every good deed not only hastens the redemption and brings it closer, but serves as an actual part of the redemption.

Kabbalah, along with hasidic thought, describes in great length how every physical object possesses a Godly spark that sustains and vivifies each created object. The spark serves as the "soul" of the object, as it were (although in a much more limited form than in the case of a living creature's soul— whereas a human's soul is that part of him that enables life, movement, speech, and exercising will, the spark merely sustains the physical existence of the object). So dependent is each creature on this spark of divinity that without it, the object could not exist. But it is the physical dimension assumed by the object, as it occupies spatial-temporal coordinates, that conceals this inner Godly spark. Thus it may be said that the Godly spark is found in exile, or is (seemingly) disattached from its source while in the object. The spark wishes to unveil its true essence, namely, that even this physical object only exists because of the divine sustaining force hidden within it. Alas, the spark loses the battle to the object's outer material shell. It feels lost and abandoned. It feels caged in its physical husk, unable to feel its attachment to its source in holiness and spirituality. It waits to be redeemed. This spark needs to be freed from its material prison. This is done when the Jew utilizes that object for a Godly purpose, in accordance with the divine will. For instance, when a Jew drinks a glass of water and recites the blessing "Blessed be you O Lord our God, through Whose word everything came into existence," the Jew redeems and frees the spiritual spark lurking in the water.

This objective of refining material existence, which is accomplished via the uplifting of sparks of holiness, has a specific order which must be followed. Every single Jew has his own portion in the world that he is obligated to refine and elevate.

And it is this portion of the world that shares an intrinsic relationship with his soul and can only be perfected by him and no one else.

Generally speaking, in the Kabbalah it is explained that the world subdivides into six hundred thousand lots, or areas, each one in turn subdividing into many smaller parts. Correspondingly, the Jewish people possesses six hundred thousand *collective* souls, which is why at the giving of the Torah at Sinai six hundred thousand Jewish souls were present, representing the Jewish nation in its entirety, past, present, and future. Each one of these six hundred thousand in turn breaks down into millions of smaller soul fragments. Each of these fragments is qualitatively a full soul in its own right, since the soul loses none of its intensity as a result of breaking off from its source. It is much like the flame of a candle, to which the soul is often compared; a candle can light an infinite number of other candles, each sharing its exact characteristics. The hierarchy of souls is like the branches of a tree; although the branches can be distinguished individually, they are nevertheless connected and are parts of a larger tree. Each individual living today is ultimately connected with one of the six hundred thousand general souls that were present at the giving of the Torah at Sinai.

Every soul has its own individual plot of creation intrinsic to it. The soul's duty is to unearth the Godliness from its designated portion and express its real nature. This constitutes the entire purpose of a soul's descent to earth. The soul did not descend into a body only for itself, but rather to create profit from the Torah, that is, to transform the world into a dwelling place for God.

The Almighty leads every single individual, sometimes in the most inexplicable of circumstances, to the specific area designated for His elevation. At times a person, when he arrives at a place unexpectedly, tries his best to immediately return to his previous destination. But it is important to recognize that when one finds oneself at an unplanned destination, his arrival in this place is no coincidence. It is appropriate to say a blessing on a piece of fruit, pray one of the obligatory prayers of the day, or study a passage of Torah, since it was not coincidental. Similarly, the individuals one encounters in commerce and trade, school and the university, the health club and restaurants may be part of those he is meant to influence. Thus, opportunities to spread *Yiddishkeit* among Jews and ethical monotheism among non-Jews should never be missed.

Most people hold the opinion that one's freedom of choice applies specifically to where one goes, what one does, who one marries, and so on. However, this goes against the notion that one has no choice whatsoever as to the places one travels or the circumstances that fall into one's lap. Rather, what is within man's ability to choose and decide is this: once one has reached a certain destination or come into contact with a certain object, or person, one can choose what *to do* in that place or with that object. You can go to sleep in this place and ignore the divine providence that brought you hence, or you can do something constructive and positive, based on God's law as found in the Torah. You can fulfill the purpose of creation by doing something as simple as washing your hands for bread and reciting the grace after meals, thus elevating this location and unearthing the true character of the place. An individual possesses the ability to bring within God's jurisdiction each place in which he finds himself. But where one goes and whom one comes into contact with is outside of one's control. Thus one is not in control of where one is born, to which family one is born, whether one is male or female, who one marries, or where one lives. All of these things are preordained. The only determining factor in all these choices is the Almighty, Who, in His infinite wisdom, guides each individual to the specific portion with which he is spiritually connected.

Every single action and every single activity performed by the individual, wherever he finds himself, is an actual part of the redemption.

This is the true state of affairs, and it is to he who denies its validity that the *Mishnah* addresses itself when it says, "Woe to the people because of their affront (to the Torah) for whoever does not occupy himself with the Torah is called 'censured' " (*Ethics of the Fathers* 6:2). The Talmud goes even further by equating a generation in whose lifetime the Temple is not rebuilt with the generation in whose time the Temple was destroyed (*Yoma* 1:1).

The relationship between one who does work to achieve the ultimate objective of Torah study and the one who does not can be gained from a talmudic passage:

> Rabbi Shimon, Rebbe's (Rabbi Yehudah the Prince) son, and Bar Kapara were once sitting and studying a certain lesson together when a difficulty about a certain passage arose, and Rabbi Shimon said to Bar Kapara, "This matter needs Rebbe [to explain it]," and Bar Kapara replied, "What could Rebbe possibly be able to explain about this" ("There is not a single teacher in the world who understands this verse"—Rashi). R. Shimon went and repeated Bar Kapara's statement to his father, [at which] the latter became angry. [*Moed Katan* 16a]

Subsequently, Bar Kapara was censured for thirty days. In other words, Bar Kapara was insulting the knowledge of a great scholar, and he was punished with censorship—one step before excommunication—because censorship is the punishment given to all who devalue something of importance and deny the truth of a matter. And so, too, the individual who underestimates the true value and potency of Torah and denies its ability to conquer the coarseness of the physical world is censured.

It can now be even more fully appreciated why the belief in the coming of the Messiah is a cardinal tenet of Judaism. The coming of the Messiah is not merely a reward that will be granted to the Jews in recompense for their steadfast loyalty to God throughout three millennia. Neither is it a gift from God in exchange for all that the Jews have suffered through their long history. Rather, the Messiah is part and parcel of that steadfast loyalty and divine worship that the Jews have been practicing for as long as they have been a nation. It is a recognition of this inherent relationship between the Messiah and Jewish practice that brings the Jew to a greater appreciation, and thus a more wholesome fulfillment, of God's laws.

When it comes to the belief in the Messiah, it is insufficient merely to *believe* that one day he will arrive, but one must actually *await* his coming, as Maimonides writes, "I shall wait every single day for his arrival" (Daily Prayer Service, *Ani Maamin,* no. 12). Just as any soldier who finds himself in battle waits, not only to put his training to use, but ultimately to completely destroy his enemy in the final battle and to assert the mastery of his country over his foes, so too we await with great excitement and longing for the final day of redemption, when the Messiah will dispel the last remnants of darkness and God will dwell openly in His creation. It is only when one views his actions as part of a higher and greater plan, when one sees each individual effort as profoundly significant in the higher scheme of things, that one will yearn and pine to reach the ultimate objective. One's very heart and soul will cry out for the victory of light over darkness.

Thus, the belief in the coming of the Messiah gives life, energy, and perspective on the study of Torah and the fulfillment of its commandments, along with an immense sense of satisfaction and pleasure in one's individual participation in ushering in the day "when God will be king over the whole earth" (Zechariah 14:9).

9

STRENGTH AND LIGHT FROM DESPAIR AND DARKNESS

The beginning of every business involves an investment. *Investment* is the temporary loss of capital whose purpose it is to generate such a significant future return so as not only to recover the initial investment, but to generate a much larger sum of money. Stated in other words, every business first involves a sacrifice and what appears, superficially, as a loss of funds. Of course, this initial sacrifice can remain so, and the money can be utterly lost. But the real intention behind this investment is to generate an enormous gain many times the original investment. As Scripture itself states, "He who scatters can receive a manifold return" (Proverbs 11:24).

This same concept exists within the God–man relationship. Rabbi Yechiel ben Shlomo Halperin, author of *Seder Hadorot,* demonstrates God's ambition in sending a soul down from heaven. In his book *Erkei Hakinuyim,* under the heading of business, he explains that the entire descent of the soul into the body is an investment. At first the whole process of sending a soul down from heaven into a physical body seems to be both a sacrifice and a loss. Before the soul descends into this material world, it stands at the very pinnacle of spirituality and Godliness. As the Talmud states, "The soul is carved from underneath God's glorious throne" (see Isaiah 51:1). From this great spiritual plateau, the soul descends into a physical body, which also incorporates within it an animal soul and an evil inclination. In other words, from the highest revelations of Godliness and holiness, the soul descends to the abysmal depths of a world of darkness and evil, the antithesis of holiness.

Imagine a prince who grows up eating the fanciest foods, wearing the finest silk, and with servants at his feet to fulfill his every desire suddenly being deported to a labor camp infested with rats and vermin. This, and many more times this agony, is what the soul feels upon its descent to earth. For the soul, this is the ultimate in humiliation and degradation. Nevertheless, explains Rabbi Halperin, this descent should be viewed as an investment designed to yield great profit many times the investment of the original descent. For the soul will take an active part in constructing a dwelling place for God in the lower worlds, thus elevating the soul's position far in excess of its original state prior to its descent.

The purpose of the descent of the soul into the body, as explained in *Etz Hayyim,* by Rabbi Hayyim Vital, the foremost disciple of Rabbi Isaac Luria, is to perfect the physical body and man's animal soul. For it was God's wish to have His dwelling place specifically in the lowest of worlds, which, although full of darkness, could be transformed into a home for the Almighty. This transformation could not take place in the higher worlds, notwithstanding their exalted status. It was only in this world for which the higher creative process was initiated and that God's ultimate objective could be achieved.

But why was this world chosen by God for His home? In *Etz Hayyim,* it is explained that it is specifically this world that could yield the greatest return on God's initial investment. The profit gained in this world after causing the soul to descend from the heavens is what is known as *Yitron haor habo min hahoshekh,* the greater light that emerges from the midst of the darkness.

Anyone who has ever experienced tragedy and grief will appreciate just how great the joy that follows the tragedy can be. Imagine a newlywed husband and wife who are separated at the beginning of World War II, each thinking that the other is dead. Suddenly, after years of torture, loneliness, starvation, and pain, they discover that the other is alive. Can one imagine the magnitude of joy they would have experienced upon their reunion? It is specifically when one is immersed in a world that is void of all that is precious and beautiful that one can truly appreciate when the beauty returns to one's life.

Now imagine the predicament of the soul. Before its descent into the physical realm, it enjoys close proximity with God, only to be torn away from its source and submerged in a totally foreign environment. It is in an environment so contrary to its natural habitat that the soul feels utterly bereft of the former beauty that surrounded it. The soul feels pain and misery. In its new home, in order to have the most minute experience of holiness, the soul must fight its archnemesis, the animal soul, whose objectives and desires are quite contrary to its own. Yet, it is here, immersed in the heart of *klippah,* where the soul begs and longs to return to its former glory, that it can generate an infinite light. While fighting to overcome the constraints of darkness, the soul learns to harness its infinite powers and cause "light to emerge even from amidst the darkness" (see Ecclesiastes 2:13).

Thus we have here a significant "investment" and initial loss in the form of the descent of the soul into the body. Nonetheless, through this investment emerges an inestimable profit—an infinite light that could not have existed before the descent of the soul. In demonstration of this principle on a more human plane, anyone who has lived through a traumatic ordeal can testify to the fact that it is through the most trying circumstances that man's infinite character emerges. Prior to one's being tested with hardship, how could one be said to possess the qualities of fortitude, stamina, or strength. Just as an olive emits its bountiful oil only through being squeezed, such is the soul of man. This attribute of "the light that comes from the darkness" is accomplished by the soul passing through the test of fire—being caged in a physical body, but ultimately refining and elevating the physical. This includes even the animal soul and a person's portion in the world, as discussed earlier. Whereas before the descent of the soul the body and the animal soul were covered in darkness and knew no light, the *neshamah* (soul) instills within them Godliness, which dispels the darkness.

Jewish mystical disciplines speak of the world being divided into many parts, corresponding to the number of Jewish souls. Every soul has its portion in the world, which is its duty and its inheritance to refine and purify. Collectively, all Jewish souls elevate and transform the entire world.

This refinement is brought about through many different means. For example, when a person strolls through the street with thoughts of Torah on his mind, he brings about holiness into the entire area in which he is walking. Whereas prior to his stroll this area was a part of the world (*olam* in Hebrew, etymologically derived from the root word *helem,* meaning "hidden and concealed"), now the area radiates with the Godly light of the Torah. Every time a person gives *tzedakah* (charity) from money he earned in business or work, he is refining many elements of the world at once. Money is always connected with many different causes and efforts.

Think of an individual who owns a factory. The factory consists of industrial equipment that was made elsewhere. Parts for these industrial machines were made in a third factory, in which there worked a certain employee who eats his lunch in order to have the energy to operate and build these machines, and so on. As one might imagine, literally thousands of people from all walks of life have contributed in some way to this factory owner's ability to run his factory and thus create wealth. So, when this factory owner then gives a tenth or even a twentieth of his earnings to *tzedakah,* in accordance with Jewish law, he thereby elevates the food the worker was eating for lunch, the materials used to make the machinery, and so on, all the way up the ladder to include his very own body, which worked to make the wealth from which he supports the poor. Therefore a plethora of creation is consecrated to a higher good in one fell swoop.

It is for this reason that *tzedakah* is said to be "equivalent to all of the *mitzvot* of the *Torah*" (*Bava Batra* 9a). For whereas as each individual *mitzvah* sets out to refine a single part of the human anatomy, e.g., *tefillin*—the mind and the emotions, kosher food—the mouth and stomach, and Torah study—the higher faculties of intellect, it is *tzedakah* that refines and uplifts the body in its entirety. For man must utilize his every limb, his every muscle, and his every talent in being successful in the business sector. It follows that when he gives a portion of those earnings to charity, he elevates all of his faculties at once, and much more. *Tzedakah* is an all-inclusive *mitzvah*.

Birurim, the edification of the world, contains esoteric secrets beyond human grasp. It is only the Almighty, in His infinite wisdom, who has allocated and understands which person refines what portion of creation and through which means. What is certain, though, is this: there remains no portion of this world that is outside mankind's duty of working with the land and cultivating it. Thus, every single activity related to Torah and *mitzvot* must be connected with a physical object and a tangible concept because the Torah "is not in the heavens" (Deuteronomy 30:12). It was given here, in this world, for the purpose of making this world a holier place.

Should a person question which part of the world is his to refine, the Baal Shem Tov answered with his interpretation on the verse, "From God follows all the steps of man" (Psalms 37:23). He took "the steps of man" literally; when a Jew reaches a certain destination, he does so with divine providence. God brings every individual to the place that is his to perfect and to the sparks that are spiritually bound to his soul. The Baal Shem Tov also emphasized that an individual should never fret when he loses his way while traveling. It is God's intention to bring him to a place where he will perform even one Godly deed and thereby elevate the spark that was his from the beginning of time.

This was the message the Baal Shem Tov brought into the world and the legacy he left behind. He instilled within the Jewish world the conviction that, come what may, everything, from greatest to smallest, is guided by the hand of God. Nothing is chance or coincidence. Everything is part of a divine plan for the dispersed souls of Israel to develop the entire creation.

To continue with the analogy of a business investment, generally speaking, the more profit a businessman wishes to earn, the greater his investment must be. Thus, when a businessman invests huge sums of his fortune into a particular business venture, it is due to his desire to reap a phenomenal return. The same applies with the descent of the soul into the body. There are different degrees of investment. A soul en-clothed in a body during the time when, for example, the First Temple stood found a far more enlightened and a far more spiritual earth. The Jews all dwelled in the holy land of Israel, prophecy existed along with ten daily miracles in the Temple, which could be witnessed by all the earth's inhabitants. Closer to our time even, a soul forced to descend to pre-World War II Europe found a thriving Judaism and an incredibly high level of Torah scholarship. In such times, although there still is no comparison with physical earth compared to the soul's place in heaven, the investment was not as great as present.

But the world in which we live today, when Jews are dispersed throughout the world, with war plaguing the nation of Israel and the world at large, in an age when Godliness is enveloped by a double darkness, the investment of the soul is all the greater. Likewise, the gains are far greater than in previous generations.

What is this great reward that we are meant to reap from exile? The Talmud says in *Zevahim* (87b), "The reason for God putting the Jews into exile between the nations of the world was for them to win converts." The meaning of this statement is this: Externally it would appear that the exile is a punishment for the sins of Israel. Internally, however, the exile is not a punishment at all. Rather, the exile, like everything in creation, serves a divine purpose—that the Jewish people "win over converts." Is this referring literally to Gentiles who convert to Judaism?

Rabbi Shneur Zalman, in the *Tanya,* rejects this literal inter-pretation. After all, how many converts has Judaism gained from the nations of the world throughout the exile? A few thousand? Was it really worth two thousand years of exile, persecutions, crusades, inquisitions, and holocausts for a handful of converts? He explains that the intention here is not to win human converts to Judaism, but to convert the spiritual sparks. In the esoteric vernacular, these *nitzutzot* (sparks of divinity that sustain material existence) are referred to as "converts" that dwell between the nations. For every time we elevate them back to holiness, we are converting and re-deeming them from their mundane physical cage. It is for this reason that God exiled the Jews between the nations of the world; through the study of Torah and performance of the *mitzvot* for the sake of heaven, they should raise these spiritual sparks and convert them to holiness in the same fashion that a non-Jew converts to Judaism and becomes a member of a holy nation.

Clearly, then, the purpose of the exile is not to punish Israel but to gain profit while in exile. We must raise the spiritual sparks without which the messianic redemption cannot follow.

Following this same line of reasoning, the darker the exile becomes and the greater the difficulties and travail faced by the Jewish people in overcoming the darkness, the greater the harvest must be. In the language of the *Mishnah* this reads, "The reward is commensurate with the travail" (*Ethics of the Fathers* 5:21). Likewise, this great reward cannot be earned without an even greater temporary loss and investment, represented here by the immersion of the soul in a much darker world.

How can one honestly accept that with every additional act of Torah and *mitzvot* one refines the world and brings the messianic redemption closer, when one sees on a daily basis how the morality of the world seems to be sinking? It seems as though every day there is less light and more darkness. If the world is being refined through every deed one performs, then one should see more light and a higher ethical and spiritual standard operating in the world. Yet the reality seems to be the reverse.

The world is indeed on a path of refinement and spiritual uplift, which is an ongoing and never-ending process. But the reason why one sees more darkness than light is that, whereas in the previous generations the portions of the world that were refined by those giants of piety and righteousness were the higher, more spiritual parts of our world, today one is polishing up the last bits, which also happen to be the lowest! After all, Jews today have moved beyond the confines of the synagogue and the *yeshivah*. Jews are engaged in all aspects of material life, from the highest to the lowest.

Today, Jews participate in fields that would have been unthinkable just a hundred years ago. Jews are in television, broadcasting, the theater, politics, fashion design, and so on. In short, Jews today operate in parts of the world that have never been instilled with holiness. Were our grandfathers in Poland given the opportunity to make a *berakhah* while doing a trade on Wall Street? And was any *yeshivah* head ever given the opportunity to visit the palaces of the rulers of the world and teach them that God desires moral politics? Yet today, American presidents have been influenced to issue Congressional enactments encouraging an adherence to the seven Noachide laws. We are reaching parts of the world, which, while dark, are the final stages in readying the world for a messianic epoch.

As the historical process continues and generations come and go, each generation is assigned to refine a lower part of the world. Therefore, the very fact that the world can become darker and darker is a testimony to the fact that the portions with more light have already been completed and what is left to be illuminated are the last bits of darkness. While the previous generations who did not experience exile refined the land of Israel, the sacrifices brought in the Temple, and all those things readily associated with holiness, one's job today is to elevate the spiritual sparks in the lands of the nations of the world amid a darkness so thick that it can almost be touched.

One can look forward to the final elevation of the last few spiritual sparks, whose completion will finally usher in a messianic redemption. In that time, ''God will be king over the entire earth'' (Zechariah 14:9).

10

MOSES AND MATHEMATICS
MAKE A MESSIAH

Every Hebrew letter possesses a numerical equivalent, and the sum total of all the letters of a word is known as the *gematria*, or numerical equivalent, of the word.

The very first time the Messiah is mentioned in the Torah is in the blessing of Jacob to his children. In the Book of Genesis, Jacob blesses his son Judah with the words, "The scepter shall not depart from Judah, nor the ruler's staff from between his feet, until *Shiloh* comes. And unto him shall be the obedience of peoples" (Genesis 49:10). Commenting on the words "until Shiloh comes," Rashi, the classical biblical commentator whose intention it was to define the simple, rather than the allegorical, meaning of the verse, writes, "This means the messianic king, for the kingdom is his, and thus does Onkelos render it [that it applies to the messianic king as well]. And the aggadic interpretation [of the word *shiloh*] is *Shai Lo*, 'presents to him,' as it is stated 'Let them bring presents *(Shai)* unto him *(Lo)* that is to be feared' (Psalm 76:12)." There are other commentators as well who explain this verse as a reference to the messianic king. Rabbeinu Yaakov ben Asher, the *Baal Haturim*, explains that the words "until Shiloh comes" has the numerical equivalent of "Moshiah" (Hebrew for Messiah), both equal to 358. He goes on to explain that the word *Shiloh*, without the word *yavoh*, "will come," is also the numerical equivalent of Moshe (Moses), a total of 345. Thus is it also explained in the *Zohar* and the *Likutei Torah,* by Rabbi Isaac Luria.

At first there seems to be no difference in interpretation between Rashi and the *Baal Haturim.* Both men explain the verse as a reference to the Messiah. But when we delve into their interpretations, we see that the *Baal Haturim* says something different than Rashi and the other commentators. According to Rashi and those who concur with his interpretation, the reference to the Messiah is in the word *Shiloh,* whereas according to the *Baal Haturim, Shiloh* does not refer to the Messiah but to our master Moses. The allusion to the Messiah is only when we join the two words, *"Yavo Shiloh,"* "until *Shiloh* comes."

Why is it that the word *Shiloh* refers to Moses, while the words *Yavo Shiloh,* "until *Shiloh* shall come," refers to the Messiah? In Jewish writings, the word *"Yavo,"* "will come," is numerically equivalent with the word *Ehad,* "one" or "oneness," which is 13. Thus, most amusingly, what emerges is that the word *Moshe* combined with the word *Ehad,* one, gives us the numerical equivalent of Messiah.

To simplify matters, what we shall investigate is why it is that when we take the word *Moshe* and add to it the word *Ehad,* we arrive at the numerical equivalent of *Moshiah?* Why is it that "Moses" plus "one" equals the Messiah? What intrinsic relationship, if any, exists between these three concepts?

As for the relationship between our master Moses and the Messiah, it seems simple enough. The *Midrash (Midrash Rabbah, Parashat Shemot)* states, "Moses is the first redeemer and the last redeemer." The intended meaning of the *Midrash* with this phrase is that the ultimate redemption, set to take place at the end of days, is also connected with Moses. This presents a difficulty, for it is a fact that the final redemption will be through the Messiah, not Moses. Furthermore, Moses is a member of the tribe of Levy, while the Messiah will be a king from the tribe of Judah. What then is the explanation for the final redemption coming about through Moses? Although Moses will not actually be the final redeemer, the potential for the final redemption sprouts from the special power of Moses. Since Moses was the one who redeemed the Jewish people from

Egypt, he thereby also initiated a potential for the Jews to be liberated at the end of days from the longest exile. In actuality, however, the redemption will come about through the Messiah.

Moses was most connected with the Torah. So attached was Moses with the Torah that it is even united with his name, as the Talmud (*Shabbat* 99a) emphasized when commenting on the verse, "Remember the Torah of Moses my servant." Moses' entire being was permeated with Torah. He received it, studied it, taught it, lived it, and left it as a legacy to all Jewish generations till the end of time. Now this unique relationship between Moses and Torah will be duplicated by the Messiah.

In "Laws of Kings and Wars" (chap. 11), Maimonides explains that the important quality that will distinguish the Messiah from all other individuals that have lived before him is "his great mastery of Torah." As with Moses, the Messiah and the Torah will be inseparable. This also indicates how the final redemption is absolutely dependent on the Torah. It is in the merit of the Torah that the final redemption will be brought about. It began with the first redemption when Moses, who received the Torah at Sinai, took the Jews out of Egypt, and it will end with the final redemption, which will be carried out by the Messiah, but with the potential created by Moses, since Moses was the one who actually received the Torah. Stated in other words, since it was Moses who received the Torah at Sinai, and it is in the merit of the Torah that the ultimate redemption will take place, it is indirectly through Moses that the final redemption will come about.

Based on this interpretation, we can mediate between the seeming discrepancy of the interpretations of Rashi and the *Baal Haturim* on the word *Shiloh*. Although Rashi maintains that *Shiloh* is a reference to *Moshiah*, (Messiah) while the *Baal Haturim* holds that it refers to *Moses*, in essence they are saying the same thing.

The concept of the Messiah itself can be divided into two parts: (1) the potential for the Messiah and (2) the actual redemption and era of the Messiah. Although the redemption itself will come about through the Messiah, the potential for the Messiah emanates from Moses. This can be seen even in the

interpretation of the *Baal Haturim* himself. As quoted earlier,
he states that *Shiloh* is the numerical equivalent of Moses, while
"yavo Shiloh," *"Shiloh* will come," is the numerical equivalent
of *Moshiah* (Messiah). This means to say that when one adds the
concept of Moses, i.e., the potential for the redemption, with
"shall come," i.e., the *actual* redemption, which is what "shall
come" implies, one arrives at the full concept of the Messiah.
Without the words "shall come," i.e., without the actualization of the messianic redemption, one is left only with the
potential for the redemption, which is connected with Moses,
who allowed the ability to be redeemed. Yet, when this
potential is actualized, as exemplified in the word *"Yavo,"* one
arrives at the actual concept of Messiah, both in name and
numerical value.

Stated in other words, the potential for the Messiah, as is
exemplified in the word *Moshiah* is, on its own, incomplete. In
order for this potential for the messianic redemption to be
translated into the actual, something must be added. It is here
that one may utilize the second half of the *Baal Haturim*'s
words. The word *"yavo"* has the same numerical equivalent as
Ehad, meaning "one." Thus, Moses without "one" leaves only
the potential for the Messiah, while Moses plus "one" equals
the actualization of the messianic redemption. Simply written:
Moses + 1 = *Moshiah.*

The single most important and famous statement about the
unity of God within the Torah and the very test of Jewishness
is the *Shema.* This verse from Deuteronomy has been immortalized by both young school children, who must master it as
one of the very first Jewish sayings they learn, and by thousands of Jewish martyrs throughout the ages who have died
with these words on their lips. The *Shema* seems simple
enough: "Hear O Israel, the Lord is our God, the Lord is One"
(Deuteronomy 6:4). But on this most basic of Jewish verses, a
famous question is asked: Why does the verse say "God is
One"? It could have used an expression far more befitting the
Almighty, such as "God is *yahid, Unique, Singular, the Only."*
The difference between the two words is great, and, superficially, it would appear that "unique" is far more fitting.

The *Shema* is a statement about God's unity and is designed to express how there is only one God. But, the words "God is One" do not negate the possibility for other gods. On the contrary, the word *one* implies that others may follow it, only that this entity described as being "one" is the first among many. This is borne out by the fact that the number one is used in the process of counting. An illustration of this is the six days of creation. At the conclusion of the first day, it says in the Book of Genesis, "And it was night and it was day, day *one*" (Genesis 1:5). Immediately thereafter there follows day two, and then day three, and so on. Thus the word *one* not only fails to deny the existence of other similar entities, but it even seems to imply that alternative, albeit secondary, gods do exist.

On the other hand, the word *unique* implies there is no other existence besides God. He is unique and there is nothing else like Him. He is singular, *yahid,* and besides Him there is no other entity. For example, when we say that a child is an only child or that a person has only a single child, this immediately excludes the existence of other children. Why, then, when the Torah wishes to emphasize the indivisible unity of God and the fact that there is no other God beside Him, does it state that "God is one" and not "God is the only"?

There are two levels in the unity of God, known in the Kabbalah as *yihudah ilaah* and *yihudah tataah,* the higher and lower unities, respectively. The lower level of divine unity is achieved through the utter nullification of the world's existence to God. This comes about through human contemplation into the greatness of God, understanding His sublimity and infinite nature. As a consequence of this contemplation, the significance of the world's existence becomes diminished in the eye of the mind, until it becomes totally unimportant and is nullified completely. After all, a finite world, with all its material pleasures, when held up against the truly Infinite, can seem quite pathetic. Thus, a person is unimpressed by the existence of this complex and surrealistic world in the face of God's unity because, although the world may indeed exist, when compared with God, it is utterly unimpressive and absent.

The reason why this contemplation is referred to as *yihudah tataah,* the lower form of unity, is because it fails to see all of existence within God's unity, as a part of God's Being. This meditative discipline is so overwhelmed by the enormity of God's being that it chooses to deny and ignore the world's existence when confronted with God's impressive presence. This mindset cannot accept such a lowly world as having any significance in relation to God, much less be an actual part of Him.

But the highest level in the unity of God is not when the individual negates the world's existence, but when one understands that although the world does exist and appears as an independent entity, behind it all is God. Scratch the surface of the world, dispel its misleading darkness, and you will find God. It is this realization that the world is nothing more than an extension of Godliness that convinces man that there is no need to negate the world's existence in order to assert God. Since its true nature is Godliness, the existence of the world poses no threat to God's unity.

Achieving the latter form of divine unity is much harder than the former. The difference is obvious. The reason for the supremacy of the second unity over the first is that the first unity is not wholesome. The fact remains that the confrontation between the existence of the world and the unity of God has not been addressed, but ignored. It is as if the world continues to pose a problem, but we turn a blind eye to it, since the problem that is posed is utterly insignificant compared to God's greatness. So when the first individual is asked, "If God is 'one,' how is there a world that exists outside of Him?" his response is simply this: "God is infinite; the world is transient and finite. Therefore, although the world is there, it is unimportant and can be said not to exist. Thus, the truth is that there is only God." On other hand, in the latter unity the world poses no threat to God's unity and there is no need to nullify or ignore its existence, since it poses no contradiction to God's oneness. If it is true that the world is an extension of Godliness and what we see to be an independent existence is only an illusion caused by the concealment of God, then in truth the world is part and parcel with God.

This can be compared to the different attitudes taken by Jewish communities the world over to the existence of Gentile communities and non-Jewish culture. The purpose of the Jews as laid out in the giving of Torah at Sinai was to be a chosen people. Chosen for what? Does God play favorites? Was God's choosing of the Jewish people a statement of his desire for them to serve Him alone, without the participation of the other nations of the earth. To be sure, this was not the purpose. The Jewish people were chosen for a mission and that mission was to bring the knowledge of the one God and the demands He makes of man to all corners of the globe. This takes the form of the Noachide code—the Bible's universal code of universal ethics and morality, known as the Seven Noachide Laws, which entail prohibitions on idolatry, blasphemy, murder, sexual immorality, kidnapping, sadistic treatment of animals, and a postivite commandment to set up courts of law and uphold justice—as outlined by the Talmud and codified by Maimonides (*Laws of Kings and War,* chap. 9). What has happened, though, is that through rampant anti-Semitism the Jews have become suspicious of their non-Jewish neighbors and over the past two millennia have chosen to live in very sheltered, isolated, and ghettoized living conditions. This has had a dual effect. On the one hand, it has definitely served to preserve Jewish identity and the Jewish way of life. On the other hand, it has made the Jews utterly ineffective in their role of bringing Godly values to the Gentile nations. At the root of this problem lies the question of how one should view the non-Jewish parts of this world? Does one ignore them, deny their existence, and make brazen statements about how, when compared to true Torah values, non-Jewish culture is utterly worthless and valueless?

Is the world Godly? Or is only the synagogue Godly? Should Judaism devote its attention to developing the Godliness in Western culture, or should it be ignored and berated for being *goyish?* If one chooses to view the unity of God as an all-encompassing unity that includes all aspects of the world, then with joy and confidence one can set about the task of not only bringing Godliness to the non-Jewish peoples but unearthing their latent Godly potential. If one chooses the former attitude toward Godly unity, then it is obvious that one should stick to oneself and concentrate on enhancing revealed Godliness, building more *yeshivahs* and synagogues only, and not uncovering latent holiness.

The difference between these two outlooks also finds expression in deed. Following the logic inherent in the former outlook, there is a need to distance oneself from the material world and to lock oneself up in the Torah, prayer, and *mitzvot*. One cannot synthesize the world's existence with Godliness because they are antithetical concerns. The more one engages in worldly experience, the further he finds himself from holiness. The only path by which to reach unity with God is through negating worldly existence totally and utterly. This would make a strong case for religious worship consisting primarily of meditation, celibacy, material abstention, and all the other forms of withdrawal.

Indeed, this is the path that has traditionally embraced the transcendentalist views of God. Those religions that advocate God's transcendence of the world and His limited interaction with a world far beneath Him also advocate that man reciprocate by withdrawing, in whatever degree possible, from earthly existence. This popular *weltanschauung* was immortalized in the philosophy of Descartes and other protagonists of the Cartesian school.

Conversely, if we follow the latter approach to God's unity, one that can be described as *panentheism*, or that God is both fully immanent, while also maintaining a transcendental being and the world is *part* of God (as opposed to Spinoza's pantheism, which advocates that the world *is* God), there is no need to run away from or invalidate it. A Jew can be part of everyday society—participate in the financial community, the medical profession, the fashion world—and this will not serve to create a chasm between him and holiness. On the contrary, it will give him the opportunity to manifest the latent holiness in such ordinary activities as eating, drinking, and working—in short, in every human endeavor.

This is what Maimonides meant when he used the words "Know him in all your ways" (Maimonides, *Shemoneh Perakim*). A person should never see a contradiction and conflict between pursuing a life of business and fulfilling the Torah and *mitzvot*. The goal of every Jew should be to achieve synthesis between the holy and the everyday. Through this, the unity of

God is wholesome and encompasses every object, every emotion, and every atom so that the entire world proclaims the oneness and unity of the Almighty.

This too is the difference between referring to God as *Yahid*, "singular" and "only," and *Ehad*, "one." Referring to God as single and only nullifies the world's existence. The statement implies that the world is canceled out by the unique and overwhelming presence of God. Of course, this is not the desired state of Godly unity. The whole beauty of Godly unity is that it encompasses the whole world, which is created and sustained by God constantly, thus conveying the impression that the world as it appears today is a part of God. For this reason the Torah expresses God's unity with the word *ehad*, "one."

There is a well-known interpretation of the word *ehad* as referring to all of empirical reality. The word *ehad* may be broken down to the Hebrew letters *Aleph*, whose numerical equivalent is one, *Het*, whose numerical equivalent is eight, and *Dalet*, whose numerical equivalent is four. *Het* is said to represent the Seven Heavens and the one earth, thus begetting eight. *Dalet*, four, is said to refer to the four corners of the globe. The statement connecting the letter, then, is this: The entire world represented by the *Het* and the *Dalet* pose no conflict with the *Aleph*, which stands for *Aloofo Shel Olam*, the One Creator of the world. In the word *ehad* itself, the intrinsic unity of God and His creation is expressed.

Thus, the purpose of using the word *ehad* within the *Shema* is to express the highest consonance between God and His world and express the realization that God can be found in every sector of human life.

The difficulty, of course, with this realization is that although one might be willing to accept it in theory, one somehow doesn't feel it to be so. Every time one glances upon the outside world, one perceives an independent entity that stands in complete contradiction to its origin and does not serve as a testimony to a Creator. One doesn't see God or feel Him in the world. Rather one must be taught this concept in order to accept it.

And here is where the purpose of the Judaism and the Jewish

people comes into its own. The Jewish nation has a mission to remove the false veil that conceals the truth of the world's nature and to allow God to shine through the darkness and concealment. And with every passing *mitzvah* one does, and every moment of time one uses for the study of Torah, one thereby expresses how all of spacial-temporal existence can be reclaimed into the perimeter of holiness. It is seen retroactively how the world was never really separated from Godliness in the first place. Thus one literally removes the concealment from the Godly spark that exists within every physical object and allows the truth to glow.

Unfortunately, during the exile, permission is not granted for the human eye to see how every single one of the *mitzvot* brings about a transformation of earthly reality. But when the Messiah comes, when the world is refined to the point where it becomes transparent and the Godly sparks shine through, one will see how not a single action proved fruitless. "Then we will all see together how the Lord God speaks [reveals Himself]" (Isaiah 40:5).

But from where does a Jew derive this ability? If it be true that the world was created with the Godliness hidden and concealed, and in fact expressed in the definition of the word *olam,* or "hidden," in the very first place, how does the Jew have the power to overturn this concealment and express the world's true character? The answer is that this incomprehensible capacity was given through the Torah at Mount Sinai. Up to the giving of the Torah at Mount Sinai, it was impossible to reveal the Godly nature of the world.

Before Sinai, as the *Midrash* says, commenting on the verse, "The heavens are the Lord's, but the earth He has bequeathed to man (Psalm 115:16)," there was a divine edict "that the spiritual realm will not descend to the material world and the material world will not ascend to the spiritual world" (*Exodus Rabbah* 12:3). The spiritual and physical domains were totally divided without any possibility for synthesis. The amazing transformation that took place at the giving of the Torah was when this edict was annulled and for the very first time the spiritual and physical domains met. God came down to Mount Sinai and Moses, a human, ascended to the heavens. Here for the first time was a meeting between the Godly and the physical, and the effects of the giving of the Torah were also noticeable. Moses henceforth was referred to as a *Godly man*, and God left part of His holiness on earth in the form of the Torah and the *mitzvot*. Through this unique event, the Jewish people were given the ability to consecrate physical objects by using them in divine worship and infusing them with holiness.

Stated in other words, if redemption be nothing more than the true character of the world being expressed for all to see, then the possibility for redemption came about through Moses when he received the Torah. It was Moses who took down the barriers between heaven and earth, thus enabling a Jew to bring about heaven on earth.

The *Midrash* expresses this point aptly: "Abraham, our forefather, caused God's presence to descend from the seventh heaven to the sixth, Isaac caused the divine presence to descend from the sixth heaven to the fifth, Jacob from the fifth to the fourth . . . until Moses came along and finally drew the *Shekhinah* down to earth" (*Song of Songs Rabbah* 5:1). It was Moses who gave all of the world the ability to work toward *ehad*, the unification of God and His world.

What is missing is the actualization of the word *ehad*, the manifestation and revelation of the world as being Godly. Thus a unique equation is formulated: Moses, who gave the potential to express the true nature of the world and its Godly character, plus the word *ehad*, equals *Moshiah*. When the power of Moses is actualized through the work of the Jewish people in the fulfillment of Torah and *mitzvot*, then and only then will the final redemption come about through the messianic redeemer, and in that time God's promise, found in Scripture, will be fulfilled, "and the glory of God shall be revealed and all shall see with their physical eyes how God shows Himself" (Isaiah 40:5).

11

A HUMAN BODY IN HEAVEN?

When God instructed Moses to go down to Egypt and redeem the Jewish people, Moses initially refused, stating, "Send by the one you will send," meaning "Send someone more appropriate" (Exodus 4:13). Who was Moses referring to as "more appropriate"? The *Midrash* gives two possibilities: One is the Messiah, as the *Midrash* states, "In the hand of your Messiah who will ultimately redeem them." A second interpretation, found in *Pirkei d'Rabbi Eliezer* 40, maintains that Moses was referring to Elijah. In the words of this *midrash,* "In the hand of he whom you are destined to send at the end of days, as it is stated, 'Behold I send you Elijah the prophet.' "

Moses did not wish to redeem the Jews from Egypt and requested from God that the redemption come about either through the Messiah or Elijah the prophet. But how could Moses refuse? God comes to him with a personal request, asking him to undertake the task of redeeming the Jews from their long and tortuous exile in Egypt. Yet Moses declines to fulfill the wish of the Master of the world.

The reason why Moses refused was that he wished the redemption of the Jews from Egypt to be the final and ultimate redemption as well. Moses knew that should he accept the task of Jewish redeemer from Egypt, there would still follow an exile from the land of Israel, necessitating a future redemption through Elijah or the Messiah. He therefore suggested that this redemption from Egypt be carried out through one of those future redeemers, transforming the transient Exodus from Egypt into the epoch of the Messiah. Moses wished for the Jews to march into Israel and remain there forever. But God did not accede to his request and refused to make the redemption from Egypt the complete and final redemption.

There are many striking similarities between the redemption from Egypt and the ultimate redemption. The purpose of both is to bring the Jews to a great and glorious revelation of God. Egypt was a pagan and idolatrous land. Moreover, idolatry was actually built into the Egyptian ecosystem. Since all early cultures and societies were dependent on life-giving water that rained from the heavens, this created an innate dependency between human beings and God, who resides in the heavens. (Indeed prayers for rain existed in many early cultures.) Man undertook a subservience to God and a dependency on His life-sustaining facilities. The exception to this rule was Egypt. Egypt has no rain and subsists due to the Nile river overflowing its banks and irrigating the fields; hence, the Egyptians chose to deify the Nile rather than worship the invisible God. Egypt was a culture completely drowned in pagan values and false Gods. Thus the miracles wrought at the redemption of the Jews from Egypt in the form of the ten plagues, the splitting of the Red Sea, and ultimately the revelation of God at Sinai were not only in order to free the Jews from their oppressors, but to utterly crush the Egyptian culture through a glorious display of Godly intervention. After God revealed Himself through the miracles of the exile from Egypt, no Egyptian could ever take the deity of the Nile river seriously or deny God's existence. The same thing will happen in the ultimate redemption. As the prophet foretold, "As in the days of your exodus from Egypt, I will show you wonders" (Micah 7:15).

Nevertheless, there is also an important difference between the redemption from Egypt and the final redemption. The Godly revelation that took place in Egypt was brought about through God Himself. The importance attached to this fact is that whether or not the Jews were worthy of this revelation and redemption, it was God who chose to intervene in the state of affairs and make it known, for all the world to see, that He is the ruler of the universe. Thus it was God who chose to radiate His light. The world's Godly awareness came about from above.

In the ultimate redemption, however, the opposite will occur. The revelation of Godliness will not be from ''above'' as it was in Egypt, but from ''below.'' It will be brought about through the inhabitants of the world itself. Through three thousand years of Torah study and observance, the Jews will have refined the world to the point where it radiates Godliness. When the Messiah comes, we will witness the collective revelation of the Godly light glowing from the world itself.

For this reason, the redemption from Egypt was only a temporary redemption and will have to be augmented by the ultimate redemption. Since the revelation of Godliness came from above, the moment that revelation ceased, the world, which had awakened to a new reality during the revelation, immediately returned to its former state. It was not the world that changed but rather the world that was illuminated from a lofty source. This can be compared to a dark room that is suddenly illuminated when someone turns on the lights. As long as the light remains on, the room is illuminated. But the moment the light goes off, it becomes dark again. Likewise, at the redemption from Egypt, the world's natural order was only interrupted momentarily from the heavens. But the final redemption will be eternal and everlasting, since it will be caused by a transformation in the world itself. In line with our previous analogy, this can be compared to a room constructed of precious gems that glow in the dark. Whether or not one turns on a light bulb, there will always be light in the room, for the light is independent of an external source.

It was for this reason that God, in His infinite wisdom, did not concur with Moses to allow the redemption from Egypt to become the final redemption. For at the redemption from Egypt, the world had not yet been worked upon and sufficiently infused with holiness. It would take generations of keeping Torah and *mitzvot* that had not yet even been given, before the world could be sufficiently developed. And God's desire was for the world to become Godly through man's activities and chores.

To achieve a deeper understanding of this important concept, it is necessary to examine the difference between Moses our master and Elijah the prophet. What distinguishes Elijah the prophet from all other human beings who have ever lived is that fact that he did not die but ascended to heaven in a chariot of fire. All the other prophets and righteous men died and were buried in the ground, but the body of Elijah the prophet arose together with his soul into the heavens. Why did Elijah merit this incredible feat, and none of the other prophets or righteous men? The explanation given is that Elijah the prophet had refined his corporal body to such an extent that it matched the spirituality of the heavens exactly. The fact that it was a physical body posed no contradiction to it entering the heavens.

Before we elaborate on this point, we must deal with a pressing matter. Our praise and glorification of Elijah amid all the other prophets is acceptable, so long as we exclude Moses from this assessment. But we know that Moses did not merit ascending to heaven in a chariot of fire, but died and was buried in *Gai*. Of course, this seems to imply that Moses did not achieve the spiritual perfection of Elijah.

But the Torah states explicitly that "no other prophet like Moses has arisen in Israel who knew God face to face" (Deuteronomy 34:10). The Talmud explains the difference between the prophecy of Moses and that of all other prophets (*Yevamot* 49b). The prophetic visions of the average prophet could be compared to looking into a frosty glass. The effect of the opaqueness of the glass was to obscure the prophecy. But the prophetic vision of Moses was comparable to looking through a crystal-clear or translucent glass. A clear glass is something that does not distort or obscure the image being seen through it in any way. One sees the object on the other side of the glass the way it really is. This was the prophecy of Moses. He had reached such a transcendent level of prophecy that God did not need to obscure or distort the lofty ideas and concepts that he prophesied in order to make them tangible to a mortal. Amid

Moses' physical body he still was able to view the Godly world unhindered. On the other hand, all other prophets looked into an unclear glass. They did not see a vision the way it really was. What they saw was a vague representation of the object through which it became more palpable to the human mind and its senses.

Thus the prophecies of all the other prophets centered around allegory and parables that the prophets would later be forced to decipher in order to make sense of their prophetic vision. For example, the prophet Jeremiah foresaw the siege of Jerusalem and the destruction of the First Temple. But the actual prophetic visions were only symbolic of their inner content. The first vision that Jeremiah saw was "a rod of an almond tree" (Jeremiah 1:11). From this he was to understand that the siege of Jerusalem would last a mere three weeks before the city would be destroyed, just as an almond takes a mere twenty-one days to grow. Next Jeremiah saw "a seething pot; and the face thereof is from the north" (Jeremiah 1:13–14). From this Jeremiah was to understand that "out of the north shall break forth the evil upon the entire land" and that Jerusalem would be subject to a terrible siege that would devour the city's inhabitants, just as a sealed pot cooks all the food inside.

Thus one can appreciate the magnitude of difference between the prophecy of Moses, who saw Godly essence, and all other prophets, who saw mere icons and shadows.

Sifri says something similar. "All prophets prophesied with the word *Ko,* 'thus,' as in 'Thus sayeth the Lord.' But Moses prophesied with the word *Zeh,* 'this,' as in 'This is the thing that God hath commanded.' " The difference between the words *Ko* and *Zeh* is similar to the difference between a frosted glass and a clear glass, as explained above. When someone says *Zeh,* "this," he is speaking about and pointing to the object directly. One points with one's finger and exclaims, "This is what I'm referring to." But when someone cannot see the object itself but is rather speaking about something in general terms, he says, "Thus," as in "Thus (or in more modern terminology, such) is the thing. It is the way I am explaining it," but it cannot be seen. So, once again we see the qualitative

divide that separated the prophecy of Moses and all other
prophets.

Based on this explanation, how could it be that Elijah, who
had a far lower level of prophecy than Moses, merited that his
body should ascend to heaven in a chariot, but Moses did not?
Was Elijah then on a higher spiritual plane than Moses?

We might have been able to answer that when the Torah
speaks of Moses' unparalleled virtue; specifically it refers to his
soul. His body, however, was inferior to that of Elijah. Thus,
Elijah was able to ascend the heaven with his body, but not
Moses.

However, we find that Maimonides, in discussing the essential differences between the prophecy of Moses and the other
prophets, writes:

> In the midst of being communicated their prophecies, all
> other prophets were overcome by great dread and fear, and
> their bodies would shudder. Moses, however, was not like this.
> This is what the Scripture was referring to when it says that
> Moses spoke to God the way a person speaks to his friend.
> Which means to say, just as a person does not fear the words of
> his friend, so too, Moses had the ability to understand all the
> words of the prophecy he was being communicated, as if he was
> being spoken to as part of an ordinary conversation. [*Laws of the
> Essential Principles of the Torah,* chap. 7]

The reason why most prophets experienced "great dread,"
"shuddering," and total chaos in their bodily order was that
the sublimity of their prophecy completely overwhelmed their
corporeality. They physical bodies simply could not contain the
communication with God. Thus they had to divest themselves
of their physical dimension to whatever degree possible.
Moses, however, was left standing while being communicated
his prophecy. The sublimity of the prophecy did not overwhelm him at all. Of necessity we must say that the reason for
this extraordinary phenomenon was that Moses' body was so
refined as to make it a perfect receptacle to divine communication. The spiritual did not find the body of Moses an obstacle
to it. It was conducive to the holy spirit resting upon it.

Moses' body was just as exalted as that of Elijah, and much more so. The question then returns—why was it that Moses could not ascend to heaven with his coporeal being intact, as did Elijah?

People worship God primarily in two different ways: those who serve God with their bodies and those who serve God with their souls. To be sure, both of these individuals are serving God faithfully. There is only one Torah and the Torah's commandments apply to all equally. What the Torah demands of a person is the purification of his body through the Godly light of the Torah. What then is the difference between them?

The difference is one of emphasis. When those who serve God with their soul undertake the purification of the body, their principal concern is to remove the obtrusive shell of the body, thus enabling the light of the soul to shine forth through the body without any hindrance. Stated in other words, their principal concern is the revelation of the *soul's spirituality* and not the refinement of the body's crassness. But since the body interferes with this revelation when it acts as a cage to the soul, the body needs to be refined and purified. It will then no longer darken the soul's brilliance. So, in this mode of divine service, the emphasis is on the soul, with the elevation of the body serving as a utility to the soul.

On the other hand, the principal concern of those who serve God with their body is to uncover and release the Godly light that is hidden within the *physical body*. To them the radiance of the soul's light is not an end in itself, but a means by which to reveal the divine spark that exists within the body. Thus, their undertaking of refining and purifying the body of its corporeality is not merely to enable the revelation of the soul, but to elevate the body so that its own natural Godly light can shine forth. The Godly light of the soul, however, is necessary in order for this to be accomplished. So here the emphasis is on the body, with the soul serving the purposes of the body.

Thus, in the religious duty of refining the body, there are two different ways of going about it: (1) removing the concealment of the body so that it no longer serves as an obstacle to the revelation of the soul (in this model the soul is the end and the body is the means through which to achieve that end) and (2) revelation of the Godliness that exists within the body, with the soul serving as the catalyst to achieve this end (in this model the body is the end and the means through which to elevate the body is the soul).

Here we have the difference between Moses and Elijah the prophet. The central motif in the life of Moses was the incandescence of the light of the soul. This began even in Moses' infanthood. Upon observing Moses at birth, the Torah reports that his mother saw "that the child was good" (Exodus 2:2). In addition to the midrashic interpretation of "good" being a reference to the fact that the entire house filled with light at his birth, goodness is also a reference to the central concept that Moses represented.

A house symbolizes the body, since the body houses the soul. With Moses, as soon as he was born his house, or his body, was immediately filled with light. His soul immediately radiated its light through the body without any obstruction, as there would have been with another human being. If this was how it was immediately at his birth, it can be appreciated how the radiance of the light grew more intensely as well, until it culminated with Moses' unparalleled prophetic visions. It is also true that Moses' body was refined to the greatest possible extent, to the point where he could receive and retain the loftiest prophetic revelations without his ordinary bodily senses being disturbed in the slightest. Nevertheless, this did not mean that his physical body radiated with Godly light. On the contrary, the greatness of Moses was that his body never posed any impediment to the light of the soul. But Moses found his niche in serving God through the brilliance of the soul's light. Moses did not reveal the Godly light inherent in his body. To him, the body was a means through which the soul could achieve its full luminosity.

Therefore, when his soul departed from his body, the body needed burying and could not ascend to heaven in its existing form. In his lifetime Moses did not cause the body to radiate Godly light, and as such it could not ascend to heaven where it was incongruent with ethereal existence. His body was only translucent and spiritual so long as Moses' soul was enclothed within it and ablaze with Godly light. Once that light ceased, the brightness of the body ceased along with it. Therefore, it could not rise heavenward but had to be interred.

The prophet Elijah, on the other hand, was a servant of God with his body. Elijah's whole purpose was to reveal the Godly spark that exists within the physical body. Elijah worked and toiled with his body to the point where it glittered with Godliness. It did not radiate Godliness merely because of the soul embellished within it, but because the spiritual well that exists deep in the body had been unearthed.

It must be pointed out that the Godly light shown by Elijah was not nearly as high as that of Moses. No matter how refined and lofty the body becomes, it still never reaches the immensely high spiritual brightness of the soul. For this reason Elijah was of a lower prophetic status and could enjoy a lower level of prophecy than Moses. His body, too, could not contain the high revelation of the soul, as did Moses'. Nevertheless, Elijah possessed this great virtue of uncovering the Godly light buried within the body.

It was for this reason that Elijah's body did not have to be buried; he was able to ascend in a fiery chariot to heaven. Elijah refined and elevated his physical body to such an extent that it blazed with Godly light and therefore posed no barrier to the heavens. For Elijah, living in a physical body on earth was the same as being a celestial entity in heaven. His body felt equally at home in heaven and earth because he had made heaven on earth.

This difference between the virtue of Moses and that of Elijah also expresses itself in their influence on the world. Our teacher Moses brought into this world the highest Godly revelations that have ever occurred. This began while still in Egypt, with the ten plagues, continued with the splitting of the Red Sea, and reached its highest peak with the giving of the Torah, when God Himself descended on Sinai. Moses brought about such lofty Godly revelation that the *Midrash* states that "an ordinary maid saw more of God at the splitting of the sea than the greatest prophets in their visions" (see *Mekhilta* and Rashi on Exodus 15:2).

Notwithstanding this, all the Godliness generated by Moses was revelation *from above to below*. They all involved a

projection of Godliness onto the world from a source outside
the world. Thus they did nothing to refine, purify, or elevate
the world itself. The revelations induced by Moses merely
transformed the world for a very short time so that it no longer
impeded or obstructed the revelations of God on earth. At the
moment those revelations ceased, the world returned to its
previous and visibly un-Godly state. As long as God "stuck
around" for the splitting of the Red Sea, a maid-servant was
privy to the highest and most lofty revelation. But the moment
it finished, she reverted to being a simple maid. Neither she,
nor the world around her, had changed.

On the other hand, the effect that both Elijah and David had
on the world was to purify and elevate it out of its un-Godly
and physical state. They focused and concentrated their work
on revealing the latent Godliness within our world. They were
not interested in revelations from above as much as revealing
Godliness from the ground up. Their lives revolved around
digging deeply into the earth and unearthing its latent holy
character.

Stated in other words, there are two paths by which man can
meet God. The first way is for God to reveal Himself to man
from above. When this occurs, all illusions disappear and man
merits an exalted vision of the truth of existence, that there is
a God and an origin to the world and its inhabitants. What is
lacking in this occurrence is that it does not change anything
permanently. When the revelation is over, man returns unaf-
fected, to his daily chores. He may be a bit more knowledgeable
now about his own origins and the truth of the world, but he
has not lived Godliness, only seen it.

The second way that man meets God is by undertaking a
refinement and elevation of oneself to such a point that the
corporeality of material existence is shed from the body and
from the world and its intrinsic Godliness is permitted to beam
forth. This is not a revelation from above, but rather from
below. The world itself radiates Godliness.

This also marks the difference between the redemption from
Egypt and the messianic redemption. Although both of them
involve a very lofty Godly revelation, the difference is that
in Egypt the revelation came about from above, without the

world being permanently affected by it. The very fact that Egypt had to be subdued, rather than taught the truth and improved, because of their extreme impurity and unholiness, is a testimony to the fact that the redemption from Egypt did little to transform the world. It was a transient, Godly experience that left no visible trace.

Conversely, the final redemption at the end of days will be a revelation from below whereby three millennia of toil to unearth the Godly character of the world will materialize. For this reason, this revelation will be eternal and will bring about a profound transformation in the world. This new world order will be revealed through David the messianic king, who will be preceded and heralded by Elijah the prophet. It is specifically these two who were chosen for the task because it is their mode of serving God that has always concentrated on developing the latent Godliness of the body.

This explanation also gives new meaning to the verse, "And the glory of God shall be revealed, and all flesh shall see together that the mouth of God has spoken" (Isaiah 40:5). At first, the second half of the verse seems to be an outcome of the first half. Since God will be revealed, therefore all flesh shall see Him. The difficulty with this interpretation is that the verse itself seems to indicate that the two concepts are separate, that the latter half is in addition to the former.

Rabbi Menachem Schneerson explains the verse thus: "And the glory of God shall be revealed" can take place in two ways, either a revelation from above or a revelation from below. So when the verse says, "And the glory of God shall be revealed," one doesn't know what kind of revelation one is speaking of, from above or below. Therefore, the verse continues to state, "And all flesh shall see." With this the verse emphasizes that this revelation will come about through the "flesh," i.e., the body. The physical body will experience Godliness because it has been uplifted and refined to the point where it radiates Godliness.

The Baal Shem Tov once remarked that he was also capable of rising to heaven in a fiery chariot, like Elijah, but he declined to do so because he wished to fulfill the verse from Scripture, "You are dust and to dust shall you return" (Genesis 2:19). The

Baal Shem Tov was one of those who revealed the latent
Godliness of the body to the point where his body was one
with Godliness.

Hasidism, the legacy the Baal Shem Tov left behind, is all
about finding God within the world rather than causing it to
descend from heaven. In the correspondence of the Baal Shem
Tov, a story was found: "I asked the Messiah: 'When will the
Master come?' and he answered: 'By this you shall know: When
your teachings become public and revealed in the world and
your wellsprings burst forth to the farthest extremes, that
which I have taught you and you have comprehended, and they
also shall be able to perform unifications and elevations like
you, then all the *klippot* "shells" shall cease to exist and there
will be a time of good will and salvation.' . . ."

II

THE BELIEF IN THE RESURRECTION OF THE DEAD

12

WHY LEAVE THE GARDEN OF EDEN?

The thirteenth and final principle of Maimonides' Fundamental Articles of Jewish faith is the belief in the resurrection of the dead. Jewish writings stipulate that forty years after the coming of the Messiah there will be a resurrection of the dead, and all who are lying in dust will rise to new life. (Concerning great *tzaddikim,* saintly men, it is written that they will rise immediately after the Messiah's arrival.)

Perhaps due to the natural human disposition to reject such a radical concept, Maimonides goes to great length to emphasize its importance: "Resurrection of the dead is one of the fundamental principles in the Torah of our master Moses. There is neither Jewish faith nor any attachment to the Jewish faith, for an individual who does not believe in this" *(Introduction to Perek Helek).*

In his *Mishneh Torah,* too, Maimonides concludes that both the one who denies the concept of resurrection of the dead or the one who denies the coming of the Messiah are among those who have forfeited their share in *Olam Haba*—the Hereafter (*Mishneh Torah Hilkhot Teshuvah* 3:6).

Because Maimonides dealt summarily with the question of resurrection, and did not elaborate upon it as he did in regard to the other Articles of Faith, there were those among his contemporaries who criticized him for this summary treatment of this important topic. In order to dispel all doubts concerning

111

his stand on this important question, Maimonides wrote, some twenty-five years later, his *Treatise on the Resurrection of the Dead,* in which he reiterates unequivocally that belief in *Tehiyat Hameitim* is an integral and indispensable principle of Torah faith. Whereupon Maimonides cites two verses in Daniel concerning this matter, as follows:

> In truth, this Resurrection [principle], which entails the return of the soul to the body after death, was already mentioned, in no uncertain terms, by Daniel. Thus, he says, "And many of them that sleep in the dust of the earth shall awake. . . ." And the Angel said to Daniel, "But you, go to the end of all flesh] and rest; and stand in your lot at the end of the days." [Daniel 12:2–13]

Observing that he cannot do much more in this essay than reiterate that which he already stated in his commentary on the *Mishnah,* Maimonides writes,

> And I will state that the resurrection of the dead—which is widely known and recognized among our people, which is accepted by all groups among us, which is mentioned on numerous occasions in the *tefillot, Aggadot,* and supplications that were composed by the Prophets and the great Sages, who fill the pages of the Talmud and the *Midrashim*—refers to the return of the soul to the body after it had departed. Concerning this, there has never been heard any disagreement in our nation, nor does it have any [allegorical] interpretation [other than its literal meaning]. Nor is it permissible to rely upon any individual who believes otherwise.

Further on in this essay, Maimonides concludes with a similar observation:

> In conclusion, we have been informed prophetically [concerning *Tehiyat Hameitim*], whether on one or on many occasions, and it has been mentioned countless times by Sages of Israel, both of earlier and of recent times, and it has become widely publicized in our nation, and there is universal consensus concerning this, that the human soul will return to the body.

And this is the proper approach concerning the resurrection of
the dead.

This difficult concept requires enormous elaboration and
discussion, not to mention an outlining of its many facets and
stages. Notwithstanding this general need, there are two specific questions that immediately spring to mind.

First, what makes the belief in the resurrection of the dead a
cardinal article of Jewish faith? The entire Torah is true, but not
all the articles of the Torah are considered to be cardinal
principles of Jewish belief. When something is enumerated
among the cardinal Articles of Faith, the implication is that it
forms a foundation, a pillar that supports the entire structure of
Judaism. What, then, is so incredibly important about the belief
in the resurrection of the dead that all of Judaism rests upon it?

Second, the very concept of the resurrection of the dead
seems odd. Why is it necessary for a soul that has frolicked in
the Garden of Eden for thousands of years to suddenly be torn
from that wonderful abode and reenter a physical body and
repeat living on earth? Kabbalistic literature devotes much time
to describing how the souls in the Garden of Eden are constantly elevating themselves to higher and higher levels in their
knowledge of God. The Talmud (*Berakhot* 64a) finds a scriptural proof for this concept: "The righteous have no peace, not
in this world and not in the world to come, as it is written,
'They ascend from strength to strength' (Psalm 84)." What this
means is that there are elevations on a daily basis for the soul
where it enjoys a greater and higher revelation of Godliness. An
ascendance of much higher magnitude is enjoyed on each
anniversary of the day of the passing of the soul, known as
Yahrzeit. The following year the soul rises even higher.

Based on this insight, the sublimity of Godly revelation
enjoyed by the souls of our forefathers Abraham, Isaac, and
Jacob, for example, and similarly those of Moses and the great
prophets, the authors of the *Mishnah* and the Talmud, whose
souls have been in the Garden of Eden for thousands of years,
can be instantly appreciated. Why, then, is it necessary for
these souls to suddenly leave this exceptional abode and return
to this world in a physical body?

Practically speaking, it appears that resurrection of the dead is part of the reward promised by God for the observance of the Torah and its commandments. It would appear that this reward subdivides into two categories: one in the Garden of Eden, when the souls are separated from their bodies, and the other on earth, when the soul is once again enclothed in the body. The resurrection of the dead comes after the souls have already dwelled in the Garden of Eden; they must leave the Garden of Eden in order to be reenclothed in the body. We must conclude that the latter reward, in the form of the resurrection of the dead, is far greater than that of the Garden of Eden. If this were not the case, then the resurrection of the dead would be more like a punishment than a reward. But what kind of a reward is this? What could a soul possible enjoy more on earth, trapped in a physical shell, more than the Godliness in the Garden of Eden. How, in truth, is the resurrection of the dead to be considered a reward at all?

There are those who explain that the purpose of the resurrection of the dead is to provide reward, not for the soul, but for the body. Just as the soul has its own special place where it is rewarded in the Garden of Eden in its natural environment and habitat from which it was originally extracted, so too the body must return to its domain, where it too can be rewarded with the pleasures in which it delights. And being that a reward must always be qualitatively similar to its cause, the body must be returned together with the soul to the place where it earned the reward in the first place.

We find a similar thought expressed in the Talmud, where it relates how the body complains to God that it should not be punished since it was due to the soul that it sins. After all, without the soul the body is a lifeless mass. Likewise, the soul complains that it is the body that caused it to sin, for only after it materializes in the body can it commit a sin at all. The Talmud then uses an anecdote to describe how the Almighty settles this dispute: "A king chose two guardians to protect his garden. One was blind and the other a midget. What did they do? The blind man put the midget on his shoulders, and in this way they were able to eat all the fruits of the garden. The king returned, furious, and questioned them as to what had happened to his fruit. Each one explained to the king how he could not have eaten the fruits on his own due to his own deficiency. What did the king then do? He put the stout man on top of the blind man and judged them as one" (*Sanhedrin* 91a,b). So, too, says the Talmud, "God brings the soul, puts it into the body, and judges them together as one." Now, if this is said concerning punishment, it must also be the case concerning reward. Thus, if God wishes to reward the body, it must be done the way the body once existed, synthesized together with the soul. The resurrection of the dead is necessary to reward the body.

In truth, however, this explanation is insufficient. Whereas it may suffice in explaining why the soul must leave the Garden of Eden and again be reenclosed in the body, it does nothing to solve our second dilemma, namely, how it is possible that the reward for the soul enclothed in the body on this earth should be greater than its spiritual reward in the Garden of Eden. On the contrary, from this explanation it seems that the whole purpose of the resurrection of the dead is to reward the body, without any consideration for its effects on the soul.

13

WHY PERFECT THAT WHICH WILL DIE?

The resurrection of the dead is one of those concepts that best illustrates the superiority of the physical body over the soul. Although superficially the body seems not only subordinate but almost humiliatingly perverse in comparison to the purity, spirituality, and Godliness of the soul, the truth is that the body has far greater virtue than the soul. Therefore, so that the supremacy of the body over the soul be revealed in the messianic era, representing the culmination of the whole creative process, the soul will be forced to be reenclothed in the body. In this way, too, the soul will be able to benefit and share the lofty attributes of the physical body.

The knowledge of the body being superior to the soul is not surprising. The very fact that the soul is forced to leave God's environment and be enclothed in a body against its will is proof of the fact that it stands to gain from the experience. One should not underestimate the enormous decline and humiliation felt by the soul when it is forced into the body. An illustration of just how great a descent this really is may be obtained from the morning prayers.

Almost immediately upon awakening we state, "My God, the soul that You have given within me is pure. You have created it, You have formed it, You have breathed it into me and preserve it within me." A question that is posed concerning this passage is: If it is true that there is a whole procedure through which the soul comes into being, as the prayer implies, "You have created it, You have formed it, You have breathed it," why then do the words "it is pure" proceed "You have created it"? How could it be pure before it existed? The explanation given is that "You have created it" is a reference to the soul the way it exists after it has already entered the first created, albeit, spiritual world, known as *Olam Habriyah,* through which it must pass before it can descend further and reach the physical world. In other words, one should not believe that before the soul is "created" that it did not exist. Before it even began its descent through the spiritual hierarchy, the soul lingered in the highest of worlds, *Olam Haatzilut,* the world of emanation, a world whose makeup is not a *creation* of God, but an *extension* of Him. Kabbalah speaks of four "worlds," with only one actually being physical, namely, the bottom one, *Olam Haasiyah.* The three higher worlds, in order—*Atzilut, Briyah,* and *Yetzirah*—are all Godly, but in differing degree. The highest of all the worlds, *Olam Haatzilut,* bears its name because it is not considered to be a "created world." Rather, it is a world of "emanation." It is still an *emanation,* rather than a *creation* of God. As such, it is still technically considered to be part of the Godhead. The world of *Briyah,* though, bears its name because it is the beginning of something that is disconnected from the Godhead, or created. It is thus infinitely lower than *Aztilut,* although it is still a spiritual world.

This is the reason why the soul is referred to as being pure. It stands at the very highest plateau, higher than anything created. It is only after it is obligated to descend that the soul must take a quantum leap downward and reemerge in the created world. It is then that it is referred to as being a created entity. In the Hebrew language, the word *bara,* "created," a verb used in Scriptures exclusively with reference to divine activity, is explained by the commentators as referring to producing something out of nothing *(yesh me'ayin),* creation ex nihilo. As the Ramban comments, "There is no expression in Hebrew for producing something from nothing other than the word *bara,* '*created.*' Thus, the word 'created' symbolizes an object that is now unattached to God, since it is brought into existence as something from nothing. Thus, the magnitude of descent for

the soul can be appreciated. The Talmud expresses it aptly:
'The soul descends from a high mountain to a deep pit' "
(*Hagigah* 5b).

Why is this necessary? Why must the soul fall from such
unimaginable heights? The answer is that this descent is for the
purpose of a much greater ascent, later. Through the soul
descending into the body and experiencing the tension and
turmoil of being in constant battle with the evil inclination, it
merits a much higher ascent. The soul must fight for the human
organism to conform with the guidelines of Godly law amid the
conniving of the animal soul to frustrate its plans. But the
struggle bears fruit—the soul is able to ascend to an infinitely
higher level than where it existed previously.

To illustrate the concept of a descent for the purpose of a
later ascent, when the waters of a river flow without any
obstruction, they flow smoothly, calmly, and without great
force. But when one puts an obstruction in the path of the
flowing water, such as a large stone or tree trunk, the first
consequence is that the flow of the water is stalled and
sometimes stopped completely. It may even appear further
down river that the stream has completely dried up. But little
by little the water begins to gather more strength as it piles up
against the obstruction, whereupon it suddenly breaks through
the obstruction with great force and fury. So strong is the water
at this point that it will even pull the stone along with it, and it
will appear as if there had never been an obstacle in its path.
Interestingly, it is specifically the placing of the stone that
brings about the terrible strength and fury of the water after a
brief interlude in its flow.

This same principle applies to the soul. It is remarkably the
descent of the soul onto earth that brings in its wake the
strengthening of its power and heightening of its spiritual
acclaim. The impediments to holiness faced in this world, the
concealment and hiddenness of the Godly that forces the soul
to break through the darkness, serves to develop the full
infinite potential of the soul so that it rises even above its
standing in heaven. Tapping into hidden reservoirs of strength,
fortitude, and stamina, the soul flicks aside the obstruction that
the world poses to Godliness.

Another example of descent for the sake of ascent is the exile in which we find ourselves today. Exile is not a punishment for the Jewish people's misdeeds. Rather, the exile is only a preparation for the great revelations of the messianic era ahead. It is specifically through the trials and ordeals of exile that the Jew musters within himself high spiritual stamina he never knew himself to possess.

Certainly in Temple times the Jew was not called upon to unearth and reveal such deep-seated devotion and commitment in remaining observant and united with his God. Anyone who doubted God's sovereignty over the world could go to the Temple and see ten daily miracles. There was no room for doubt. To be sure, those generations had their own tests. But exchanging Judaism for materialism and craving acceptance by their non-Jewish neighbors were not among their tests. Today when Jews find themselves in Gentile lands, their thirst and desire for Godliness is heightened, and they are able to awaken greater strength to fulfill *mitzvot* and enhance their ability to draw nearer to God.

This will be better understood by way of yet another analogy. When a person finds himself in the desert or similar circumstances without water, his thirst for water is much greater than someone in the city, where water is abundant, even if objectively both of them have drunk the same amount of water that day. The very fact that the individual in the city can drink at any time he so desires causes his mind not to worry or think about water. But the person who is wandering in the desert knows that even if he wishes to drink, there is no water to be found. Because of this, he thinks about water, constantly making himself more and more thirsty.

The same is true during the times of the exile when Godliness is difficult to come by and the world's moral and ethical standards are on the decline. This causes the individual to thirst for Godly revelation and yearn for more holiness in his life.

There is a fascinating modern-day Jewish development. Thousands of people are returning to Jewish observance and struggling to bring more meaning into their lives. What is so interesting about this phenomenon is its cause. Rabbi Joseph Isaac Schneersohn of Lubavitch discusses the phenomenon of the *baal Teshuvah* (returnee) and asks what causes him to return? Could it be because of his sudden appreciation for the values of Judaism or that he thought Judaism would bring holiness into his life? Neither of these reasons can be accurate. After all, this is someone who in most cases has not grown up with Jewish observance or education. From whence shall he appreciate it? The rebbe concludes that in most cases he is not running to Judaism (which he does not know), but rather he is running away from where he is. It is not that Judaism may be attractive, but that he recognizes that his present situation is devoid of holiness and removed from Godliness. It is a sense of emptiness and despair in his life and a lack of meaning that motivates the returnee to run to God. This phenomenon could only happen in our times, when there is such a poverty of overt Godliness.

The way in which to overcome the darkness of the exile is to devote oneself tirelessly to bringing the Messiah. When one does so, one does not feel exile as this shady and awesome presence looming over him. Rather, the feeling is that one's whole being and the purpose of one's existence is to pursue this path in life, to dispel the darkness from the earth. This brings a person to feel that he is in control of his own destiny and truly free, rather than a prisoner of the exile. This was the inner meaning of the famous statement by Rabbi Yehoshua ben Levi in *Ethics of the Fathers,* where he states, "[It is stated in Scripture, 'the tablets were the work of God and the writing was the writing of God, *harut* (engraved) on the tablets.' Do not read *harut* (engraved) but rather *heirut* (freedom) for there is no free man except one who occupies himself with the study of Torah" (*Ethics of the Fathers* 6:2). The meaning of this statement is that one who sees God's unity encompassing all of existence will be liberated from the exile and the dominion of the animal soul, which lead man to feel that he is distant from God. Therefore, through a true appreciation of God's all-encompassing unity, and one's unique place within the scheme of things, one comes to know his true self, the self that is "always and united and attached to You [God]" (Prayer liturgy for Sukkot—*Hashannot*).

But all of the above is only one side of the explanation of the

virtue acquired by the soul in its descent to our world. Ultimately, this explanation is incomplete because it fails to recognize the virtue of the body and material existence. On the
contrary, this explanation dwells on the obstruction that the
physical poses to spirituality and its concealment of Godliness.
The physical serves to enhance Godliness precisely because it
obstructs it, as in the example of the stone in the river.
Accordingly, the virtue gained by the soul by being in the body
has nothing to do with the virtue of the body, but rather with
its un-Godliness.

Only a deep and proper understanding of the resurrection of
the dead will teach one the virtue of the physical realm and the
body over the spiritual realm. The resurrection of the dead
comes only after the soul has already been involved with the
body for a lifetime. Whatever gains or virtue it could possibly
have received from the body, be it from the body's positive or
negative aspects, it must have already received. The resurrection of the dead is also after the soul has reentered the Garden
of Eden, enjoying an infinitely higher level of spirituality than
it did before its descent. Here, too, it acquired whatever
attributes that are to be had in the Garden of Eden. Yet
notwithstanding this, it is still necessary for the soul to again
descend from its high standing in Eden and reinvest itself in the
body. This could only mean that the physical body, while in the
physical world, can give something to the soul that the Garden
of Eden and the highest spiritual worlds cannot.

The physical world possesses an incredibly strong Godly
presence, far higher than the Godly life force that sustains the
nonmaterial worlds. The reason is simple: the spiritual worlds
are worlds of light. In them God's radiance and splendor shine
visibly. From an analogy of the sun, we can appreciate that the
sun comprises two disparate concepts: a luminary and the light.
They are not the same. While the light of the sun may extend to
the entire solar system and the closer one is to the sun, the
greater the heat and the more intense the rays, nonetheless,
none of this light, no matter how close to the sun it may be, can
be put into a box. Why? Because it is only light and is not
source-independent. It is an extension, but not the essence of
the sun.

The same standard applies to the spiritual worlds. Because of their proximity to God, they are indeed lofty and holy. Nevertheless, they are merely a ray, an extension of God's light. They have none of God's essence. It is like the difference between the scent of an object and the object itself. The spiritual worlds are mere fragrance; they possess no tangible essence.

But our physical world is not a world of light. It is a world of essence. The reason is simple: This world was not brought into being through God radiating His light, but through God calling it forth from nothingness into a created reality. The ability to create something from nothing can only be done by God, Who is infinite. The very concept is inconceivable to the limited human mind. Thus, this world is a part not only of God's light, which of course shines naturally, but from an infinite creative act that involved God's deepest and most personal faculties. Insofar as God must constantly re-create the world in order to keep it in existence, as explained earlier, the very material of the world, what sustains it and what it is, in truth is God's essence. Our world emanates from God's deepest, most inner Self and must remain consciously involved with it in the most intimate manner. There is nothing closer to Him. In our time, though, God's sustaining life force is hidden. In the future, however, at the time of the resurrection of the dead in the messianic epoch, it will be revealed for all to see. One can only imagine what such revelation will bring. But one thing is clear. It will be infinitely higher than any revelation the world has enjoyed thus far, or any other experience that the soul could have experienced in the Garden of Eden. The messianic era will also not be a world of light. The essence of God that comprises our world will be seen.

This is the reason for the belief in the resurrection of the dead being counted among the Principal Articles of Jewish faith. Rabbi Shneur Zalman explains in the *Tanya* (chap. 37) that the purpose of the descent of the soul to earth is not really for the soul's advantage, the notion traditionally held in the Kabbalah. After all, the soul is not so bad off in the Garden of Eden. And although it, too, benefits from its descent, it would have been happy to remain right where it was. The real purpose for the descent of the soul into the body is the refinement and elevation of the body in its physical condition. The purpose of the Torah and *mitzvot* is to bring Godliness into an otherwise un-Godly world, thus consecrating all material existence. While it is true that this descent also benefits the soul, it is still not its principal purpose.

The same is true of the entire creative process. It is not the physical world that is created to serve the spiritual worlds. Rather, all the spiritual worlds were created only for the purpose of facilitating the development and nurturing of God-liness in the physical world and ultimately executing God's wish of creating a dwelling place for Himself in the lowest of all possible worlds. As explained above, this itself is accomplished through every *mitzvah* that refines a certain portion of the physical world. And through the cumulative activities of thousands of generations, we complete the polishing of the world until it is ready for the messianic redemption.

It is this knowledge that gives the individual the comfort and excitement in going about his daily religious obligations. He understands that he is working toward a glorious time and that his every activity plays an indispensable role. He understands that he is literally bringing God into his world.

But amid this sense of comfort, a discomforting and devastating thought sends a shock to the system. What good is it, one asks oneself, this ongoing elevation and sublimation of the body, when one day, in the not-too-distant future, the body will die and decay, reverting to dust and nothingness? Why labor seventy or eighty years in the refining and raising of the body to a higher state of perfection when in the final analysis the body is insignificant and transient? At least the soul goes to heaven. But the body goes to the grave!

Moreover, it seems that the ephemeral nature of life and the body is wholly part of what the body is. The Torah itself attests to the need of the body to return to the dust from whence it issued. "Dust you are, and to dust shall you return" (Genesis 2:19). The very essence of the body is evanescent, and by virtue of its natural condition it dies and decays. Therefore, even while the body is alive, it is not a 'real' existence in the Torah definition of the word, for the Torah equates all transitory existence with illusion and deceit.

This is derived from the Talmud in its discussion of the waters that were allowed to be used for ritual purification in a *mikvah*. Generally speaking, the water had to be drawn from a living spring. Among the water sources that were not to be used, the Talmud lists a "deceitful" river, *mayim hamekhaz-vot*. What exactly is a deceptive river? The Talmud defines it as any river whose waters cease their flow even once in seven years. The water's cessation indicates that this is not a living spring, a *real* river. And although now indeed it is flowing, its present state deceives the eye. It is not a "living spring," but a false and lifeless illusion.

Now, if something that expires is deceptive and valueless, what good is there in spending a lifetime in illuminating the body? Notwithstanding man's actions, it will revert to its previous darkness. This realization can be the cause of immense frustration and suck out the very life from the Jew who is dedicated to the purification of the body. It also serves to detract from one's understanding of the entire purpose of creation and the giving of the Torah. Hence, it is here that we can appreciate the central importance of the belief in the resurrection of the dead. The belief in the resurrection of the dead expresses the absolute truth that the expiration and corrosion of the body is only a temporary phenomenon. The truth of the matter is that the body is a very sublime entity, in fact an eternal one. Rabbi Shneur Zalman explains in the *Tanya* (chap. 49) that the Torah statement of God having "chosen us from every other nation and tongue" (Daily Morning Prayers) applies to the body, which "bears in its corporal state an identical resemblance to the bodies of the nations of the world" (*Tanya,* chap. 49). God did not choose the Jewish soul at Sinai, but the Jewish body.

What Rabbi Shneur Zalman means to say with this radical pronouncement is this: One cannot contend that the element of the Jew chosen by God is the soul, for what kind of choice could there possibly be with a soul. The nature of real choice is that it can only exist among identical, or at the very least, extremely similar objects. If one is told to choose between a pile of ashes and a pile of gold, is there really a choice? Must one enter into any conscious or even subconscious deliberations to determine which one to select? Real choice exists only where the objects to be chosen are alike. Thus, the quality of 'chosen' possessed by the Jew must pertain to the body and not the Jewish soul. For the Jewish soul, by virtue of its inordinately high spiritual character, made a choice between it and another spiritual form impossible. The Jewish soul is said to be a part of God Himself. What choice could there be?

What emerges from this proof is that the body is the possessor of sublime virtue and is the chosen of God. God's choice has lent to it the quality of permanence. God chose the body not for seventy or eighty years, but for all time. And although the body may expire and disintegrate, this is only a provisional state. In the messianic epoch the body will once again rise in the resurrection and will exist for ever and ever.

The belief in the resurrection of the dead forms a basic foundation of the Jewish faith. Thanks to this belief, one knows that the physical body, to which one dedicates one's entire effort in Torah and mitzvot, and for whose elevation one toils eighty or ninety years, is an eternal entity. One's struggle on behalf of the body will never be in vain. The body dies temporarily, only to reawaken to everlasting eternal life. As the famous principle of talmudic law teaches, "Any change that reverts back to its original condition is not considered to be a change at all" (Bava Kamma 67a; Sukkah 30b). Thus, the ongoing battle to purify, refine, and uplift the body and all material existence has an eternal result.

14

TO UNDERSTAND THE INFINITE

The most central question pertaining to the resurrection of the dead is this: How can the soul merit higher Godly revelations while lodged in a body in this physical world than in a disembodied and spiritual state in the Garden of Eden? This concept seems to run contrary to everything one assumes about the nature of spirituality. How could it be that "heaven" is subordinated to "earth." How can God be more on heaven than on earth? The fact that, as a reward, God will cause the soul to leave the heavens and redescend to earth indicates that indeed this world is greater. In fact, Nachmanides, in his celebrated treatise, *The Gate of Reward,* describes at length the phenomenal award that awaits the body and the soul at the time of the resurrection. He insists that this will be far superior to anything that exists today in the Garden of Eden. But how so? Is it not true that the spiritual is much higher than the physical? Is not the physical intrinsically limited? Doesn't it pose a challenge to the unity of God? Why then, in the belief in the resurrection of the dead, does Judaism insist that it is in the physical world, when the souls will be enclothed in a physical body, that they will have an infinitely greater understanding of God and revelation than in the Garden of Eden?

Moreover, this belief of the spiritual being more of a conduit to Godliness than the physical is not just human intuition. In fact, it is part and parcel of the reward promised as a result of fulfilling the *mitzvot*. Jewish mystical writings emphasize that in order for the soul to receive the reward in the Garden of Eden promised for the fulfillment of Torah and *mitzvot,* which is the Godly revelation generated by one's own activities in accordance with God's Will while on this earth, the soul must first rid itself entirely of the body. The soul must be cleansed of the body's physical needs, its material orientation, and its points of reference completely. Then and only then is it able to receive the Godly revelation in the Garden of Eden, which is, as is self-evident, a spiritual place.

So important is this need for the soul to utterly divorce itself from things physical that the *Zohar* asserts that so long as the soul has "any trace of this world upon it," any material residue or vestige, however minimal or insignificant, it cannot be permeated by the Godliness awaiting it in the Garden of Eden. The *Zohar* states emphatically that for the soul to take pleasure from the radiance of God's light in the Garden of Eden, it must first divest itself utterly from anything bodily or earthly. Only then can it bask in the divine light of the Garden of Eden.

We see, therefore, that not only is the physical an improper receptacle for the spiritual, but it actually impedes the soul from receiving God's light. And not only while on earth, but even in the Garden of Eden, after the soul has departed the body, any remnant of its bodily state serves as an impenetrable obstacle to Godliness. If this is all stated in reference to the reward that is given in the Garden of Eden in the hereafter, it applies *a fortiori* to the ultimate reward in the messianic era, when the spiritual revelation will be all the greater.

In actual fact this question breaks down into two parts. First, how can we in any way compare our physical world to the spiritual Garden of Eden in terms of each one's respective ability to contain Godliness? Second, even if we find some plausible explanation for this equality, we will still be forced to explain why the highest revelations of Godliness of all time will take place here in the physical world and not in the Garden of Eden. In short, the former half of our question pertains to the overall ability of the physical domain to serve as a conduit to Godliness, and the latter to the supposed superiority of physical domain as a receptacle to Godliness over the spiritual domain, to the extent that the soul will be forced to leave the Garden of Eden in order to fully apprehend God.

Concerning the first question of how the physical world can contain the infinite Godly revelation that will take place at the resurrection of the dead, Rabbi Menachem Mendel, author of *Derekh Mitzvotekha,* explains that the distinguishing feature of the higher spiritual worlds over our physical world is only in terms of a finite and condensed Godly light. In terms of raw revelation of God's light, the higher worlds constitute a more fitting receptacle to this light, while our world is not a channel to it at all. Thus, manifest Godliness does not reach our world and we find ourselves shrouded in darkness. But in terms of God's infinite essence, which will radiate in the times of the Messiah and the resurrection of the dead, this light is so immense, so lofty, so above our world *and* the spiritual worlds as to render the two absolutely equal in its presence. Neither our world nor the higher spiritual worlds constitutes any receptacle whatsoever to this immensely potent revelation. Thus, the spiritual worlds have no added virtue over our world in receiving the infinite revelation that will come in the times of the Messiah. If this awesome light can be revealed in the spiritual world, which is also infinitely removed from it, then it can equally be revealed in our world, which is at an equal distance from it.

After dealing with the sheer ability for the physical to absorb God's light in the messianic era, Rabbi Menachem Mendel focuses his attention on the second, more pressing issue: If the Godly light in the messianic era will be so lofty as to render the spiritual and physical domains equal, what superiority lies in our world that causes God to choose it for that revelation over the spiritual domain? Can the physical domain actually be higher than the spiritual? This issue, he says, is much more difficult and requires far deeper insight.

It is specifically the physical world in which there is laden much higher Godly virtue than the spiritual worlds, since it is the *lowest* of all worlds. In other words, the very facet of our world that makes it the lowest also makes it the highest.

One of the most important articles of Jewish mystical thought is the principle that states, "The beginning and highest is always anchored in the end and lowest part, and the lowest part is connected with the highest.'' What this means is that there is an intrinsic relationship between every beginning and every end, the highest and the lowest. The two are far better related than the middle point or any other points in the same continuum. In the eyes of Kabbalah, the highest, most lofty objects are always inherently related to the lowest, most coarse objects. Another way of saying this is that the higher something is, the lower it can fall.

One common example of this is that whenever a brick wall falls, it is the highest bricks that fall furthest from the wall. Of course, the same applies to many other instances of life. The higher someone climbs in social and political ranks, the harder they will fall. Similarly, it is specifically the greatest and most brilliant minds who are able to teach difficult academic concepts to the layman, or even schoolchildren. The higher one is, the greater the capacity to make oneself lower.

Greatness is not measured solely by one's ability to be big, but also by one's ability to be small. Being an Einstein necessitates the ability to teach Oxford professors, as well as the ability to write on the same subject in a way that be accessible to the lay audience. As it applies to God, possessing infinite power not only means the ability to create an infinite universe, but also, and especially, the ability to create a minuscule physical world. Infinite includes the possibility of being as big and as small as one likes. In fact, it takes far more skill for an artist to create a tiny masterpiece than a large one. The artist must employ his fullest skills in the precision and meticulousness necessary when working with something microscopic. Building a transistor or computer chip, or mapping the nucleus of an atom, can be far more difficult and impressive than building a skyscraper.

It is for this reason that our world, the lowest of all possible worlds, is intrinsically connected with the true Essence of God, which is infinitely higher than anything that ever was or could be. There is simply nothing that precedes God and there is nothing that transcends Him. This infinite, unlimited light has a relationship with and can be expressed only in the lowest and most mundane of all worlds. Stated somewhat more comprehensively, it is only God, the highest, most exalted Existence, who has the capacity to condescend to our world. And in this fact itself, it is God's most lofty faculties that must be employed in order to bring about this physical world. Thus, the world from its inception is involved with God's infinity. It is for this reason that the ultimate reward and culmination of the creative process will be found in this world in the form of the resurrection of the dead.

In the *Tanya* (chap. 48) Rabbi Shneur Zalman explains the difference between the finite and the infinite. "The term *reference* is understood in values where the figure 1 has a relevancy with the number 1,000,000, for it is one-millionth a part of it; but as regards a thing that is in the realm of infinity, there is no number that can be considered relative to it, for a billion or trillion do not attain the relevancy to the figure 1 in comparison with a billion or trillion, but it is veritably accounted as nothing."

To understand this basic and vital definition of infinity, let us once again use the number 1,000,000. The difference between one and a million is very great indeed. Nevertheless, there is certainly a relevancy between 1 and 1,000,000. This is very simple to prove since the number 2, or two 1's, is closer to 1,000,000 than 1. The fact that we can say that 1 is more distant from 1,000,000 than 2 shows that they both have a relevancy. By adding more 1's to the original figure we come even closer to 1,000,000. In short, therefore, although the chasm between them is immense, it is not infinite; and because the chasm is not infinite, the two numbers, however large or however small they may be, have a relevancy.

Another proof to the fact that 1 and 1,000,000 share a relevancy is from the fact that we can write 1 as a fraction of 1,000,000. In a mathematical equation 1 over 1,000,000 (1/1,000,000) expresses a new mathematical quotient: one millionth. The fact that we can describe 1 in relation to 1,000,000 in a mathematical formula proves that 1, even in the face of 1,000,000, is of significance. Of course, to divide between 1 and a 1,000,000,000 is even greater than that of 1,000,000 and is truly immense when we speak of 1 in relation to 1,000,000,000,000. At the same time, the number 1 never loses its relevance, even to those immense numbers, since it can always be expressed as a fraction of those numbers. In fact, we might even say that 1,000,000,000,000 is merely one trillion ones. So, notwithstanding how small a relevancy the number 1 may have to 1,000,000,000,000, it still has a relevancy and can still be spoken about in reference to a trillion.

But what if we have to try and speak of 1 with reference to infinity. This will be impossible and utterly meaningless. The number 1 has no relevancy to infinity whatsoever. The proof is that one cannot even use the two earlier formulations to display the relevancy between 1 and a million, or a billion, or a trillion. First, one cannot say that if one begins with 1 and adds another 1, one draws closer to infinity. No matter how many 1's one adds, one is still *infinitely removed* from infinity. So, too, if one has 3 or 4 or 5, or even if 1,000,000, one is no closer to infinity. The numbers 1 and a million or a billion or a trillion are *equally distant* from infinity, which proves that they are all *equally insignificant* in the face of infinity. And even if one begins with the number 1 and adds to it 1,000,000, one has come no closer to infinity at all. What this means is that in the presence of infinity, 1 and a million are absolutely equal, 1 and a billion are equal, and a billion and a trillion are equal. As far as infinity is concerned, they are both insignificant and cannot be expressed in any mathematical equation or be spoken of together, as if they were part of the same continuum.

Stated in simpler words, so long as we are speaking within the confines of things finite, the smallest, most limited object will always have a relevancy to the greatest and largest, albeit finite, object. This is because even the largest and greatest finite object is assembled from smaller, more limited objects. Therefore, it is simply impossible for the smallest finite object to be unrelated to the largest. But once we enter into a higher plane and speak of something limitless, the infinite, by definition, is not comprised of component parts.

To most people, the most tangible infinity is a number line. But this is a misconception. Although a number line may be nonending, it is not infinite. An entity is only infinite if it has neither an end nor a beginning, since a beginning constitutes a definition and a true infinity is totally undefined. If it has no beginning and no end, then it cannot have a middle either, or it may be said to possess an infinite number of middles. This is the same thing as saying that all its parts are exactly equal, and thus they are indistinguishable one from the other. The units or separate entities that constitute its make-up are not recognizable. They are drowned in the all-encompassing unity that characterizes the infinity. Therefore, there cannot exist a single identifiable "finite" unit within infinity. Hence, an infinite series of finite events or units is not possible. It is a contradiction in terms.

There is a uniform simplicity to an infinite entity. It is not complex in the way of something that consists of component parts. A true infinity has an consonant, indivisible character so that nothing can be related to it—it is infinite. Thus, the biggest finite object and the smallest finite object have no relevancy whatsoever to an infinite object. It is not only larger than they but is in a class by itself. It exists in a different dimension altogether. The greatest proof of this is that when one tries to add finite objects to reach the infinite, one grows no closer whatsoever to the infinite entity. Something finite has absolutely no relationship or comparison whatsoever to the infinite.

A cursory observation of the empirical world shows that all of existence subdivides into four categories: mineral and inanimate, vegetable, animal, and intellectual. This continuum of existence extends from lowest to highest. To be sure, within each category as well there are different levels. For instance, copper is of greater value, and is thus on a higher level, than simple stone. Silver is even higher than copper, and gold is higher than silver. Greater than all of these, of course, are the precious stones, which, while still part of mineral existence, are far more precious than metals.

At the same time, one cannot say that precious stones, such as diamonds and emeralds, are infinitely higher and have no relevancy with a rock. This would be totally inaccurate, for while the difference between a precious gem and a stone is great indeed, it is not infinite. The proof is that they exist on the same continuum. There is a ladder of existence that extends from the simple stone up through the less precious metals, and from the precious metals to the precious stones. This demonstrates the strong relevancy that exists among all mineral existence. Comparisons can be made between diamonds and gold, and between gold and silver, silver and brass, and so on. Although the difference in value and usage may be great, there is nonetheless a relevancy among them.

The vegetable is radically different than the mineral. It possesses a totally new dimension, called life. The vegetable expresses this life in the form of development and growth. Even the highest among the minerals do not possess these sublime properties of life and development.

But higher than the vegetable looms the animal, which has not only life in the form of growth and development, but life in the form of will and vibrance, movement and independence. Even the most developed plant is completely impoverished compared to the animal.

Standing at the very peak of created existence, far greater than any animal, is man. Man's life is qualitatively superior to that of the animal in that he has intellect. Intellect is what distinguishes man as the crown of creation. The ability to transcend instinct and impulse through rational thought and to act contrary to one's nature, to articulate and express emotion, to unite with fellow men by way of a common language—all of these attributes are unique to man. Man also has the ability, by virtue of his intellect, to recognize and serve the Ineffable. Man can exercise his freedom of choice to negate his indigenous disposition and pursue the higher things in life.

But amid all of these immense differences that exist between the different classifications of creation, they are nonetheless measurable objects that share a relevancy. Notwithstanding the sublimity of man's intellect, it is still limited. The fact is that certain animals possess intelligence as well, but we confidently maintain that man is more intelligent than animals. Thus, far from demonstrating man's infinite superiority over animals, his possession of intelligence demonstrates his affinity, his relevancy to the category beneath him. The fact that the two may be compared demonstrates their kinship. So man may be said to be superior to apes, and apes may be said to be superior to plants, and plants to minerals—thus all demonstrating the relationship that is inherent in all of created existence and the affinity that exists in all of creation subcategories. Since all of these categories are limited, their virtues and deficiencies in comparison with one another can be quantified. Anything that can be measured or quantified is, by definition, finite.

Furthermore, this relevancy continues and includes the spiritual sector as well. It would be absurd to believe that compared to angels, man and stone are equal. Just as we cannot say that compared to man, plants and stones are equal, likewise, while angels may possess far greater intelligence and overt spirituality than man, we cannot say that relative to angels, man and beast are equal. They are both finite and as such, even in the face of angelic being, man is still far greater than stone. On the contrary, it is far more plausible to say that relative to man, angels are great. We define celestial beings in contrast to man. The sublimity of angels may be their celestial intelligence. But this only serves to demonstrate their kinship with man and even animals. They may have more intelligence than both categories, but it is still limited intelligence and it is still something that is shared by man and, to a degree, animals.

Yet the gulf that separates all of creation from God is not relative but absolute. When compared to God, the loftiest celestial body and the smallest ant are absolutely equal. The chasm that exists between the angel and seraphs in heaven, on the one hand, and God, on the other, is the same chasm that exists between the dust of the ground and God. The distance in both cases is infinite.

Returning to our example above, just as in relation to infinity there is no difference between 1 and 1,000,000, likewise in relation to God, who is the only true infinite existence, there is no difference between the highest and lowest created forms. All of them are equally and infinitely removed. The best description of the relationship between God (as He exists on an infinite plane before He contracts Himself to create our world) and creation is that there is no relationship whatsoever. Nothing in creation, even the highest heavenly spheres, enjoys any proximity to God. *Tzimtzum,* or contraction, is the process whereby God undergoes a series of self-imposed condensations of His omnipresence, thus allowing for a *"makom panui"* or a place void of His presence in which a world can now be created.

The true question posed by the resurrection of the dead *is not* how God can reveal Himself in our physical world, of all places. Rather, the real question is how God can reveal Himself *anywhere,* even in the highest, most spiritual worlds. In comparison to God, the highest worlds and the lowest worlds are utterly equal. The Garden of Eden and the highest spiritual worlds are no less removed from God than the physical world. So how can God reveal Himself in any world? How can something infinite fit into something finite? Can an infinite amount of chairs fit into a ballroom? Can something infinitely smaller than God be large enough to retain His revelation?

In reference to the infinite Godly revelation that will take place in the messianic era, a revelation unlike all previous contracted and limited manifestations of God, our world is not inferior to the heavens in its ability to contain that revelation. Nor do the heavens pose any less of an impediment to the revelation of God's infinite essence. They either can or cannot contain Him equally. Whether they can or cannot serve as a receptacle to Him, they are both equal in what they can or cannot do. And if God chooses to reveal Himself in either of them, it makes no difference whether they are more spiritual or more physical; it is just as impossible in either.

With this, the difficulty of how the *physical world* can serve as a conduit to God at the great revelation that will take place at the resurrection of the dead is resolved. If the world cannot receive this revelation, then the highest spiritual worlds cannot either. And if they can, then this world can, too. Relative to God, both are removed by an absolute chasm.

15

A Tale of Three Sages and a Fool

Imagine a group comprising four individuals. The first among them is possessed of infinite intellect (of course, only theoretically). The ideas he puts forth are unlimited in depth, scope, and profundity, and they come in infinite quantity. The second individual is also a great genius who offers deep and impressive arguments and ideas. Nevertheless, he is different than the first individual because his intellect, while impressive, is limited and finite. The third individual is also intelligent, but his ideas are far more superficial and ordinary compared with the intellect of the second individual. The fourth and final individual, however, is an utter blockhead. Every idea he expresses is comical and ignorant. His thoughts are void of any logic. He possesses no rational intelligence whatsoever, other than that which permits him to communicate his stunted ideas. In short, he is an imbecile.

Although in comparison with the first individual, whose intelligence is unlimited, the latter three individuals, without any exception, are infinitely removed from him, nevertheless there is still a tremendous difference between the three. In comparing the features of the second and third individuals, although the former is the greater and wiser sage, they are still relatively equivalent in comparison with the sage of infinite intelligence. This is identical to the number scenario where 1 and 1,000,000 are identical in the face of infinity (see chap. 14).

137

They are both infinitely removed from infinity. Similarly, notwithstanding the intellectual superiority of the second sage over the third, neither of them is any closer because of their intelligence to the infinite intelligence of the first sage.

Yet, one must be extremely careful in understanding the divisions between the sages. What is the reason for the infinite chasm that separates the latter two sages from the sage of infinite intelligence? The answer that immediately springs to mind is the *intelligence itself.* Because the first sage possesses endless intelligence, this makes him infinitely ahead of his colleagues. But this formulation of the *infinite intelligence* being the distinguishing characteristic between the first sage and the latter two is absolutely wrong. In fact, the very opposite is true. The one thing that all three sages have *in common* is their intelligence. And it is this intelligence that allows one to compare and contrast the three, as well as to describe their positions in relation to each other. Had they not had this one common attribute, there would be no pretense by which to compare them at all. Their intelligence therefore does not divide them but *unites* and creates a relationship between them.

The real reason why the first sage is infinitely removed from the second two is not due to the fact that he has intelligence. Stated in other words, what distinguishes the first sage from the other two is not the *quality* of his intelligence (on the contrary, this is what he has in common with the first two), but the *quantity.* Because he has *infinitely more* intelligence, there is an uncrossable gulf between him and the others. It is how far his intelligence reaches that sets him far astride his counterparts. One looks at their limited intelligence as being insignificant compared to his infinite intelligence. And it is not because they have intelligence that they are incomparable to the first sage, but because their intelligence *ends* at a certain point. Because they quantitatively don't have *enough* intelligence, there is quantum gap between themselves and the former sage. Therefore, no matter how many wonderful ideas they offer, the first sage can offer an infinite amount more. It is for this reason that one dismisses the intelligence of the latter two sages as insignificant. Stated in simpler words, one dismisses their intelligence and considers it null and void not because of what it *contains,* but rather because of what it *lacks,* not because of what it *is,* but because of what it *isn't.* It lacks in infinite extension and quantity.

But this applies only when one is measuring the *intelligence* of the first three individuals in the party. But the moment one speaks with regard to the imbecile whose words lack any intellectual dimension whatsoever, the infinite chasm that exists between him and the first sage is due, not to his lack of *infinite* intelligence, but to his lack of *any* intelligence. In other words, he is incalculably removed from the first sage in a completely different way than his two colleagues. While the second two are distant from the first sage due to the fact that their intelligence *ends* and has *limits,* this fourth person is infinitely removed from the first sage because his intelligence *never begins* and his *ignorance is unlimited.* In simpler words, the immeasurable gulf that exists between the words of stupidity uttered by the fourth person and the infinite wisdom of the first sage is not because of the *quantity* of ideas put forth by former, but because of the *quality* of his thought. It simply lacks any depth. His immeasurable inferiority is a not a product of what he is *missing,* i.e., an infinite amount of something, but rather because of what he *has*—he possesses stupidity and dullness rather than intelligence and logic.

To sum up: Whereas the second and third sages are immeasurably removed from the sage of infinite intelligence because of what they are lacking in *quantity,* the fourth person is infinitely removed from the first because of what he is lacking in *quality.* One can draw no correlation or comparison between the first and fourth sages because, unlike the middle sages, they have nothing in common at all.

Whereas the middle two are separated by a quantitative infinite divide, the fourth person is separated by a qualitative infinite chasm. The middle two individuals, if their intelligence were suddenly to extend without end, if one were able to remove the limits on their ideas, would then be equal to the first sage. But the fourth person, even if one were to remove the limitations on his words and thoughts, even if he could think and express his personal thoughts for all eternity, would still remain infinitely removed from the first sage. All he would possess would be an infinite amount of *stupidity,* which is still a quantum leap down from intelligence. What makes him permanently removed, then, is the stupidity he possesses and not the quantity of intelligence he lacks.

Many philosophical disciplines, religions, and cultures are in the habit of defining God as the repository of all virtue, power, and greatness. To be sure, they accept that whatever man is, God is infinitely greater. Nonetheless, they define God in relation to man's greatness. Basically what they are saying is this: Any virtue possessed by man is in turn possessed by God in an infinite quantity. This is an accustomed way of defining God. What is God? Whereas man is powerful, God is all-powerful. Whereas man is knowing, God is omniscient. Whereas man is capable, God is omnipotent. Whereas man is present, God is omnipresent. Whereas man is mighty, God is Almighty. Whereas man is merciful, God is all-merciful. Whereas man may be a king, God is the King of kings . . . and so on.

By defining God in this way, the concepts of higher and lower, greater and lesser, bigger and smaller are used in reference to the Almighty. If all God represents is the most powerful, the most awesome, and the most incredible, if His definitive characteristics are the infinite quantity of everything man is, then obviously even the highest and mightiest bares a relationship with the lowest and weakest. God may be of infinite intelligence and because of that is infinitely higher than man. At the same time, this also means that God's superiority over man is only a quantitative one. Nevertheless, in that man possesses *some* intelligence, he exists on the same continuum as God, albeit at the very lowest rung of the ladder. Since man possesses some might, he shares a common feature with God.

It is amazing that people actually think they are doing God a favor when they pray to him and praise Him in the above manner by speaking of His infinite virtue. Does no one realize just how degrading this really is? Is it any wonder why Maimonides was absolutely opposed to adding more and more poetic adjectives in the daily Jewish prayers?

The reason that this view of God is so wrong, even dangerous, is that it characterizes the God–man relationship as analogous to that which exists between the middle two sages described above, and the sage of infinite intelligence. In other words, it is like stating that God transcends man infinitely not because of what God *is,* but because of what man *lacks.* The infinite chasm that separates man from God is due to man's lacking an infinite quantity of virtue.

Stated in other words, this is identical to saying that God is infinitely greater than humans, angels, and everything else; whereas angels and humans have some important qualities, God has an infinite amount of these same qualities. This would mean that God, angels, and men have something in common, i.e., virtues and attributes. Notwithstanding this consonance, there is still an infinite divide between man and God because God has an infinite amount of these attributes. Thus God's infinite superiority over man is not due to God's intrinsic nature, which is not qualitatively superior to man, but to the fact the man's powers are not endless.

But this is not the case at all. God is not merely the repository of all virtue and greatness. Rather human greatness, those things we laud most, such as intelligence, courage, mercy, love—these are all concepts created by God. In that respect they are no different than stone. Neither existed before the creation of the world. Therefore, the fact that every created being, from angels all the way down to rocks, are infinitely removed from God is not because of what we *don't possess,* namely, an infinite amount of qualities and virtues, but rather because of what we *do possess*—qualities and virtues. We are like the fourth person who because he speaks utter rubbish is infinitely removed from someone with intelligence. Because we are created, no matter how high we ascend on the ladder of existence, the most we can have is greatness and status created by God that have no association with Him whatsoever. He completely transcends all descriptions precious to man. He is qualitatively higher than anything possessed by man. Thus, the infinite gulf between God and creation is there because of what we *are,* not because of what we are not, or what we lack.

Applying this concept directly to the relationship between God and His creation, we observe how the infinite divide that exists between God and His world, even the highest of worlds, can be expressed in one of two ways:

First, if we define God as a Being that incorporates every form of virtue known to man in an infinite quantity, then God is infinitely removed from creation simply because creation is limited. God and creation may share many things in common, but ultimately creation is left in the dust, since God's greatness has no limits, whereas the creation ultimately comes to an end.

According to this superficial and flawed understanding of God, the infinite gulf separating God and man is not due to God's essence, which is not qualitatively different than that of man. On the contrary, the implication is that God and man share many things in common—they both have great virtue. It is just that God has an infinite amount of virtues that are also unlimited. It follows that being human is not what separates man from God. Rather, this is what man has in common with God. Being human means the possession of the same qualities as God. What does separate God from man on this level is the fact that man's attributes end. Man has only a certain number of attributes, and even those are limited, whereas God has an unlimited amount, all of which are inexhaustible. Clearly this perspective is identical to the example of the second and third sages, who are only separated from the first infinite sage because their wisdom is limited.

Second, even man in his highest form, with all his greatness, is infinitely removed from God precisely *because he is human* and possesses human traits. Even man's highest attributes, his intelligence, charity, emotion are qualitatively insignificant compared with God, who created these features in the first place. It is thus man's essence that divides God from man, because all of these concepts are merely creations of God and can in no way be applied to Him, just as God's creation of a stone cannot be said to have anything in common with Him. Thus it is not the fact that man's essence expires, or the fact that even man's higher virtues are limited, which provides for the infinite gulf between God and man. Rather, it is the fact that a human being, being what he is even in his greatest form, possesses only those things that are created by God and are utterly worthless, insignificant, and null in the presence of

God. This is like the fourth sage compared to the first—any idea he offers is worthless, not because it is limited, but because it isn't even intelligence. He shares nothing in common with the first sage. Likewise, the quintessence of man, from his toes to his brain, are insignificant and nonexistent when applied to the true perfection of God.

God's infinite Being transcends everything created. There is nothing in our creation that it is not catastrophically overwhelmed in the face of His glory.

16

IS IT GOOD FOR GOD TO BE IRRATIONAL?

It is common knowledge that the Torah has 613 commandments. What is not as commonly known is that all of these *mitzvot* in turn subdivide into three categories: *mishpatim, eidut,* and *hukim,* which translate as judgments, testimonials, and statutes. *Mishpatim* are those laws that can be apprehended by the rational faculties of the human mind—they are rational commandments. The category of *mishpatim* embraces all of Gods commandments, which, had it not been for the giving of the Torah at Sinai, man would probably have developed on his own. Man would have seen how these laws are indispensable to the development of society. An example of *mishpatim* are the prohibitions of murder, theft, adultery, and all other laws whose importance are comprehended by the human intellect.

Eidut, or, testimonials, are also laws that have a rational explanation insofar as they are a testimonial to an earlier event in Jewish history. This means that although one is unaware of their intrinsic explanations, one knows that they commemorate and remind one of his Jewish past and, in many cases, the miracles that God performed on his behalf. Take for example the law to eat *matzah* on Passover. No one knows the intrinsic reason why *matzah* must be eaten on Passover, save for the fact that the Jews ate *matzah* when coming out of Egypt. Thus one commemorates and relives the Exodus from Egypt by eating *matzah.* At the same time, this is not the deepest meaning behind the act. The same is true of sitting in a *sukkah,* an outdoor hut, during the festival of Sukkot. Being that God housed the Jews in huts during their wanderings through the Sinai desert, one commemorates God's benevolence by living in a *sukkah* for the seven days of the feast of Tabernacles. At the same time, the *mitzvah* possesses an unknown hidden explanation.

Finally, *hukim* are irrational commandments. They incorporate all those laws that have no rational or intelligent reason for man to keep them other than the fact that God has commanded them. As such, one must comply. A classic example of a *hok* is the Red Heifer, which was used to remove ritual impurity from those who had come into contact with the deceased. There is virtually no understanding of its curious phenomenon. As the rabbis stated regarding the Red Heiffer, "[The Almighty says] I have ordained this statute and have decreed this decree. You have no permission to question it." Thus one keeps the irrational commandments solely because one knows them to be God's will. One takes upon oneself the yoke of heaven and fulfills them without an explanation as to why they are necessary. *Hukim* incorporate commandments such as the obligation to keep kosher, to don *tefillin,* to wear *tzitzit,* and so on.

Generally speaking, then, all *mitzvot* subdivide into two categories: rational and irrational commandments. The first two categories, *mishpatim* and *eidut* being the commandments that are rational and intelligible, and the *hukim* comprising the laws that are irrational.

Rabbi Yosef Yitzchak Schneersohn explains in many of his written discourses that conventional wisdom maintains that it is desirable for one to try to fulfill the irrational commandments, whose explanation is hidden, in the same manner, with the same degree of life, enthusiasm, and excitement, with which one fulfills the rational commandments. After all, people are in the habit of "getting into" those things that they comprehend, as opposed to those things they can't appreciate. So, this seems to be quite reasonable. One should perform the irrational commandments with the same vigor as if he understood the reason. Yet, notwithstanding this conventional thought, Rabbi Yosef Yitzchak writes that the very opposite is true. The desire of a Jew should be to fulfill the rational commandments with the same degree of subjugation and subservience with which one fulfills the irrational commandments! The fulfillment of the Torah and its commandments should not be based on a rational conclusion that the Torah is sensible and thus desirable. Rather, the correct approach to Jewish observance should be that the individual bends to the yoke of heaven. A Jew is a servant to the Almighty, and a servant carries upon himself the will of his master. A servant has no will of his own. He need not understand the charges of his master. Rather, a servant serves as an extension of his master's will, regardless of whether he understands or agrees with them.

Although the Torah incorporates many commandments that are rational and agreeable to the human mind, the pretext for their fulfillment should not be what they have in common with human understanding but rather that they are all commandments of the Almighty. Even on the intelligible commandments one makes the blessing, "Blessed be you, Lord and God, who has sanctified us with His *mitzvot* and *commanded* us. . . ." This means that even these rational commandments are fulfilled not because they are compatible with one's intelligence, but because one has been commanded by the Almighty. Thus, even the *eidut* and *hukim* should be fulfilled with the same degree of acceptance of the will of heaven that serves as the pretext for the fulfillment of the irrational commandments.

Superficially it would appear that this revolutionary pronouncement pertains to the *fulfillment* of those commandments. The performance of the *hukim* should be executed with the same awe and subservience to God's will with which the *mishpatim* are performed. Nevertheless, Rabbi Menachem Schneerson (Rabbi Yosef Yitzchak Schneersohn's son-in-law) has explained on numerous occasions that his father-in-law's statement that the rational be equated with the irrational commandments does not pertain to their *fulfillment*, but to the *mitzvot themselves*. The difference between the irrational commandments and the rational commandments expresses itself not only in their fulfillment. First and foremost it expresses itself in the *mitzvot* themselves. The two are very different.

The essential difference between the two is this: A rational commandment is the will of God as it enclothes itself in human intelligence, while an irrational commandment is the will of God the way it is while it still transcends human intelligence. The difference is one of contraction. In the case of a *mishpat,* God has contracted and condensed His will, thus rendering it capable of fitting into man's mind. A *hok,* however, is the will of God before any contraction alters it. In a certain respect, an irrational commandment is therefore loftier. Its retains a close proximity to God the way He exists on an infinite plane, which is why the Talmud describes a *hok* as "a statute which *I* have ordained." Nevertheless, this in no way alters the fact that a rational commandment is, in its very essence, a part of the infinite will of God.

All of the Torah's commandments, human apprehension notwithstanding, are manifestations of God's will. Having said this, the fact that the irrational commandments are God's will is something one is prepared to accept. If one didn't accept this, there would be no pretext for their fulfillment. After all, one does not understand why they are important and perform them out of a simple acceptance of the yoke of heaven. The rational commandments, however, are understood by most people as having been commanded by God for important reasons. For instance, one is naturally led to believe that God prohibited stealing, for it would otherwise have led to the utter deterioration of society.

The truth, however, is that the rational commandments are identical to the irrational commandments. They were not commanded by God in order to preserve society or teach human beings how to behave toward one another. To believe that is to believe that the rational commandments are not ends in themselves and serve the purpose of promoting ethical behavior. But God's laws are not like governmental edicts. A government's purpose in legislating laws and setting police teams to enforce the law is indeed to uphold society. As the *Mishnah* teaches, "Rabbi Chanina, the deputy high priest, said:

Pray for the welfare of the government, for were it not for the fear of it, men would swallow one another alive'' (*Ethics of the Fathers* 3:2). God is not a means to anything. God is an end, and the same applies to His will. It is not so that because human beings feel strongly about murder, therefore God incorporates the law into His Torah. On the contrary, just as the irrational commandments are the supreme will of God, so too the intelligible commandments. The real reasons for these laws, as they exist with God, are not known.

The explanation why they do in fact make sense is that when God gave these commandments to man, He *created* an intelligible reason to exist alongside the law. For example, when God gave the commandment of sending away a mother from her nest before one takes her eggs—known as *shiluah hakan*—although the reason seems to be so as not to gravely upset the mother bird, the real reason is hidden. God desired that an intelligible reason be accompanied by this commandment, and thus He created alongside it a rational insight that makes man more receptive to its bidding. But the fact remains that one is no more knowledgeable about the real reason for this commandment than the irrational.

This is what Rabbi Yosef Yitzchak meant. Although they appear to be different, one should view the rational and irrational commandments as one and the same. They are both the intrinsic will of God. And although the rational commandments appear to have a reason, in their very essence they are the will of God, which completely transcends any human logic and apprehension. Why was it, then, that these commandments were revealed to man within the garb of human intelligence and reason? The answer is that this itself is the will of God. We might also say that God created a tangible explanation to accompany the *mitzvah* in order for a human being to better appreciate the *mitzvah* and thus enhance one's enthusiasm in its performance.

With respect to man, who is a limited creature, distinctions can be created between him and his will. But when speaking about God, who is "the most uniform simplicity," and is not made up of component parts or is synthesized together from different attributes, it is impossible to say that God's will is something separate or supplementary to His existence. Rather,

God's will is one and the same with His essence. They can never be distinguished or separated.

It is illogical to create dependency between God's existence and a preceding cause. For the most basic implication of a God is a being who is infinite, which precludes the possibility of there being anything that preceded or caused God. It follows that if God is indistinguishably united with His will, then just as nothing preceded or caused God, so too it is impossible to say that something causes or precedes God's will.

Based on this, it can be easily proved that rational commandments were not commanded by God because of the reasons one holds dear. If this were true, it would mean that the sequence of events is that first there is the realization that murder is wrong, and because God understands that it is wrong, He decides to list it among His prohibitions to man. Were this true, it would mean that there are causes that precede and bring about God's will. Actually, the reverse is true. Murder is wrong because God said so. To give any other explanation as to why murder is wrong is to imply that something precedes God's existence.

This happens to be true on a social level as well. Judaism believes emphatically that the reason why man must refrain from murder, or theft, or kidnapping is not because he believes it to be morally reprehensible, but because God commanded him not to do them. The foremost purpose of Judaism is to bring the world to ethical monotheism. Ethical monotheism is the doctrine that there is one God, that He is therefore the God of all people, and that God's primary demand upon people is that they live ethical—that is, kind, good, just—lives. Although this sounds simple, it is the most radical idea in human history, and it is the ultimate cause of the greatest hatred in history—anti-Semitism.

Ethical monotheism means that any belief in God that does not teach that God's primary demand is that we treat our fellow human beings properly will lead to evil. Throughout history, there have been those who committed evil in God's name. While they may have been believers in God, perhaps even in monotheism, they did not believe that God's primary demand is moral behavior. They believed that God's primary—and even exclusive—demand is correct faith, that God judges people on their faith rather than on their actions. Judaism holds that God judges all people on their actions far more than on their faith. In Judaism the most important question is not "How do you feel about it," as was the overriding concern, say, in the "sixties" generation, but "What are you going to do about it." In this respect, one can almost call Judaism "religious human-ism."

On the other hand, Judaism also repeats incessantly to the secular world that just as God without ethics leads to evil, ethics that eliminate God as their basis will also lead to evil. If there is no God, then good and evil simply do not exist. What exists are subjective opinions regarding desired and undesired behavior. If there is no God, what we call good and evil or right and wrong are merely euphemisms for personal taste. If one don't like stealing, he would label it "wrong." But another person may enjoy stealing and label it "right." But that is all it is—a label for personal taste.

A perfect case in point is Nazi Germany, one of the most scientifically and culturally advanced civilizations that ever was. Yet they were responsible for the systematic murder of twelve million innocent people. What is most amazing about the Third Reich, though, is that they also had laws against murder. Theirs was not at all an anarchist, lawless society. So how could they murder six million Jews? Very simple. The law against murder was made, not by God, but by the Nazis themselves. Thus, they had the right to designate who was protected under the law and who was not. That this is true is borne out by the following two illustrations.

Gideon Hausner, the chief prosecutor in the Eichmann trial in Jerusalem, was asked which feature of Eichmann he found the most reprehensible and frightening. He said unquestionably that it was the fact that Eichmann was a completely rational and sane man. That a human being who is mentally balanced and has a deep revulsion for the murder of other human beings can suddenly relegate an entire people to the standing of "subhu-man" and "fit for extermination" is incomprehensible.

Another story relating to the Holocaust involves a cremato-rium operator at the Dachau concentration camp. He performed his duties faithfully for two-and-a-half years. But one day he came home and shot himself. It was not in remorse for his actions. The note he left behind spells out clearly that this was not the case. It appears that on the day of his suicide, he arrived home from "work" to discover that his favorite French poodle had been run over by a car. Neighbors who had witnessed the event related that it was no accident. The motorist had seen the dog but had not bothered to stop. Shortly thereafter he wrote a note proclaiming how he could not continue in a world of such insensitivity and cruelty, and then he pulled the trigger.

It may also be argued, although rarely, if ever, admitted, that the systematic elimination of so-called lower species is completely consonant with the most Godless doctrine of all, the very theory that made secular humanism possible—evolution.

Witness the following quotations: "The more civilized so-called Caucasian races have beaten the Turkish hollow in the struggle for existence. Looking to the world at no very distant date, what an endless number of the lower races will have been eliminated by the higher civilized races throughout the world." Compare this with the rationale for euthanasia: "In nature there is no pity for the lesser creatures when they are destroyed so that the fittest may survive. Going against nature brings ruin to man. It is only Jewish impudence to demand that we overcome nature." Were these statements written by the same author? The author of the former was a scientist. His name: Charles Darwin. The author of the latter statement was a political leader who lived by Darwin's evolutionary ideology. His name: Adolph Hitler.

Sir Arthur Keith, one of Britain's leading scientists in the World War II era, had just been through the war, enduring with other Britons the awful suffering visited by Hitler on England and the world. He wrote the following statement, his understanding of the real nature of evolution:

> To see evolutionary measures and tribal morality being applied vigorously to the affairs of a great modern nation, we must turn again to Germany of 1942. We see Hitler devoutly convinced that evolution produced the only real basis for a national policy. . . . The means he adopted to secure the destiny of his

race and people [was] organized slaughter. . . . Such conduct is highly immoral. . . . Yet Germany justifies it; it is consonant with tribal or evolutionary morality. Germany has reverted to the tribal past, and is demonstrating to the world . . . the methods of evolution. . . . The German Fuhrer, as I have consistently maintained, is an evolutionist; he has consciously sought to make the practice of Germany conform to the theory of evolution. . . . It was often said in 1914 that Darwin's doctrine of evolution has bred war in Europe, particularly in Germany. . . . In 1935, a committee of psychologists, representing thirty nations, issued a manifesto in which it was stated that "war is the necessary outcome of Darwin's theory." [*Essays on Human Evolution*, p. 26]

Note the significance of Charles Darwin giving his most major work on evolution, "The Origin of Species by Natural Selection," the provocative subtitle, "The Preservation of Favoured Races in the Struggle for Life." Though in his book the discussion centered on races of plants and animals, he also included the various races of men in the same concept. If the criterion is mere power, and men may eat animals because they gained power by accidental evolution, then the murder of weak innocents "in the struggle for life" is but a logical result of the theory of evolution, which can recognize no distinction between cattle slaughter-houses and the German murder-factories, except the degree of "accidental evolutionary development."

Thomas Huxley, the man most responsible for the widespread acceptance of evolutionary doctrine, remarked, "No rational man cognizant of the facts believes that the average negro is the equal, still less the superior, of the white man."

With this kind of evolutionary thinking essentially universal, it is no wonder that the concepts of race were so important in the development of the master-race idea. George Gaylord Simpson, a leading evolutionist, writes that "evolution does not necessarily proceed at the same rate in different populations, so that among many groups of animals it is possible to find some species that have evolved more slowly, hence are now more primitive, as regards some particular trait or even over-all. It is natural to ask—as many have asked—whether among human races there may not similarly be some that are more primitive in one way or another or in general. It is indeed possible to find single characteristics that are probably more advanced or more primitive in one race than in another."

So, to put it in the starkest manner possible, if there is no God, one cannot say that the Nazis were wrong. All one may say is, "I don't like what they did." If there is nothing higher than man from which there emanates a moral will and standard, then the Nazis were not evil.

For the humanist, man and society are the arbitors of morality. But what about when society sanctions murder or declares it good? The humanist response to why murder is wrong, that it is rationally wrong, is this: "If you murder me, then I, in the form of my relatives and next-of-kin, will murder you, and we will all kill each other." This is the classical humanist response to why murder is immoral. The problem with this argument is that if a person knows that he can get away with murder, if you can, for instance, murder someone without being seen or caught, then the argument is totally shattered. Hitler knew that one could get away with murder, so did Stalin, and so do half the murderers in this world. What happens to the rationalist argument then? It is thus imperative that one comes to the realization that murder is wrong because God said so, not because man *feels* it to be so. There is an absolute standard of morality at work in the universe that precludes any possibility for moral relativism.

Now, it may be asked that if all *mitzvot* are humanly irrational, since they are the manifestation of the infinite will of God, why then are there *mitzvot* that carry with them a tangible explanation? As stated earlier, the difference between the rational and irrational *mitzvot* is that whereas they are both part of God's transcendent will, it was also God's will that certain commandments be rationally comprehended by man. Just as God willed for them to be performed by man, so too He willed them to be understood by man. He thus created alongside them a tangible explanation.

But why is all of this so important? Why is it essential that man recognize how decrees, even the *mishpatim,* are irrational? What positive outcome is there from this knowledge? The very opposite should be true. When a directive/instruction contains with it an important reason, it appears to enhance and upgrade the directive. The reason transforms it from being merely a command or order into something significant for its own sake. Although it may be important to execute a directive because of the very fact that it has been commanded by someone from above, it becomes even more necessary when one understands the reason for its fulfillment. Why seek to degrade, as it were, the rational commandments by removing the rationale from behind them? Why state that reason is not intrinsic to the commandment, but rather is a creation alongside it? By emphasizing that these *mitzvot,* too, are the will of God and nothing more, it appears as if one is sucking out the life and beauty from them, as well as the individual's enthusiasm in completing them.

Taking this a question a step further, when a person is given a command he cannot understand, his first thought is not that he has been given this command merely in order to fulfill the irrational will of the party giving the command. Rather, he thinks to himself that there is an important reason and that he is too young or unable to understand, at this juncture in time, the reason for the instruction; with the passage of time it will all become known.

Take, for example, a science student who is instructed by his professor to perform a scientific experiment that is tedious and cumbersome, bearing no overt relationship to the student's work. Although it makes no sense, the student will fulfill the request, not because it is the professor's decrees, but because of the rationale: My professor is far more experienced and intelligent than I, and if he tells me to do this experiment, then there must be a reason for it, although it is not intelligible to me at this moment.

In fact, this is what most people are accustomed to hearing from rabbis and other teachers of Judaism when they discuss the irrational commandments. The teachers try to dissuade people from thinking that the irrational commandments have no explanation. Rather, man, due to his lowly state, is unable to comprehend God's sublime motives. And the reason why these teachers of Judaism make this contention is because they think that they are enhancing the commandments in the eyes of the masses by stating that they do in fact have a concealed purpose.

In Hasidism, it is believed that the irrational commandments definitively have no rational or intelligent explanation whatsoever. They are, in their very essence, *decrees.* It is not just that man cannot comprehend them now. They will never be comprehended because they are nothing but the manifestation of God's supreme will, which cannot be rationalized. Furthermore, even those commandments that are logical are also, in essence, decrees with no justification whatsoever, other than the fact that they are God's will. The fact that they have a rational, intelligible reason is also part of God's decree. Thus, all the *mitzvot* are *absolute* commandments and, in relation to man, are just.

There are two ways to perceive the irrelevance between an infinite and finite object, or as it applies here, between the creation and God. The first way of thinking is that virtue, power, brilliance, greatness, and all other important things are the best way to define God. Since they are so lofty, He is the repository of all of these things and in an infinite quantity. Man also possesses these qualities, but, whereas man's greatness is limited, just as man himself is finite, Gods greatness is infinite. Thus, we speak not only of God being powerful but all-powerful, not only of God being knowing but all-knowing, not only of God being potent but omnipotent. This understanding is terribly flawed since greatness and virtue are concepts created by God. God Himself is infinite and has no limitations whatsoever and cannot be consigned to the human points of reference since He created those points of reference. In relation to God, one cannot speak of higher or lower, greater and lesser.

This faulty reasoning is made by every individual who struggles to find great and noble reasons to accompany God's commandments. For if one understands God as being the highest, greatest, most powerful existence, then so too when one speaks about other related Godly subjects, such as His commandments, must one find a reason to make them important as well. They too must be brilliant, sensitive, caring, and merciful. One is led to believe that through such rationalization one lends virtue to God and His Torah. Thus, when teachers of Judaism, who believe that God is perceived in terms of greatness, come across His irrational commandments, they state that no one should believe that they are not great, wonderful, and deep. Rather, the explanation is that the reasons are so deep that they must remain hidden. Thus, because one uses references of higher and lower in describing God, one applies them to His commandments as well, thinking that in this way he elevates God's *mitzvot* to a higher status by attributing to them profound explanations.

However, in truth God is infinite, beyond any created reference that could even describe how He transcends that point of reference. Being that God has no restrictions or bounds, when we say that God's commandments have no reason, this itself brings out their illustriousness, not their shallowness. If they were to have a reason, if they were to be considered great by our human standards, then they would really be vacuous and low. They would not even be united with God. For even if the *mitzvot* were connected with a reason or some rationale, even if this would be an infinite reason both in quality and quantity, it would still be limited, as explained. But the will of God, which is the essence of all commandments, completely transcends the very idea of intelligence. After all, intelligence is a very limiting factor and God cannot be limited.

God's *mitzvot* are decrees, simply the will of the Creator. They are the will of a true, infinite, and simple Existence who completely transcends any limitations and has no relevancy to anything human or worldly. Thus, when a Jew fulfills a commandment, even a rational commandment, for no other purpose than the fact that God has commanded it, he is transporting himself far higher than merely doing something moral, proper or worthy. He is now, via the fulfillment of the *mitzvah,* connecting himself with the only true infinite existence that totally transcends anything created.

It is for this reason that *mitzvah* derives from the root word *tzavta,* meaning to connect and bind. A *mitzvah* binds a Jew with God. Thus, not only the fulfillment of the rational and irrational commandments, but the acceptance of them as the will of God, elevates the Jew to the most sublime heights by connecting him to the Almighty, Who is neither high nor low, great or small, but simply infinite.

17

A Miniature Horse Must Be Hidden Somewhere

There is a story about a group of simple, unlettered farmers who heard about the news that was sweeping Russia. There was a radical new invention—a train. They could not believe their ears—a carriage that rides on its own without being pulled by horses! A wagon pulled by horses was something plausible to them; they had seen it themselves. But a horseless carriage seemed impossible.

After the news had reached them, the farmers sat together discussing this wondrous event. Each one offered a different explanation as to how it could be feasible. When no explanation sufficed, the farmers unanimously drew the only possible conclusion: It must be a hoax. There simply cannot be a carriage that travels independent of horses. Rather, hidden somewhere deep within the locomotive there must be a team of horses pulling the carriage. Some sinister charlatans must have something up their sleeves. The farmers then agreed that upon seeing the carriage for the very first time, they would expose the shysters by finding the horses hidden somewhere within the train.

When the farmers heard that in a few days' time a train would indeed be coming through their village, they all waited by the platform a few hours before the train was due. Upon arrival, they began searching it from top to bottom. Where were the horses? They knew that they were hidden somewhere in the train. However, they could not find any compartment large enough to place a horse, especially a team of horses capable of pulling the carriage. Could they have guessed wrong? There were no horses to be found, since there was no place to house them. Once again they assembled and reached the only possible conclusion. It was true that there were no big horses pulling the train. For if there were, where could they be? There wasn't any crevice large enough to hide a standard-sized horse. Rather, somewhere in that train there must be a very small, miniature-sized horse, and it was this horse that was pulling the train!

This anecdote provides a response for the human mind whenever it is confronted with something that transcends its comprehension, something larger than it. Human intelligence is prepared to accept the fact that there are things that are superior to it. What it cannot accept is that there exists something superior to intelligence and completely different than intelligence. While the human mind is prepared to accept that there are things on a more elevated plane and perhaps even infinitely higher than it, at the same time even those things are confined to the acceptable parameters of intelligence and logic, just as in the story. The farmers were prepared to accept that this train was radically different from anything they had seen before. It certainly did not possess the horses that they were accustomed to. *But, somewhere, there had to be a miniature horse.*

So, too, the human mind must use its previous experiences and channels of its own consciousness to apprehend those things that transcend it.

Rabbi Yosef Yitzhak Schneersohn of Lubavitch taught that, contrary to conventional wisdom, the rational commandments are to be viewed as being the same as the irrational commandments. Furthermore, Rabbi Menachem Schneerson explains this as applying not only to how the rational commandments should be fulfilled. One should not make the mistake of believing that because the rational commandments are intelligible, they are essentially different, and possibly more important, than the irrational commandments. Rather, in their very essence they are decrees. The intelligible reason that comes along with them are also part of the divine will, so that man can understand them, but this is not their intrinsic reason. One should not be led to believe that the rational reason for the commandments is anything more than a garment into which the commandments have been enclothed.

Why go to such great lengths to emphasize that God's will completely defies all intelligence? Why take even the rational commandments and prove that they too were unintelligible? Is it not true that everything in the world only assumes significance when it is grasped and appreciated? Why detract from the significance of God's commandments by going to the greatest lengths to emphasize that they do not have a reason? If somebody finds the *mitzvah* of charity exciting, sensitive, moral, and holy because he understands its rationale, why remove this from him?

All adjectives, such as importance, holy, intelligent, and wonderful, are concepts created by God. Each one demarcates something higher or lower in relation to something else, and thus it is impossible to use them as descriptions for the Creator. God has no relationship or relevance to any of other points of reference, and thus He cannot be said to be great. So, too, we cannot ask questions concerning the relevance and importance of His *mitzvot*. Questions of importance cannot be applied to God or His will, which is infinite. God's infinite will transcends utterly every notion of significance possessed by mortal beings.

There are things, such as God's will, that a mind can accept to so utterly transcend any human points of reference as to render them incapable of comparison to anything a human being can possibly conjure up. But to the average mind, this remains only theoretical and never practical. As the human mind fights this pressure to conceive of something that transcends human intelligence, it finds no point of departure. From where should it embark, from where should it begin in its understanding of God? Even extrapolation and abstract thought must begin somewhere. In fact it is plainly impossible. It is like asking the mind to be unintellectual. We are asking the mind to completely divorce itself of all its points of reference, of all the arguments, debates, and analogies it uses for logical deduction. It is stating that one cannot use any of these methods to apprehend God. In fact, one cannot use any means at all. Thus the mind returns and continues to question, Why must we continue to emphasize a certain object that cannot be rationally apprehended?

It is here that the parable of the train and small horse comes into its own. Just as the farmers who are only aware of one reality cannot even understand what it means for a train to move by means of its own steam, so too the human mind cannot admit any importance and refuses utterly to recognize something that transcends intellectual apprehension.

In chapter 9 of the second section of *Tanya,* Rabbi Shneur Zalman explains that the gulf that separates human intelligence and God is so immense that one cannot even state accurately that God is higher than intelligence. This is analogous to a student who has just absorbed a very deep philosophical insight. When asked to explain what he has just studied, the student responds that it is so deep that it cannot be grasped with the human hand. This is, of course, a singularly silly description. Had we been speaking within the confines of things that are physically tangible and apprehensible by sensory perception, then it might have applied. There are those physical objects that are so fine that they cannot be grasped with human hands. For example, if someone had seen fire for the first time and was asked to describe it, he might say that it is so sublime that it could not be grasped with a hand. One simply cannot capture it. A similar description might be given to a beautiful melody or a sweet scent, which, while physical, transcends human touch. But the one thing that all of these three—fire, sound, and smell—have in common is that they are tangible objects that exist in the physical domain. Thus, they all share the same points of reference. The only thing that distinguishes them from each other is their degree of corporeality. Some of them are palpable enough to be touched and captured, while others are not. But to describe intelligence as something that can't be touched is absurd. There is no relevancy whatsoever between the sense of touch and intellectual thought. They exist in different realms of experience. They cannot be accurately applied to one another.

Likewise, comments Rabbi Shneur Zalman, if someone were

to describe God as transcending intelligence, this would be as absurd as defining intelligence as transcending the sense of touch.

To better understand this concept, we may use an analogy of two people of very different degrees of intelligence. The intelligence of the first is very material and coarse. The extent of his comprehension begins and ends with his sense of touch. He only accepts the existence of those things that can be felt. If one were to approach this individual and inform him of a completely new entity that had just been introduced into the universe called intelligence or knowledge, his first questions would be: What kind of a substance is it? Is it soft or hard? Is it rough or smooth? Is it big or small? When one answers that it cannot be described as being any of these things, he will reach the only conclusion he can: This new substance, known as intelligence, simply does not exist. If it cannot be defined within the realm of his experience, he rejects its presence. After all, he only has his own points of reference at his disposal to judge information that he is supplied.

On the other side stands another man who possesses much finer intellect. When one tells him about this new entity known as intelligence, and describes how it cannot be touched or felt—he will accept our description as well as the existence of intelligence. But he will make the same mistake as the first individual, above. Just as the former rejects the existence of intelligence because it exists outside his reality, his points of reference, this latter individual accepts the existence of intelligence precisely because *he can use his points of reference to define it.* He will rationalize the existence of intelligence with the following thoughts: "So what's the big deal if intelligence cannot be touched. Isn't it true that fire can't be grabbed either? And what about sound and scent, which are even more intangible than fire, for they can't even be seen! They can't be described as being hard or soft either, and yet they exist." And he concludes that, likewise, there must be something even higher that cannot be touched, seen, heard, or smelled. It must be this object concerning whose existence he is now being informed.

One can already see the mistake being made even by this

individual. To him, intelligence is a physical entity that can be compared and apprehended through references to fire, sound, and scent. And although he accepts that intelligence is far higher and more refined than these lower objects, still there is a relevancy. But even for this individual to properly accept that intelligence is an entity bordering on the spiritual that cannot be compared with anything in the empirical world, not even the higher things such as sound and scent, is impossible. To him as to his counterpart, that which cannot be defined by using material points of reference cannot be defined or understood at all.

While this may only be an illustration, this type of thinking is actually rather universal. There is a story of a man who once came to the celebrated Rabbi Yosef Rosen of Dvinsk, better known as the Rogatchaver Gaon, one of the leading Jewish minds of pre-war Europe. The visitor had read the statement of Maimonides that the stars and higher constellations possess intelligence. He traveled a very long distance to the Rogatchaver to ask him how could this be possible and told him that although he is a believing and observant Jew, he found it extremely difficult to accept this statement of Maimonides. After all, how could stars have intelligence? The Rogatchaver, who was known for his sharpish tongue, looked the man in the eye and said to him, "Bullock! And how intelligence rests within the grey matter of your brain *is* understandable to you?" In other words, the man was willing to accept the existence of his own intelligence without even considering how absurd even that possibility seemed within the cells of the human organism. What he couldn't accept was how an inanimate object such as a star burning hydrogen gas could possess intelligence.

This matches almost exactly what transpires when the human mind is told that there exists a Godly entity that utterly transcends rational confines. One takes for granted that everything that is true to our reality, whether it is understood or not, is the best way by which to apprehend something higher.

In truth the two people in the anecdote and the one in the story are not really different people at all, but the same individual. All have the exact same way of going about their arguments and their rationalizations. They are one and the same person because they reflect the deficiency in all people, indeed, the very shortcomings of being human. Thus they represent the human race itself. Every created being is unable to negate the constraints of its own existence. One simply cannot divorce oneself from the points of reference used to define one's existence. And while an entity is willing to accept that there is something higher than itself, even something that totally transcends whatever *it* is, even this supremacy will be seen subconsciously within the same coordinates and parameters as human existence. No wonder then that one finds oneself naturally gravitating toward descriptions of God being big, great, awesome, and mighty—things that we believe make something worthy and noble.

Returning to the anecdote of the small horse, the farmers simply could not accept that a train traveled on its own. What's more, they even preferred to accept the existence of complete absurdity—a miniature horse—rather than something radically different to their realm of experience. The same thing is true of our approach to understanding God.

If a person's intelligence is coarse and crude, he might immediately dismiss all of spirituality as an impossibility. He will argue that anything that exists outside the parameters of verifiable earthy experience simply doesn't exist, just as the first individual in our previous anecdote immediately dismisses the existence of intelligence because it cannot be touched, felt, or sensed. Similarly, this same type of individual would dismiss the spiritual and Godly realm completely.

But notwithstanding the superficial approach of this person, even someone possessed of a more refined and engaging intellect—who would accept the existence of a spiritual entity that transcends intelligence—would still define God as "a higher form of intelligence." Here we have the explanation of why this bizarre method to describe God is used so universally. Most people see God as being fantastically higher than intelligence, but nonetheless a form of *higher* intelligence. Since one sees intelligence as being one's highest and most sublime faculty, one is generous enough to define God with one's greatest asset! So God is up there at the highest point of the continuum of intelligence.

This, then, is the natural process by which our minds perceive Godliness. Since God has created intelligence and the references of higher and lower, greater and inferior, one can accept these concepts not as relative values, but as absolutes, and one should get in the habit of applying them in all cases. One doesn't see that there was a time when even these concepts did not exist and thus cannot be applied to those things that existed before the creation of the world. Perforce it must be this way. For if one doesn't use even these to understand the world, or that which transcends the world, one is left with absolutely nothing. Unfortunately, when one is told to accept that the *mitzvot* are God's intrinsic will and have no relevancy whatsoever to intelligent reasoning, it is hard to accept this and one struggles to find reasons in order to enhance their value. One simply finds the task of divorcing God from one's own set of values too difficult.

All human attributes, such as intelligence, are concepts created by God, and He transcends them utterly. He bears no relationship to created entities. Thus, the only way to truly express the infinite quality of God is in terms of His infinite will. To accept and fulfill the Almighty's *mitzvot* because they are the embodiment of the supreme Will is to be connected with the infinite God. To rationalize them is to remain imprisoned in the constraining environment of limited human experience.

Thus when a Jew fulfills a *mitzvah,* even if it is a rational commandment, because God has decreed it so and not due to one's own feeble understanding, he connects and binds himself with the Infinite God and elevates himself to a state he could never possibly reach on his own.

18

GOD CAN BE SMALL TOO

In the weekly *Shabbat* prayers we conclude the prayer *Hakol Yoduha,* "All shall praise you," with the following words: "There is none comparable to you and none apart from you. There is none comparable to you, Lord our God—in this world."

The seeming implication of these words is that there is nothing *in this world* that is in any way comparable to the Almighty, and there is nothing that can exist without Him. But again, in which realm does all of this apply? In *this* world.

What is the meaning of this proclamation of there being nothing comparable to God in *this* world? Does this then mean that in the higher worlds there is something that is comparable to God? Is there any angel or winged seraph of heaven that can be equated with God's sublimity or omnipotence? Obviously not. So why end the statement with the words "in this world"?

Moreover, the equal insignificance of the higher worlds and the lower worlds in comparison to God is not an article of faith, but something that can be rationally proved, as was the subject of the foregoing chapters. Why do we emphasize in the Sabbath prayers how nothing can be compared to God in *our* world, when the same is equally true of the spiritual worlds? In fact, it would seem that a far more appropriate statement of praise would be that there is none comparable to God in the *highest spiritual* worlds. The fantastic attribute of an infinite quantity is not that 1 is tiny and insignificant in comparison to it, but that even a billion or a trillion is minuscule in relation to it. Likewise, it would have seemed far better to praise God saying that "there is none like You not only in this world, but even in the highest worlds." Why, then, is there no mention of the spiritual realm in this prayer, nor is the insignificance of our own world mentioned?

No matter how high and lofty a finite object may be, it is as distant from the infinite as the smallest and most insignificant finite object. Furthermore, not only is the loftiness and sublimity of a created being totally unimpressive and as if nonexistent when compared to God; *even the lowliness and boundaries* of a created object are nonexistent and pose no limitations with respect to God. This second statement is of pivotal importance and will ultimately provide the reason for the necessity of the resurrection of the dead.

A limitation is the inability to be or do something larger than what one is capable. One cannot buy a mansion for which one does not have financial backing, and one cannot lift a weight that is beyond the capacity of one's strength. Similarly, one cannot build a home in a cloud, since this too is beyond any human capacity. Limitations also imply the inability to condescend, become smaller, than one's existence allows. Thus, just as one cannot live in heaven, one cannot live in a mousehole either. One simply cannot descend to that level. So, the fact that one is large and human and cannot enter into a mousehole does not demonstrate one's greatness, but rather one's weakness, one's limitation.

The more limited an object is, the more difficult it is for a higher object to descend to its level. The *deficiency* of the object beneath it is *significant* compared to the higher object, since it is also limited. Because the deficiency and the small size of that object beneath it are *weighty,* it thus cannot condense itself sufficiently. It has the inability to make itself small enough to descend and fit into the smaller object. And the greater the deficiency and lowliness of the inferior object, the greater the need for the larger body to be capable enough to descend to it. Thus it becomes more and more difficult for the superior entity to connect with the inferior. Condensing itself sufficiently sometimes stretches the capacity of the higher object. In other words, it is *too limited* to contract itself and become small as it would like to do.

However, something that has no limitations whatsoever not only can be as big and as great as it wishes, but as small and as tiny as it wants. Because everything is utterly insignificant compared to the infinite, big and small are exactly equal. So included in this knowledge that "the highest and lowest creatures are all equal before God" is the fact that it is just as easy for God to communicate with an ant as it is with the angels of heaven. Moreover, it is just as easy for God to communicate with the dust of the earth as it is with a human. Big or small pose no barriers for an all-powerful being.

Imagine a group of three physicists, all with differing levels of intelligence. The first is a very average physicist, the second is a renowned expert in his field, and the third possesses infinite intelligence and has an infinite knowledge of all aspects of physics. Each one of them is asked to teach the general theory of relativity to three different classes of people. As an average physicist with an average mind, the first physicist is able to teach something as complicated and difficult as relativity only to students who are basically as smart as he. He cannot teach those who are smarter and better informed than he, because he won't be able to answer their questions. But he also cannot teach people very much inferior to him, since he is not creative enough to think of methods by which to communicate to them. His intelligence is too limiting in both directions. To be sure, since he is a professor and a specialist in his field, and he must teach uninitiated students, notwithstanding who they are, he must descend to their level. After all, they are on a lower intellectual plane than he. They are students and he is the professor. But being that this is a limited descent and there is no great qualitative intellectual difference between the students and himself, he is able to accomplish the task. But if we were to ask him to teach the theory of relativity to high school students, or kindergarten children, he will find this utterly impossible. He simply cannot descend to a level where he can articulate himself to people with such a small intellectual capacity. Finding the words to express such difficult concepts to people so inferior to his intelligence stretches his intellectual prowess beyond its capacity.

The second professor, who is a great genius and renowned expert in his field, will find it possible, although with considerable strain, to teach very young students and maybe even kindergartners the essential points of the theory of relativity, and have them absorb it as well. Since he has a great mind and he also understands his subject exceedingly well, just as he can publish new insights into the theory and teach the greatest minds in the field, he can also find creative insights that allow him to descend and teach the smallest minds. For example, he might enter the kindergarten and tell the children about a man who is standing on the moon and believes that the earth revolves around the moon, rather than the opposite. He will tell the students that essentially this observation is not erroneous inasmuch as it is made relative to his vantage point. But, even this great genius will be completely incapable of teaching students with retarded minds and stunted intellect. One can't ask the professor to *give* people intelligence. Rather, within his own field he has the ability to reach great extremes, from Oxford dons to children. But to overcome the impenetrable barrier of a brute mind he cannot do.

Yet the third professor, who possesses infinite intelligence and an infinite knowledge of his subject, will find it possible to teach even the densest minds. For him to teach the highest IQ's and utter half-wits is all the same. Both are so infinitely distant from his own understanding that it makes absolutely no difference whom he teaches. As long as one presents him a skull with a brain inside, even a pinhead, he can communicate the theory. He finds no difficulty whatsoever in going up and down the whole continuum of human intelligence with the greatest of ease. Neither the greatest minds, nor the weakest, neither the largest nor the smallest, stretches his ability in the slightest.

In this analogy, it is not only the sublimity of a finite objects that is nullified to God, but even their *shortcomings and inadequacies* that are nullified to God and are as nought. Just as God is not intimidated or obstructed by the highest things in creation, neither is He intimidated or hindered by the lowest things. In the finite world not only the ability to progress but the ability to descend is also limited. Just as a professor possessed of average intelligence cannot become an infinitely great scholar, neither can he teach lofty ideas to school children. To the professor of infinite wisdom, high and low are both equal. Not only can this professor deal with the very difficult questions, contradictions, and inconsistencies that the greatest of professors pose to him, but he can also overcome the deficiencies inherent in the intellectual vacuums of babes and the mentally handicapped and communicate to them the loftiest ideas. Real infinity is the ability to be as big as one wants and also the ability to be as small as one wants; it works in both directions.

Nevertheless, even this professor of infinite knowledge and wisdom has a red line over which even he cannot pass. The moment he is asked to teach physics, or even the fact that $2 + 2 = 4$, to a block of wood, he raises his hands in defeat, for he is not infinite in *everything*—he is only infinite in intelligence. Therefore his intelligence cannot penetrate something void of a brain. Although he can fit into the smallest keyhole of any mind, he cannot break through the door. He cannot impart a mind. He must at least have something in common with the object he is teaching. But this descent, to teach physics to a stone, is so far beneath him and so qualitatively inferior to his essence that the descent is no longer insignificant. In other words, the deficiency of the stone has assumed relevance. The condescension for this infinite mind to reach an inanimate object is so significant that he cannot even begin. Here he is confronted with a barrier that cannot be penetrated.

This illustration, in the words of one of the thirteen principles by which the talmudic law is formulated, "is singled out not only to teach concerning its own case, but is to be applied to the whole of the general law" (see *Sifra*, Introduction). The fact that in the presence of an inanimate object the infinite sage finds it impossible to articulate himself and convey his teaching, reveals to us that he is not truly infinite, because the moment he is required to leave the domain where *he is infinite* and become infinite on some other plain, he finds himself totally helpless. Had he been truly infinite, then he could make even a stone understand.

The fact that there is a limitation on the ability of this infinite sage to descend beyond a certain point also proves that in essence *no descent* is truly and fully insignificant to him. Rather, the descent to a child is easy and effortless and he is therefore able to execute it. But it is still a *descent* for him. He must change himself for a certain time in order to communicate with something lower. The fact that the sage reaches a certain point beyond which he cannot cross proves decisively that he is not infinite and, by extension, nothing is truly insignificant to the point that it is nonexistent. Were he truly infinite, he could transcend all barriers.

The only true infinity is God. He is the existence for whom nothing is too big or too small. There is nothing He cannot do, and there is no barrier He cannot penetrate. God is fully capable of communication with an object that is totally outside the realm of intellectual thought. This is because, in the face of a *true* infinity, not only is the greatest professor and the youngest schoolboy equal, but both are just as equal to a block of wood. All three are infinitely removed, in all ways and on all levels, from God. The professor is no closer to God than the boy, or even the block of wood. Thus, if God can communicate with a human, He can communicate with wood. There is absolutely no difference between them and none poses any obstruction to His ability.

Hence, the purpose of the *Shabbat* morning prayers where we say "There is nothing comparable to you in this world" is to convey how even the smallness and shortcomings of our world poses no barrier to God whatsoever. Even this physical world, which represents the antithesis of everything spiritual and holy and is utterly tiny and infinitesimal in comparison to the higher spiritual worlds, does not impede God's ability to do with it as He pleases. Just as God can communicate intelligence to stone, so too can He reveal Godliness in an un-Godly world. God can reveal Himself in a physical world. The constraints of our very limited world constitute no impediment on God's ability to do with it as He likes. Thus, "there is nothing comparable to You"—there is no limitation in our world that God cannot transcend. Our world and its hindrances are utterly insignificant and as if nonexistent in relation to God.

How is it possible in the time of the resurrection of the dead that God's infinite light would be revealed here in our physical world to souls enclothed in a body? Seemingly the two are contradictory, if not impossible. The *Zohar* teaches that in order to receive the sublime Godly revelations of the Garden of Eden after the body expires, the soul must divorce itself completely of "any vestige of the material world." If a complete renunciation of all material existence is necessary in order to be privy to even limited Godly revelation in the Garden of Eden, then how can there be an infinite Godly revelation to be experienced first, by the body, and second, while here on earth?

Because the Garden of Eden enjoys a lofty, but limited, Godly light, it cannot cope with the limitations of the body. Since the light is not infinite, the limitations of the body and the material world pose a significant barrier that cannot be penetrated by the light of Eden. It simply cannot descend to something that is its antithesis. It is like the great professor who cannot teach a stone. Therefore, in order for the soul to bask in the Godliness in the Garden of Eden, it must first divest itself of all physical residue.

But, in the epoch of the Messiah, God's *infinite* light will be revealed. Because it is truly infinite in all dimensions, it will be able to descend to the lowest possible objects, even those that pose a contradiction to it. Even the material world and the body, which today conceal the Godliness of the world, will be reached by this revelation. Our world, the lowest of all possible worlds, will prove a perfectly suitable receptacle to God's infinite presence, since the smallest and most limited entity is utterly insignificant and null in relation to true infinity.

One vital question still remains. Why was our world specifically chosen for this revelation? If the smallest and the greatest are absolutely equal in light of God's infinity, then surely it is just as good to have the revelation in the Garden of Eden as it here on earth. Why, then, is it necessary for the souls of all the righteous and all those people who have died over thousands of years to uproot themselves from the Garden of Eden, where they now reside, and return to our physical world? This question into the very nature and need for the resurrection of the dead begs for an answer.

19

WHY GOD WILL REVEAL HIMSELF ON EARTH

God, who is the only true infinity in all characteristics, transcending everything known to man, finds it effortless to communicate with an inanimate object. With God the possibilities are literally endless. Nothing is outside His sphere of ability. Compared to the sage of infinite wisdom, God is the One true infinity. Furthermore, the difference between God and the infinitely intelligent professor will exist not only in their ability to communicate intelligence to inferior receptors, such as human beings or stone, but also in the way in which the idea is communicated. When the professor of infinite wisdom condescends to the level a human of very inferior intelligence, the concept he ends up communicating is not the same concept that exists in his own mind. It has been altered, even slightly, and is now different. It has been contracted and tailored to fit the capacity of the recipient. Were the sage to communicate the idea the way *he* understands it, he would completely overwhelm the small, limited grasp of his disciple.

For example, if the professor were required to communicate the theory of relativity to a schoolchild, he could not start throwing difficult equations and diagrams at the young pupil. Rather, he would be required to think of some creative method by which to communicate the essential principles. He might tell a tale of two trains approaching each other, one blowing its whistle. A passenger on the other trains hears that the pitch of

175

the whistle is different before and after the trains pass. Although this in essence would convey relativity's essential principles, it is so contracted that the student may not even recognize that what he has just heard is a revolutionary scientific principle. Surely the professor himself, when he ponders the theory, does not think of trains and whistles. But when he teaches the theory, he must contract his thinking to suit his pupil. Thus, although he is infinite, there is a change in his thinking before and after the transmission.

On the other hand, God's infinite light is not only unlimited in terms of *where* it can be revealed, but also in terms of *how* it is revealed. Since God's light is truly infinite in every sense of the word, it has the ability to reveal its full intensity, without any contractions whatsoever, to even the lowest and qualitatively inferior of receptacles.

In truth these two things—the ability to transmit to something lower and the way in which something is transmitted—are both interdependent. The communication skills of this infinitely wise professor is not dependent solely on *his* ability to teach, but also upon the capacity of the pupil to receive. Proof to this effect can be brought from the fact that when faced with an inanimate object, which has no intellectual dimension, the sage is useless. All his great teaching ability is to no avail. And even when the professor does find an appropriate receptacle, it will still be the *receiving capacity of the receptacle* that will dictate how the professor will teach. If it is a child he is tutoring, then he will be forced to contract his knowledge and use analogies, parables, fables, and other forms of tempering his thoughts. To a student with greater intellectual prowess, the professor will be able to teach more, but not completely, on his own level of thought.

But why is all of this necessary? If in truth this sage is of infinite wisdom, why does the material he is teaching differ with each individual student? In other words, why is his teaching dependent not entirely on *his* own ability but on his *students'* capabilities. The answer is that the sage is not truly infinite. If he were infinite, it would make absolutely no difference whom he was teaching. Rather, the only determining factor would be his own communication skills. But since he is limited, the descent to students lower than himself "disturbs" his ability to communicate. Therefore, communication between the sage and his student, between something higher and lower, is dependent both on the teacher and the student, the donor and the recipient, and there is an interdependency between the ability to communicate and the form the communication will take.

But theoretically, if this sage were completely infinite from every dimension and every angle, it would make no difference who the receptacle was. A true infinity would be able to overcome both obstacles. First, he could teach even a stone, and second, he would teach the idea to the stone the way it exists in his own mind without having to tailor it to the capacity of the receiver.

This matches exactly the ability for God to reveal Himself in our world. Since God's light is truly infinite, it is not limited in where it can be revealed, nor in the way in which it reveals itself. Thus, it is completely able to be manifest even in the lowest of all worlds, without any contractions or limitations.

This then is the greatness of the Godly revelation that will take place in the messianic era. The Godliness that exists at present in the Garden of Eden is limited and therefore can only be revealed in a receptacle fit to contain it, i.e., a spiritual world. Moreover, even the Godly light that does exist in that world must be contracted and condensed to fit into the spiritual realm, for the Garden of Eden is not infinite. But in the World-to-Come, where God's infinite light will shine, there will be no need for a fitting receptacle. God's light will not be limited to appearing only in a spiritual realm that is conducive to its presence.

Why will the infinite revelation at the end of days take place in the physical world? God is equally comfortable and able to reveal himself in the physical as well as the spiritual. So why not choose the spiritual realm?

One of the most important explanations for this phenomenon found in hasidic thought is this: the purpose for the creation of the world was for God to have a dwelling place. The connotation of a home or dwelling place is somewhere where the dweller feels totally at home and acts himself, without conforming to societal standards or expectations. Stated in simpler words, a dwelling is all about one thing—revelation. Not just any revelation, but unrestrained and absolute revelation. God's creative act, therefore, was a process of revelation. God desired that the full scope of His infinite essence be revealed without any restrictions. There was one catch, however. He desired that this revelation come about through man. By giving man a Torah and a code of laws by which to live, God gave man the incredible ability to expose the true underlying nature of the world—that it is all part of God.

This objective will be realized with the advent of the messianic era. In that time God's infinite Self will shine forth unhindered. The entire purpose of that epoch will be for God to dwell comfortably and openly in our world and for God's true infinite character to be manifest.

For this reason, the revelation must be in the physical world, because only through Godliness being revealed in this world can it be seen that God is truly infinite. It is only through a manifestation in the physical domain that God's true infinite Essence can be noticed and proclaimed as being truly infinite. If God's infinite Essence would be revealed in the spiritual realm, it could be interpreted as being due to the fact that the spiritual is more of a ''receptacle'' for Godliness than the physical. This perception would in turn conceal a full manifestation of God's infinite ability. But when God reveals Himself *fully,* without any hesitation or contraction, in the physical world, it is revealed for all to see that, relative to God, the spiritual is no closer than the physical. So the fullest possible manifestation of the infinite nature of God's light can be accomplished only in the physical world. In the messianic epoch it will be seen how God's light is so utterly transcendent that even the physical poses no obstacle or barrier to its revelation.

The Godly light in the Garden of Eden is essentially a reward for the study of Torah, while the infinite Godly light of the messianic era is a reward for the fulfillment of *mitzvot.* The same qualitative differences that exist in these two kinds of reward also exist between the Torah and *mitzvot* themselves. The Torah is the embodiment of Godly intellect, while the *mitzvot* are the embodiment of Godly will. Throughout kabbalistic writings, it is explained that will is superior to intellect. How many times have we heard someone say, "I know this sounds crazy, but I'm going to do it anyway." Although the idea contradicts the individual's intelligence, since will dominates the intelligence, he finds a method of doing it anyway. Will is said to be a manifestation of God's infinity, while His intellect is a more contracted manifestation of God. To say that God is a higher intelligence is erroneous. This mistakes a channel of Godly revelation, or God revealing Himself as a certain concept, for God Himself. God is truly above the concept of intelligence, which is in fact a created property.

Since Godly intellect is a limited revelation, it can be apprehended by the human mind, which is a proper receptacle to it. The Torah cannot be studied by the foot, which does not match it. Since it is not an infinite revelation, it can only be grasped by those things that suit it. Godly intellect, which is a contracted revelation of God, requires a spiritual vessel in which it can be revealed. It finds this in the form of the mind.

But divine will, which is truly infinite, does not require any spiritual vessel for its revelation, and thus it is capable of being revealed even in the physical performance of the *mitzvot*. This infinite light can be revealed through the hands. On the contrary, it is specifically through its materialization through ordinary mundane chores performed via the lowest of human faculties that the infinite nature of the divine will is manifest.

Thus, the reward for the study of Torah, like the study of the Torah itself, is a limited divine revelation. And just as the light of the Torah requires a spiritual vessel for its manifestation, so too the reward for Torah can only be had in the Garden of Eden. But the reward for the observance of the *mitzvot,* like the will of God, which is embellished in the *mitzvot,* will be infinite and will take place specifically in the physical world, just as the *mitzvot* themselves necessitate physical deed in their performance.

Like everything of holiness that is interconnected, the *mitzvot* have an element of "Torah" included within them. The rational explanation that accompanies many *mitzvot* can be referred to as the "Torah" in the *mitzvot*. It is the part of the *mitzvah* that, like the Torah, can be apprehended by human intelligence. Likewise, in the Torah, too, there is an element that may be referred to as the *"mitzvot"* in Torah. This element is the *halakhah,* the final and conclusive outcome of how one must act. After all the logical and rational debate of the Torah, one reaches the actual *law.* This is similar to the irrational will of God, since it no longer incorporates a rational dimension. Rather, the *halakhot* are instructions on how one must live in accordance with God's will.

An example of this can be taken from the Talmud, in *Megillah,* which explains that the laws, the *halakhot,* of the Torah are called *"kitra,"* the Crown of Torah. Thus, whereas all parts of the Torah are a manifestation of Godly intellect, the *halakhot,* the laws, are considered to be God's will, which transcend the intellect and are therefore referred to as the crown of the Torah. Just as the crown sits on top of the head, so too the *halakhot,* which are God's will, sit atop the Godly intellect, which is the Torah.

This also explains the meaning behind the continuation of the Talmud's discussion, when it says, "Whosoever studies the laws of the Torah on a daily basis is assured of life in the World-to-Come." The World-to-Come is the infinite Godly revelation that will radiate in the messianic era as a reward for the fulfillment of the *mitzvot,* which are God's infinite will. The *halakhot,* too, are the segment of the Torah that represents God's will. Therefore, as a direct consequence for the study of *halakhot,* the individual is guaranteed a place in the World-to-Come, a front-row seat at the infinite manifestation of God's light, which he helped reveal through the study of *halakhah.*

For this reason also, the *halakhot* take precedence over all other areas of the Torah. This includes even those *halakhot* that do not apply in contemporary times, such as the laws dealing with the sacrificial service in the Temple, or the laws pertaining to the destruction of the nation of Amalek (which cannot be performed because Amalek cannot be identified in contemporary times), or the laws pertaining to the kings of Israel (which cannot be fulfilled since there is no king). As the great kabbalist, Rabbi Isaac Luriah, explains, it is incumbent upon every soul to go through many reincarnations throughout many different time periods until it is able to fulfill all 613 commandments. For it is only through the fulfillment of *all* of God's commandments that God's will is completed. The same is true not only of the *fulfillment* of the *mitzvot,* but also of their study. One is obligated to study all of *halakhah,* which similarly is the embodiment of God's will. It is imperative that one study all of the *halakhot,* even those that are not relevant to Jewish life today. Since one cannot execute them in deed, studying the *halakhot* is the only way to bring God's will to its full completion in contemporary times.

This is also one of the very special reasons for studying the *Yad Hahazakah,* also known as the *Mishneh Torah,* the famous code of Jewish law compiled by Maimonides. This is the only compilation in Jewish literature where all the laws of the Torah are presented. When one studies the entire *Mishneh Torah,* thus reviewing all the laws of the Torah, both those that apply to today and those that apply only to Temple times, one reaches the "Crown" of Torah. One attains the fulfillment of God's will in its entirety. And it is this completion and this fulfillment that will bring about the messianic redemption and the rebuilding of the Third Temple. It is no coincidence therefore that Maimonides ends the *Mishneh Torah* with the laws pertaining to the Messiah and the messianic era. The very last law in the *Mishneh Torah* reads, "And in that time there will neither famine nor war, neither jealousy nor strife.— Blessings will be abundant, comforts within the reach of all. The one preoccupation of the whole world will be to know the Lord. Hence, Israelite nations will be very wise; they will know the things that are now concealed and will attain an understanding of their Creator to the utmost capacity of the human mind, as it is written, 'For the earth shall be filled with the knowledge of the Lord as the waters cover the ocean floor (Isaiah 11:9)' " (*Laws of Kings* 12:5). This was to be the outcome, the reward of completing the study of all the laws of the Torah.

III

WHAT WILL HAPPEN IN THE MESSIANIC ERA

20

DETAILS OF THE RESURRECTION OF THE DEAD

The Talmud (*Berakhot* 49a) lists the chronology of events in the messianic era as involving first and foremost the building of the Temple, then the ingathering of all Jewish exiles from the corners of the globe, and finally the resurrection of the dead. The *Zohar* says more specifically that there will be forty years between the ingathering of exiles and the resurrection (*Zohar* 1:139a).

The resurrection will be in the land of Israel. This applies both for those buried inside and outside of Israel. As far as the people buried in the land of Israel are concerned, it will be quite simple. Their souls will be reinvested in their bodies and they will rise. But the people buried outside Israel will only have their souls returned to them once their bodies reach the land of Israel. This of course will necessitate a means by which the bodies can arrive in the land of Israel. How will this occur?

The Talmud discusses this problem by beginning with a question on a statement made by one of the sages. "Rabbi Eliezer said, 'The deceased who are buried outside Israel will not be resurrected.' " Rabbi Eliezer brings a scriptural proof to support his claim. But what of the righteous individuals who are buried outside the Land? Will they not rise? "Rabbi Elai answered, 'Their bodies will roll to Israel (Rashi: Their bones will roll all the way to Israel and there life will be reinstilled within them).' " But the Talmud objects. Surely the rolling of the bones will cause unnecessary pain to the righteous. "Abaye answered that tunnels will be made for them to walk underground (Rashi: And they will stand up and walk through them until they reach the land of Israel and break through the ground and emerge)" (*Ketubot* 111a).

What emerges from this discussion is that the first statement of Rabbi Eliezer, that those buried outside Israel will not be resurrected, is modified. The new meaning of the statement is that they will not be resurrected until their bodies reach the land of Israel. And even the righteous who will walk through the tunnels to reach the land of Israel are still considered to have been resurrected in Israel, since their individual souls will be returned to them only when they break through the ground and emerge in the land of Israel. Thus we may assume that the place of burial has no effect on *who* will be resurrected, but it does affect *where* the resurrection will take place.

In short, those who are buried in the land of Israel will be resurrected there. Those who are buried outside Israel will necessitate transfer to Israel before being resurrected. This transfer will come about through rolling and will be painful. But the righteous will be given life and special passageways with which to reach Israel, which will spare them the pain.

As far as who within the Jewish people will merit resurrection, we have the assurance of the *mishnah* that "all of Israel have a portion in the World-to-Come" (*Sanhedrin*, chap. 11). And although Maimonides lists certain groups of people who lose their share through grave sin (see *Laws of Repentance,* chap. 3), the *Midrash Talpiot* explains that what this means is that they lost *their own merit* of partaking in the World-to-Come. But God, in His infinite mercy, has allocated "charitable funds for those with insufficient merit" from which they can partake and join the ranks of those who will be resurrected.

An interesting difficulty arises as a result of the belief in reincarnation. Judaism believes that a soul must return to earth as many times as it takes to fulfill all 613 commandments. It is the *mitzvot* that refine and elevate the soul. In order for the soul to be perfect, it must return as many times as it takes in as many body as it takes until all the *mitzvot* are fulfilled.

But what of the souls that have already occupied a body

previously on earth? How will they accommodate more than one person? The *Zohar* itself asks this question: "R. Chizkiya asked, 'If you say that all bodies will be rise from the dust and live, then what will be with those bodies whose soul first inhabited a different body in a previous age?" (*Zohar* 1:131a).

Rabbi Isaac Luria (the *Ari*) answers that every time an individual refines a certain element or dimension of the soul, then that part of the soul becomes his own and it will be that portion that will be reinvested in *his* body at the resurrection. In other words, as mentioned above, every *mitzvah* refines and elevates the soul in a different way, and depending on what part of the soul is elevated by a given person, that part of the soul will be attached to his body forever.

Rabbi Menachem Schneerson adds that one should not make the mistaken assumption, based on the *Ari*'s words, that there will be some people who will be missing whole portions of their soul. Every soul is in fact made up of various parts that include aspects that mirror one another and are thus complete entities unto themselves. For instance, all the Jewish souls collectively are said to make up the one soul of the first man. Every soul is an entity unto itself, but it also subdivides into smaller fragments, which become a separate entity unto themselves, but can still be said to be part of a larger whole. A soul is thus like a branch of a tree, which, if broken off from its source, can still grow when planted and become a completely independent tree. Nevertheless, there are higher, more significant parts of the tree, and lower, less significant parts. The same applies to the world of the souls. Adam was the collective soul of all who would live. Still, the *Midrash* says that the souls of the leaders of Israel are connected with Adam's head, the lay people with his lower features, and so on (see *Exodus Rabbah*, chap. 40). The same applies to the resurrection. The souls will subdivide into different fragmentary parts that still comprise a complete and perfect soul on their own. But the division will be decided by which body refined which fragment of the soul.

What will we be like at the reawakening? The way in which a person dies is the same way in which he will arise. If a person died blind, he will awake blind. If a person died mute, he will awake mute. According to the *Midrash*, God says, "Let them arise the same way in which they expired and after their awakening I shall heal them" (*Midrash Rabbah* 95; *Zohar* 3:91a).

The *Zohar* expresses a similar thought: "In the time when Israel will be resurrected from the earth, there will be many blind and mute people and other defects, but then God will illuminate them with the great intensity of the sun and heal them" (*Zohar* 1:203b). This idea is based on a talmudic statement that at creation God hid the full radiation of the sun and saved its healing power for the righteous in the World-to-Come (*Nedarim* 8b).

It should be mentioned that it is the body one possesses now that will be resurrected, not some other body. And although the body decays and rots, there always remains one bone, known as the *eitzim luz,* at the very top of the spinal column, that does not rot or decay. From there the Almighty will rebuild the remainder of the body. He will knead the bone in "the dew of life" and build the body from there (*Zohar* 2:28b).

How people will be dressed upon being resurrected is disputed in the Talmud. According to one authority, everyone will rise dressed in their shrouds. "R. Nathan said: The clothes with which a man is buried rises with him." But according to Rebbe (Rabbi Yehudah Hanasi), the people will arise in the normative attire they were accustomed to while alive. If Rebbe is indeed correct, then the resurrection should prove to be a very colorful occasion since there will be fifty-five hundred years of dress on display simultaneously.

The exact order of those being resurrected is as follows: First those buried in Israel will rise, followed by those buried outside Israel, and followed by Moses' generation of Jews who were exiled from Egypt (*Kilayim* 9:3). Interestingly, according to at least one authority in the Talmud, the forefathers Abraham, Isaac, and Jacob (or, as they are referred to in the talmudic passage, "those who sleep in Chebron") will be resurrected last, in order that they awake joyously to the sight of all of their righteous and pious children who have merited resurrection as well *(Avkat Ruchel)*.

An important proviso to the above is that within the respective regions, it will be the righteous who will merit being resurrected first (*Zohar* 2:140a). Within the righteous themselves, it will be those who excelled in Torah who will rise before those who excelled in *mitzvot* (*Zohar* 2:182a). According to one *midrash,* the order of the resurrection of the righteous will be alphabetical order, with the exception of those who possess the quality of humility, they will precede everyone else (see *Ohev Yisrael, Likutim Parshah Berakhah*).

What will happen to the people who are still alive at the time of the resurrection? Will they live or die? Rabbenu Saadia Gaon writes that this subject is in great confusion, since no scriptural verses or rabbinic pronouncements have been said on the matter (*Emunot Vedei'ot* 47).

Rabbi Menachem Schneerson, however, points out that now that there is the merit of the revelation of the *Zohar,* we have a clear pronouncement on the subject.

> It is concerning this time that it is written: "See now that I, even I, am He, and there is no god with me; I kill, and I make alive" (Deuteronomy 32:39). The double "I, I" indicates the absoluteness of the divine presence in the messianic time, when the "other side" shall be vanquished and be no more seen; and even death, which until that time was connected with the "other side," will thenceforth be from Him directly, for those who have not yet experienced physical death, and He will raise them immediately; for nothing of that filth of sin, which is the cause of death, will remain in the world, and there will be a new world, fashioned and perfected by the hands of the Holy One, blessed be He. [*Zohar* 2:108b]

Thus we see clearly that all those who are alive will experience momentary death so there will be no continuation of the transgressions that have stained the world or a vestige of it in the World-to-Come. But the Almighty will resurrect everyone immediately.

Will there be a Judgment Day after the resurrection of the dead? There are three differing opinions on the subject.

1. According to Nachmanides and others, there will indeed be a grand Judgment Day after the resurrection, in which all

human beings will be judged according to their merits (Ramban, *Gate of Reward*).

2. Every human being is judged directly after death, and thus there is no need for a special Day of Judgment. The repeated reference to such a day and its connection with the resurrection is really a reference to a Day of *Retribution* and Revenge (Abarbanel in *Maayanei Hayeshua* 8:7).

3. Rabbi Isaac Luria writes: "And if one shall ask, 'After this soul has passed through many days of atonement (Yom Kippur) as well as physical suffering and cleansing as well as extensive spiritual cleansing [after death], why must it again [in the time of the resurrection] be subjected to another judgment on the great Day of Judgment?' The answer is that this Day of Judgment is only for the non-Jewish nations."

According to Jewish tradition, upon a person's death his soul must first go to the *Gehenna* for cleansing, which is unlike the Christian concept of Hell. Hell, or purgatory, is a place for damnation, where a soul remains suffering for all eternity in recompense for its sins. Jewish tradition, however, rejects any belief in a place where a soul suffers for the sake of suffering. It does, however, speak of a place where a soul can be for up to twelve months, depending on how badly soiled it is, where it is cleansed and purified of the blackness that is sin. Although the process is said to be painful, the purpose is to prepare the soul for eternal bliss in the Garden of Eden, which it cannot enter until its stains are removed.

But what will happen with those who will be alive at the time of the resurrection and will only be put to death momentarily. Since they will not have sufficient time to be spiritually cleansed in the *Gehenna* and the like, will they have to pass through the Judgment Day? One of the responses given is that the magnitude of their cleansing will be heightened to such ferocious intensity that it will be equal to having been cleansed for a very long time, and thus they too will be ready to enter the World-to-Come. Of course, all of these issues are highly esoteric; the truth is known to God alone.

There is much debate as to what life will be like after the resurrection. The dispute centers around how one defines the

World-to-Come. Does it indicate the Garden of Eden, which would make it a spiritual domain, or does it indicate the world in the age of the Messiah after the resurrection of the dead, which makes it a physical domain? Simply stated, the great majority of commentators concur with the latter. They envision a world as described by the Talmud, a world radically different from our own, a world void of all eating, drinking, cohabitation, business dealings, jealousy, hatred, or war. There will be eternal life, whose purpose it will be to give all human beings the ability to devote all of their energies to comprehending God and basking in the radiance of His light. No one shall ever return to the grave.

There is, however, one important dissenter.

21

MAIMONIDES AND THE RATIONALIST APPROACH TO MESSIANISM

Some of the most important questions of what will take place in the messianic era—how long will the messianic epoch last, will people live forever, will there be a radical transformation in nature, will the Messiah die, what will life be like—are a subject of dispute between two of the greatest medieval Jewish scholars: Maimonides (Rabbi Moshe ben Maimon) and Nachmanides (Rabbi Moshe ben Nachman). To begin, Maimonides devotes much attention to the subject of the Messiah throughout his writings. This encompasses lengthy discussions on the subject in his commentary on the *Mishnah,* notably in his *Introduction to Helek,* epistles to various Jewish communities around the world, and especially his *Mishneh Torah (Laws of Kings and Wars).* In each of these places he always demonstrates the importance of the belief in the Messiah to those who underestimate its value in Judaism. He writes:

> Anyone who does not believe in him, or does not await his coming, denies not only the statements of the other prophets, but also those of the Torah and of Moshe, our teacher, for the Torah attests to his coming, stating, "And God will bring back your captivity." There is also a reference to the Messiah in the passage concerning Bilaam (Numbers 24:17–18), who prophesies about the two anointed kings: the first anointed king, David, who saved Israel from her oppressors, and the final anointed king who will arise from among his descendants and save Israel

193

at the end of days . . . as the passage states: "I see it, but not now." "I see it, but not now"—This refers to David; "I perceive it, but not in the near future"—This refers to the Messiah. "A star shall go forth from Jacob"—This refers to David; "and a staff shall arise in Israel"—This refers to the Messiah. "He shall crush all of Moab's princes"—This refers to David (as it is written [II Samuel 8:2], "He smote Moab and measured them with a line"); "he shall dominate all of Seth's descendants"—This refers to the Messiah (about whom it is written, "He will rule from sea to sea" [Zechariah 9:10]).

The centrality of the Messiah in Judaism according to Maimonides is so strong that he even says, "The final goal is the attaining of the World-to-Come, and it is to it that all our efforts must be directed."

Nevertheless, Maimonides understands the dangers inherent in being overzealous. He warns how careful one must be before accepting a certain individual as the Messiah. In his *Epistle to Yemen* he rebukes a scholar for mistakenly accepting a man who was not great in learning as the Messiah:

> But I am astonished that you, a scholar who has carefully studied the doctrine of the rabbis, are inclined to repose faith in him. Do you not know, my brother, that the Messiah is a very eminent prophet, more illustrious than all the prophets after Moses! Now if we dare not put trust in a man's pretensions to prophecy if he does not excel in wisdom, how much less must we take seriously the claims of an ignoramus that he is the Messiah?

Likewise, Maimonides warns of the danger of mistakenly accepting a given event as ushering the messianic redemption, when in fact it has not yet arrived. "Remember that even the date of the termination of the Egyptian exile was not precisely known and gave rise to differences of opinion." Although God fixed its duration in Scripture as being four hundred years, there were disputes as to when the four hundred years began and when it ended. One group had miscalculated it by thirty years.

A band of Israelites left Egypt because they believed that their
exile had ended. The Egyptians slew and destroyed them, and
the subjugation of the Israelites who remained was consequently
aggravated. . . . Now if such uncertainty prevailed in regard to
the date of emancipation from the Egyptian bondage, the term
of which was fixed, it is much more so with respect to the date
of the final redemption, the prolonged and protracted duration
of which appalled and dismayed our inspired seers. [*Epistle to
Yemen*]

Thus, Maimonides fears that the Jews of the subsequent
generations could be led to make the same mistake as their
predecessors. It is partly due to this reason that Maimonides
devotes so much energy to clarifying the messianic ideal. He
understands that due to its sublimity and difficulty, the idea of
the Messiah has become meaningless to a great many contemporaries. He feels a need to clarify a concept, which, he says,
has fallen into chaos and disarray.

In *Introduction to Helek* Maimonides writes:

I have thought fit to speak here concerning many principles
belonging to fundamental articles of faith which are of very
great importance. Know that the theologians are divided in
opinion as to the good which man reaps from the performance
of these precepts which God enjoined upon us by the hand of
Moses our teacher; and that they also differ among themselves
with regard to the evil which will overtake us if we transgress
them. Their differences on these questions are very great and in
proportion to the differences between their respective intel-
lects. As a consequence, people's opinions have fallen into such
great confusion that you can scarcely in any way find anyone
possessing clear and certain ideas on this subject: neither can
you alight upon any portion of it which has been transmitted to
any person without abundant error.

Maimonides then begins to explain all of the different errors
that people make concerning the messianic era, errors based on
literal interpretations of biblical and rabbinic texts. One class of
people holds that "the hoped-for good will be the Garden of
Eden, a place where people eat and drink without toil or

faintness." They imagine "houses of costly stones . . . couches of silk and rivers flowing with wine and perfumed oil." Another class "firmly believes and imagines that the hoped-for good will be the days of the Messiah." They think that when that time comes, all men will be kings forever. Their bodily frames will be mighty and they will inhabit the whole earth unto eternity. According to their imagination, that Messiah will live as long as the Creator, and at that epoch the earth will bring forth garments ready woven and bread ready baked, and many other impossible things like these. "A fourth class consists of those who believe that the good which we shall reap from obedience to the law will consist in the repose of the body and attainment in the world of all worldly wishes, as for example, the fertility of lands, abundant wealth, abundance of children, long life, bodily health and security, enjoying the sway of a king, and prevailing over the oppressor."

The common feature of all these views is their focusing on material gratification as the ultimate goal of religious observance. The popular notion of messianism was but one instance of this preoccupation with gratifying one's need for power, wealth, or sensual pleasure. It was a collective fantasy born of repression and deprivation. Maimonides goes to great lengths to combat this literalism in the minds of the majority of the community. Maimonides, for no ulterior motive, wished to return the focus of the Jewish world to regard the worship of God as the ultimate goal of Judaism. Thus he emphasized throughout his writings about the Messiah that the fundamental order of the natural world would not change or be compromised after his advent.

Both prophetic and talmudic references to the messianic era indicated a world that would return to the kind of existence the Jews enjoyed while wandering through the desert after their redemption from Egypt. This was an existence in which no physical effort needed to be exerted for physical sustenance. Clothing grew on backs, the "well of Miriam" followed the Jews in the desert, bread *(mannah)* rained from heaven, and shelter in the form of protective clouds followed the Jews wherever they went. The interaction of the Jews with the material world was virtually nonexistent. The same fundamental changes would take place if the statements of the Prophets and the Talmud regarding the epoch of the Messiah would come true.

But Maimonides rejected these prophetic pronouncements as merely allegorical and disputed this notion vigorously. According to Maimonides, the ultimate purpose of the Torah, ignored by all the aforementioned views, is the World-to-Come, i.e., the immortality of the soul.

To understand the Maimonidean notion of the messianic era requires an examination of who the Messiah would be.

In *Laws of Kings and Wars* Maimonides lists the qualifications for the messiahship.

> If a king shall arise from the House of David who delves deeply in the study of the Torah and observes its *mitzvot* like David, his ancestor; if he, by his personal excellence within the realm of Torah, will compel all of Israel to walk in the way of the Torah, and reinforce the breaches in its observance among the entire Jewish people; and if he will fight the wars of God, thus removing all obstacles to Torah observance in the world at large, we may, with assurance, consider him the Messiah. If he succeeds in the above . . . builds the *Beit Hamikdash* (Temple) on its site, and gathers in the dispersed remnant of Israel, he is definitely the Messiah. At this stage, when it becomes possible to observe the Torah and its *mitzvot* in their totality, the era of the Messiah will have actually begun. [*Laws of Kings and Wars* 11:4]

Note that Maimonides goes to great lengths to emphasize the natural very human side of the Messiah. In another instance he further expands upon the nonmiraculous qualifications for the messiahship. Maimonides was well aware of the average public opinion of who the Messiah would be, which was ridden with supernatural powers. To an extent, this may have been influenced by the Christian culture in which the Jews were submerged. But more important, it added a dimension of romanticism and glory to the messianic figure. Thus Maimonides writes:

> One should not entertain the notion that the messianic king must work miracles and wonders, bring about new phenomena

within the world, resurrect the dead, or perform other similar deeds. This is definitely not true. A proof can be brought from the fact that Rabbi Akiva, one of the greatest sages of the *Mishnah,* was one of the supporters of King Ben Kozeba, and would describe him as the messianic king. . . . The sages did not ask him for any signs or wonders. [*Introduction to Helek*]

He reemphasizes the point again in *Laws of Kings and Wars:*

Do not think that the king Messiah will have to perform signs and wonders, bring anything new into being, revive the dead, or do similar things. It is not so. Rabbi Akiva was a great sage, a teacher of the *Mishnah,* yet he was also the armor-bearer of Ben Kozeba. He affirmed that the latter was the king Messiah; he and all the wise men of his generation shared this belief until Ben Kozeba was slain in [his] iniquity, when it became known that he was not the Messiah. Yet the rabbis had not asked him for a sign or token. The general principle is: this Law of ours with its statutes and ordinances [is not subject to change]. It is forever and all eternity; it is not to be added to or to be taken away from. [*Laws of Kings and Wars* 11:3]

According to Maimonides, the Messiah will restore the monarchy, build the Temple, and gather in the Jewish people, thus creating an environment in which the Jewish people will be able to observe the Torah and its *mitzvot* in a perfect manner. Furthermore, he will remove any obstacles to this end in the world at large. As a consequence, the Jewish people will "be free [to involve themselves] in Torah and its wisdom [without any pressures or disturbances]. At that time there will be neither famine nor war . . . [and] the occupation of the entire world will be solely to know God" (*Laws of Kings and Wars* 12:4–5).

Thus we see throughout the Maimonidean messianic vision how the natural order of the world prevails: the Jewish people and the world at large will be elevated to a perfect state of knowledge and practice. This is the purpose of the Messiah's coming.

In order to convince his readers that knowledge and love of God for their own sakes constituted the ultimate purpose of the commandments as well as the messianic era, Maimonides offers a new perspective on the material benefits promised in the Torah and rabbinic literature:

> As regards the promises and threats alluded to in the Torah, their interpretation is that which I shall now tell you. It says to you, "If you obey these precepts, I will help you to a further obedience of them and perfection in the performance of them. And I shall remove all hindrances from you. . . ." For it is impossible for man to do the service of God when sick or hungry or thirsty or in trouble and this is why the Torah promises the removal of all these disabilities and gives man also the promise of health and quietude until such a time as he shall have attained perfection of knowledge and be worthy of the life of the World-to-Come. The final aim of the Torah is not that the earth should be fertile, that people should live long, and that bodies should be healthy. It simply helps us to the performance of its precepts by holding out the promise of all these things. [*Introduction to Helek*]

Throughout his messianic writings, Maimonides strives to accomplish two things. First and foremost, he seeks to alter the Jewish world's attitude toward their faith by making the knowledge and love of God the ultimate goal. He tries to make *olam haba,* the *spiritual* World-to-Come, the highest good in the hierarchy of rewards that Judaism promises its adherents and to make all other goods subservient to it. To this extent, Maimonides goes to the incredible extreme of subordinating even the messianic age to *Olam Haba,* domain of the souls. Nevertheless, he emphasizes that even so, one should not underestimate the instrumental value of messianisim, since it offers conditions that free man of mundane worries and distractions so that he can devote himself to the single-minded pursuit of knowledge of God.

> In the days of the World-to-Come, knowledge, wisdom and truth will increase, as it is said, "For the earth will be full of the knowledge of the Lord" (Isaiah 11:9), and it is said, "They will no more teach everyone his brother and everyone his neighbor" (Jeremiah 31:34), and further, "I will remove the heart of stone from your flesh" (Ezekiel 36:26). [*Laws of Repentance*]

He further writes concerning this point:

> The days of the Messiah are not ardently longed for on account of the plentiful vegetation, and the riches which they will bring in their train, nor in order that we may ride on horses, nor that we may drink to the accompaniment of various kinds of musical instruments, as is thought by those people who are confused in their ideas on such things. No! the prophets and saints wished and ardently desired [the days of the Messiah] because it implies the coming together of the virtuous, with choice deeds of goodness and knowledge, and the justice of the king, the greatness of his wisdom and his nearness to his Creator, as it is said: "The Lord said unto me, thou art my son; this day have I begotten thee." . . . And because it implies obedience to all the laws of Moses, without interference or disquietude or constraint, . . . as it is promised in the words, "And they shall teach no more every man his neighbor and every man his brother saying, Know the Lord; for they shall all know me from the least of them unto the greatest of them." "And I will take away the stony heart from your flesh." And there are many more similar verses on like themes. [*Introduction to Helek*]

Second, he strives to neutralize what might be mistaken as religious fantasy. He seems to try to counteract the people's exaggerated expectations fostered by biblical and midrashic literature and naturalize the concept of messianism by interpreting it in terms of regular patterns of nature. Wherever possible, he seems to try to make the content of messianic beliefs consistent with the order of nature by allegorizing prophetic and rabbinic statements that in their literal sense place messianism beyond the natural order.

Maimonides wrote that the Messiah himself will be mortal and that the longevity that people will enjoy in the messianic era will be a perfectly natural consequence of the conditions that will then prevail. In perhaps his most astounding pronouncement concerning the messianic age, Maimonides wrote:

> But the Messiah will die but people will live for 1,000 years. The Messiah will die, and his son and son's son will reign in his stead. God has clearly declared his death in the words, "He shall not fail nor be discouraged, till he have set judgment in the earth." His kingdom will endure a very long time and the lives

of men will be long also, because longevity is a consequence of
the removal of sorrows and cares. Let not the fact of the
duration of his kingdom for thousands of years seem strange to
you, for the sages have said that when a number of good things
come together, it is not an easy thing for them to separate again.
[*Introduction to Helek*]

Maimonides explains how the length of days that people will
enjoy during the messianic era need not imply a miraculous
change in the natural order. When human society is free of
violence, when people are not burdened psychologically by
anxieties resulting from scarcity and the struggle for survival,
and when people become conscious of their true human purpose, i.e., to know God, "then that society will be stable and
ordered and its members will enjoy satisfying and lengthy
lives."

Even amid his attempts to naturalize the messianic era,
Maimonides nevertheless does not altogether allegorize the
powers traditionally ascribed to the messianic figure:

His [the Messiah's] name will be great and fill the earth to its
uttermost bounds. It will be a greater name than that of King
Solomon and mightier. The nations will make peace with him
and lands will obey him by reason of his great rectitude and the
wonders that will come to light by his means. Any one that rises
up against him God will destroy and make him fall into his hand.
[*Introduction to Helek*]

And again in *Laws of Repentance* Maimonides adds:

Because the king who will arise from the seed of David will
possess more wisdom than Solomon and will be a great prophet,
approaching Moses, our teacher, he will teach the whole of the
Jewish people and instruct them in the way of God; and all
nations will come to hear him, as it is said, And at the end of days
it shall come to pass that the Mount of the Lord's house shall be
established as the top of the mountains [Micah 4:1; Isaiah 2:2].
[*Mishneh Torah, Hilkhot Teshuvah* 9:8–10]

But even amid this seeming concession to a more miraculous
aspect of the Messiah's influence over the nations of the earth,
Maimonides immediately adds:

So far as existing things are concerned, there will be no difference whatever between now and then, except that Israel will possess the kingdom. And this is the sense of the rabbis' statement: "There is no difference between this world and the days of the Messiah except the subjugation of the kingdoms alone." In his days there will be both the strong and the weak in their relations to others. But verily in those days the gaining of their livelihood will be so easy to men that they will do the lightest possible labor and reap great benefit. It is this that is meant by the remark of the rabbis, "The land of Israel will one day produce cakes ready baked, and garments of fine silk." For when one finds a thing easily and without labor, people are in the habit of saying, "So and so found bread ready baked, and a meal ready cooked." [*Introduction to Helek*]

In numerous other pronouncements concerning the messianic era, Maimonides repeatedly allegorizes the messianic prophecies and reinterprets them as depicting a natural state of affairs. Thus he sets out the following principles in regard to the era of redemption:

One should not entertain the notion that in the era of the Messiah any element of the natural order will be nullified, or that there will be innovations in the work of creation. Rather, the world will continue according to its pattern. Though Isaiah states, "The wolf will dwell with the lamb . . . ," these words are an allegory and a riddle, meaning that Israel will dwell securely together with the wicked haters of Israel who are likened to wolves and leopards. . . . In this era, all nations will return to the true faith and no longer rob or destroy. . . . Similarly, other prophecies of this nature concerning the Messiah are analogies. In the era of the messianic king, everyone will realize what was implied by these analogies and allusions. Our sages taught (*Berakhot* 34b): There will be no difference between the current age and the epoch of the Messiah save for our emancipation from subjugation to the gentile kingdoms. [*Laws of Kings and Wars* 12:1–2]

The only miraculous power, aside from the subjugation of his enemies, which Maimonides ascribes to the Messiah, is that, by virtue of possessing *ruah hakodesh,* the Holy Spirit, he will be able to determine who among the descendants of the tribe of Levi are priests and who are ordinary Levites. Then the Temple can be rebuilt and the sacrificial service reinstituted.

> The king Messiah will arise and restore the kingdom of David to its former state and original sovereignty. He will rebuild the sanctuary and gather the dispersed of Israel. All the ancient laws will be reinstituted in his days; sacrifices will again be offered; the sabbatical and jubilee years will again be observed in accordance with the commandments set forth in the Torah. [*Laws of Kings and Wars* 11:1]

Primarily, however, Maimonides sees the messianic king's functions as being both temporal and spiritual. He must provide social and political stability and security, but also establish the sovereignty of the Torah over his entire kingdom. Because he is an instrument for extending the rule of the Torah, he may not use his power for the sake of personal aggrandizement.

> The king Messiah will receive one-thirteenth of all the provinces to be conquered by Israel. This is the share that will be assigned to him and his descendants forever. [*Laws of Kings and Wars* 4:8]

Essentially, then, Maimonides sees the messianic king not as a messenger announcing a new revelation or radical change in the natural order, nor as a harbinger of an end to history. Rather, the Messiah seems simply to be the ideal embodiment of the halakhic conception of the king, who will fulfill the essential purpose of all kings by reestablishing a national kingdom governed by the Law of Moses. Maimonides' description of the Messiah thus parallels his conception of messianism as the means of an ideal fulfillment and implementation of the Torah. He therefore emphasizes that the Torah will in no way be abrogated during the messianic age, but indeed will be restored in its entirety.

Thus Maimonides allows for the possibility that new Jewish kings or governments may arise in the land of Israel before the coming of the Messiah himself. The Messiah is thus not pictured as a prophetic figure performing spectacular miracles, but rather as one among a series of kings who will follow him and perhaps also precede him. What distinguishes the messianic king from all other kings, however, is his success in restoring Jewish national life in all its aspects and the dissemination of the knowledge of God throughout the world through teaching and the abolishment of idolatry.

In equating the Messiah with other Jewish kings, Maimonides even enters into a discussion of the possibility of his failure:

> But if he does not meet with full success, or is slain, it is obvious that he is not the Messiah promised in the Torah. He is to be regarded like all the other whole-hearted and worthy kings of the House of David who died and whom the Holy One, blessed be He, raised up to test the multitude, as it is written: "And some of them that are wise shall stumble, to refine among them, and to purify, and to make white, even to the time of the end; for it is yet for the time appointed" (Daniel 11:35). [*Laws of Kings and Wars* 11:4]

Messianism, then, is simply the fulfillment of the biblical promise that the Jewish people will be given the historical opportunity to observe the entire Torah. This promise, as interpreted by Maimonides, does not presuppose an end to history as we know it. Maimonides claims that this somewhat less romantic view of the messianic epoch has always been the Jewish view of that time:

> The sages and prophets did not long for the days of the Messiah that Israel might exercise dominion over the world, or rule over the heathens, or be exalted by the nations, or that it might eat and drink and rejoice. Rather, their aspiration was that [the Jewish people] be free [to involve themselves] in Torah and its wisdom, without anyone to oppress or disturb them, and thus be found worthy of life in the World-to-Come. [*Laws of Kings and Wars* 12:4]

Whenever material well-being is promised or hoped for in Judaism, it is not regarded as an end in itself, but rather as a means for furthering knowledge and love of God. Messianic times are ideal and desirable because the conditions that will prevail will be conducive to becoming worthy for life in the World-to-Come. It is realism and not materialism that accounts for Judaism's concern for material well-being. Human beings cannot devote themselves to the pursuit of knowledge or disinterested worship of God when they are overburdened with physical and psychological concerns. This understanding also accounts for some of the better-known promises of the messianic era, such as the stability and peace of the world at large.

> In that era, there will be neither famine nor war, neither jealousy nor strife. Blessings will be abundant, comforts within the reach of all. The one preoccupation of the whole world will be to know the Lord. Hence Israelites nations will be very wise, they will know the things that are now concealed and will attain an understanding of their Creator to the utmost capacity of the human kind. [*Laws of Kings and Wars* 12:5]

This change in the stability and material perfection of the world will benefit the non-Jewish nations as well. If they observe the Noachide laws, the fundamental principles incumbent upon all human beings according to *halakhah,* and subjugate themselves to God's authority, they too will share in this world of the future. They must keep the Bible's universal code of universal ethics and morality, known as the Seven Noachide Laws, which entail prohibitions on idolatry, blasphemy, murder, sexual immorality, kidnapping, sadistic treatment of animals, and a postitive commandment to set up courts of law and uphold justice. But there is a very important precondition to these laws insofar as they necessitate an acceptance of Sinaitic revelation as the exclusive source for validating obedience to the Noachide laws.

> A heathen who accepts the seven commandments and who serves them scrupulously is a "righteous heathen," and will have a portion in the World-to-Come, provided that he accepts them and performs them because the Holy One, blessed be He, commanded them in the Law and made known through Moses our teacher, that the observance thereof had been enjoined

upon the descendants of Noah even before the Law was given.
But if his observance thereof is based upon a reasoned conclusion he is not deemed a resident alien, or one of the pious of the
gentiles, but one of their wise men. [*Laws of Kings and Wars*
8:11]

In fact, the teaching and dissemination of these Noachide
commandments comprised, in the opinion of Maimonides, one
of the integral components of the messianic ideal. The Noachide commandments, which among other things prohibit
idolatry and enjoin certain fundamental norms of social justice,
comprised what Maimonides believed to be the essential conditions necessary for a universal monotheistic world order. The
obligation to enforce them was unconditional and thus could
not be confined to the geographical borders of Israel and its
surroundings. In the times of the Messiah the laws would
spread throughout the world to be adopted by all nations.

What is possibly one of the most interesting facets concerning the non-Jewish role in the messianic era is the role that
the major non-Jewish religions play in educating the heathen
world about the Messiah before his arrival. After making it clear
that his interpretation of the emergence of the two religions is
based more on speculation than on knowledge, since the
limitations of human understanding preclude the possibility of
acquiring knowledge of God's ways in history, Maimonides
explains how he saw in Christianity and Islam a connection
between the restoration of Israel's sovereignty and the universal triumph of monotheism. Since the two religions have
exposed vast numbers of people to the biblical world of
concepts and ideas, they have created a plausible framework
for Judaism's reemergence in history as the dominant monotheistic religion.

Even of Jesus of Nazareth, who imagined that he was the
Messiah, but was put to death by the court, Daniel had prophesied, as it is written: And the children of the violent among thy
people shall lift themselves up to establish the vision; but they
shall stumble [Daniel 11:14]. For has there ever been a greater

stumbling than this? All the prophets affirmed that the Messiah would redeem Israel, save them, gather their dispersed, and confirm the commandments. But he caused Israel to be destroyed by the sword, their remnants to be dispersed and humiliated. He was instrumental in changing the Torah and causing the world to err and serve another beside God.

But it is beyond the human mind to fathom the designs of the Creator; for our ways are not His ways, neither are our thoughts His thoughts. All these matters relating to Jesus of Nazareth and the Ishmaelite [Muhammad] who came after him, only served to clear the way for King Messiah, to prepare the whole world to worship God with one accord, as it is written: For then will I turn to the peoples a pure language, that they may all call upon the name of the Lord to serve Him with one consent [Zephaniah 3:9]. Thus the messianic hope, the Torah, and the commandments have become familiar topics—topics of conversation [among the inhabitants] of the far isles and many peoples, uncircumcised of heart and flesh. They are discussing these matters and the commandments of the Torah. Some say: "Those commandments were true, but have lost their validity and are no longer binding." Others declare that they had an esoteric meaning and were not intended to be taken literally, that the Messiah has already come and revealed their occult significance. But when the true King Messiah will appear and succeed, be exalted and lifted up, they will forthwith recant and realize that they have inherited naught but lies from their fathers, that their prophets and forbears led them astray. [*Laws of Kings and Wars* 11:4; this passage was deleted from most of the editions published since the Venice edition of 1574]

What emerges from this discussion of the Maimonidean view of messianism is this: The age of the Messiah is not the final and loftiest stage in the historical process. Rather, it is a precursor to what *is* the final and loftiest stage in the creative process— when all bodies will die and we will live an ethereal existence in the World-to-Come. Note that according to Maimonides, the World-to-Come does not refer to the messianic era. Rather, it refers to the heavenly realm and the Garden of Eden. Maimonides is of the opinion that ultimately the spiritual transcends the physical and it is toward this spiritual existence that we are all headed and that constitutes the final reward. Only in a spiritual guise, uninhibited by the body, can the soul finally attain a knowledge of God:

> In the World-to-Come, our souls will attain the secrets of the Creator just as or even more than the stars and the celestial spheres achieve those secrets. Similarly, the rabbis of blessed memory said: "In the World-to-Come, there will be neither eating nor drinking. All there will be is that the righteous will sit with their crowns upon their heads, and they will delight in the Glory of the Divine Presence." [*Introduction to Helek*]
>
> In the World-to-Come, there is no physical body or any material substance. There are only bodiless souls of the righteous like the ministering angels. Since there are no material substances in that world, there is neither eating nor drinking nor anything required by the bodies of the human beings on earth. None of the conditions occur there that are incidental to physical bodies in this world, such as sitting, standing, sleeping, seeing, grief, merriment, and their like. . . . When the Sages mentioned that "the righteous sit," it is only an allegorical expression that means that the souls of the righteous exist there without labor or effort. Similarly, the sages' expression of "their crowns on their heads" means that the knowledge they have acquired is with them. [*Laws of Repentance* 8:8]

Thus, Maimonides sees all corporeal references pertaining the World-to-Come as mere allegory. The World-to-Come is a world of souls, and it is this spiritual domain that constitutes the final good that God offers.

Notwithstanding the rationalism of the Maimonidean approach to the subject of the Messiah, and notwithstanding the fact that in his view the messianic age is not the culmination of the historical process, the seriousness with which Maimonides deals with the subject of the Messiah is beyond question. Aside from his earlier quoted statements of the heresy of those who deny the coming of the Messiah, he devoted significant portions of his epistles to Jewish communities around the world, encouraging the suffering masses of Israel never to lose hope in his arrival. Notwithstanding the advances of the Gentile nations amid the lowliness of Israel and notwithstanding how improbable, indeed impossible, the advent of the Messiah would ever seem, one could rest assured beyond the shadow of a doubt that God would keep His promise and send the Messiah.

This is how matters stand regarding the era of the Messiah, may he speedily come. For while the Gentiles believe that our nation will never constitute an independent state, nor will it ever rise above its present condition, and all the astrologers, diviners, and augurs concur in this opinion, God will prove their views and beliefs false, and will order the advent of the Messiah. [*Epistle to Yemen*]

22

THE MESSIAH IN OUR TIME

I t may cause dismay and serve as somewhat of a disappoint-
ment that, in the opinion of Maimonides, the messianic era
will not be all that miraculous. This does not in any way
lessen the magnitude of change that will embrace the world at
that time. On the contrary, the Maimonidean theory provides a
highly probable scenario in which the messianic era can easily
follow the extraordinary changes that are already part of
modern-day society. Contemporary Jewish thinkers, such as
Rabbi Aryeh Kaplan in his book *The Real Messiah,* address how
Maimonidean naturalism affords a view of the messianic era
that is highly compatible with the technological and social
revolutions that have transformed our world over the past two
hundred years.

It is a foundation of Judaism that the messianic age can
miraculously begin any day. When Rabbi Yehoshua ben Levi
asked Elijah when the Messiah would come, he answered with
the verse (Psalm 95:17), "Today—if you hearken to His voice"
(*Sanhedrin* 98a). What follows is a hypothetical scenario, based
on the above statements of Maimonides, in which the world
can slip into a messianic age in a totally natural way, perhaps
without even realizing it at first.

Kaplan's vision is compelling. If one looks with an unpreju-
diced eye at the world today, he will see an age where almost
all the Jewish prophecies regarding the prelude to the messianic

211

age are coming to pass. Even the most doubtful skeptic cannot help wondering how this could be mere coincidence. The man with clear vision can truly see the hand of God at work.

The ultimate goal of the historic process is the perfection of society. Since everything was created by God, all must eventually be perfected. This is even true of man's mundane world, which was created as an arena for our service toward God. Over the past two hundred years, an unprecedented acceleration in man's achievements has occurred. A man of two thousand years ago would find the world of two hundred years ago different, but not unimaginatively so. But the man of two hundred years ago, if transported to today's society, would find himself in a world beyond his wildest imagination.

We are witnessing a steady perfection of mankind's civilization—a world where the dread plagues that decimated entire civilizations no longer exist (and while there is AIDS, it can still be prevented, albeit with a large measure of social restraint, if care is taken, unlike the terrible plagues of the past); where man communicates instantaneously with all parts of the world and flies in hours to the most distant lands; where man totally dominates his environment and is waited upon by a host of electrical servants. Where the world's superpowers devote their resources not merely to overpowering weaker nations, but to foreign aid, giving away tens of billions of dollars per year to alleviate the suffering of populations the world over; where atoms are smashed, giving man energy and ability beyond his wildest dreams; where space travel is not an impossible dream but an everyday occurrence. Over the past two centuries man has conquered his world as never before.

This thought is expressed aptly by Rabbi Y. B. Soloveitchik in his *"Lonely Man of Faith,"* where he portrays man's control over nature as being one of the imperatives given to "majestic man." He writes that one of the most striking elements and one of the central dilemmas of modernity is that majestic man has achieved unparalleled success in his attempts to explain and control nature. And while Soloveitchik uses the point to emphasize that man has shifted away from his other imperative, namely, the development of "a covenantal faith community," it cannot be ignored that of all this startling progress must mean something for the world of the future. The past hundred years or so have brought about an increase in knowledge unsurpassed in all human history and the accomplishments have been truly amazing.

What does it all mean? Why is all this happening now? In all the thousands of years of human civilization, there were many great men of genius. Why could they not bring about the revolution of knowledge that we are now experiencing? Why did it have to wait until this century? And what is it all leading to? Is there a relationship between all of these things and the prophecies that tell of the arrival of the messianic era? The above coming together in such a short space of time could be mere coincidence. But in truth, it has all been foretold.

The present technological revolution has been predicted. Almost two thousand years ago, the *Zohar* (1:117a) predicted, "In the 600th year of the sixth millennium, the gates of wisdom on high and the wellsprings of lower wisdom will be opened. This will prepare the world to enter the seventh millennium, just as a man prepares himself toward sunset on Friday for the Sabbath. It is the same here. And a mnemonic for this is (Genesis 7:11), 'In the 600th year . . . all the foundations of the great deep were split.' "

Here we see a clear prediction that in the Jewish year 5600 (or 1840), the wellsprings of lower wisdom would be opened and there would be a sudden expansion of secular knowledge. Although the year 1840 did not yield any major scientific breakthrough, the date corresponds, with almost uncanny accuracy, the onset of our present scientific revolution.

The correlation between the technological breakthrough and the messianic era is very straightforward. In order that man devote himself totally toward his ultimate goal, other forms of work must be eliminated or, at the very least, curtailed. Technology provides a means for man to achieve mastery over creation with the utmost alacrity, thus enabling him to devote his time and energy to pursuing the knowledge of God and thus bringing perfection to himself and his world. Therefore, disease will have to be eliminated, as has been predicted by the prophet Isaiah: "The eyes of the blind will be opened, the ears of the deaf shall be unstopped; then shall the lame man leap as a hart and the tongue of the dumb shall sing" (Isaiah 35:5).

Many such miracles are predicted, such as "grapes as large as hen's eggs, and grains of wheat as big as a fist" (*Ketubot* 111b). All this can be possible with a technology not far removed from that of today. Indeed, when Rabban Gamaliel spoke of these predicted miracles, he stated that they would not involve any change in the laws of nature; they are allusions to a highly advanced technology. Thus, so little labor will be needed to process agricultural products that clothing and loaves of bread will seem to grow on trees.

With the proliferation of the technological revolution, the curse of Adam will be largely eliminated (Genesis 3:19): "With the sweat of your brow you shall eat bread. . . ." Thus Maimonides writes that people will speak of these developments as if they are happening miraculously on their own, but indeed are rational developments. Similarly, as we learn the secrets of life processes it will become possible to make trees bear fruit continually (*Shabbat* 30b, according to the interpretation of Maimonides on *Sanhedrin* 10:1).

The tradition may have even anticipated the tremendous destructive powers of our modern technology. Thus, we have the teaching of Rabbi Elazar that the messianic age will begin in a generation with the power to destroy itself (*Song of Songs Rabbah* 2:29).

The technological miracles of the pre-messianic age might also bring about an even more profound social revolution. The total abolishment of war might not seem to be such a miraculous occurrence. Quite possibly due to the fact that nations will know of the destructive power of modern-day armaments, they themselves will abolish all hostilities on an international scale, just as the prophet Isaiah predicted (Isaiah 2:4): "Nation shall not lift up sword against nation, neither shall they practice war any more." As stated earlier, Maimonides sees the prophecy of "The wolf shall dwell with the lamb, and the leopard shall lie down with the kid" (Isaiah 11:6) as referring allegorically to the peace and harmony between nations. True to this tradition, Rabbi Nachman of Breslov states that man will realize the foolishness of war, just as he has already realized that of pagan idolatry (*Sihot Maharan, Avodat Hashem,* no. 99). Surely, the fall of the Berlin Wall, the end of the Cold War, and the complete disintegration of the Soviet Union—the arch nemesis of the Jews and the State of Israel—could not have been predicted even half a decade ago. That all this has occurred in such a short space of time indicates a supernatural undercurrent, guiding these developments in accordance with corresponding prophecies of old. One cannot forever remain blind to the hand of God in history, replacing it with social observations of the flaws of Communism and the like. China is also Communist, and has been almost as long as the Soviet Union. Yet, there is no indication that the regime will disintegrate or be overthrown by a freedom movement any time soon. Surely, no expert is willing to risk his credibility by allotting a time framework for the demise of Communism in China. The very recent occurrences inside the former Soviet Union and the influx of Russian Jews to Israel that are the direct result of Communism's decline must be examined by each of us so that its higher messianic implications are not missed.

On an individual level, the changes in the messianic epoch will be even greater. When nations "beat their swords into plowshares," the hundreds of billions of dollars used for war and defense can be diverted to the perfection of society. There will be a standard of social justice exemplified by the prophecy, "The Lord has sworn. . . . Surely I will no more give your corn to be food for your enemies, and strangers will not drink your wine for which they have not labored" (Isaiah 62:8). This is also the spirit of the prophecy, "To bind up the broken hearted, to proclaim liberty to the captives, and untie those who are bound" (Isaiah 61:1).

But the prophets have also foretold that these advances in the premessianic age will not be without cost. The rapid changes on both a technological and sociological level will result in a great social upheaval. The cataclysmic changes will result in considerable suffering, often referred to as the *Hevlei Mashiah* or Birthpangs of the Messiah. If the Messiah comes with miracles, these "birthpangs" may be avoided, but the great changes involved in his coming in the manner adopted by Maimonides may make these terrible travails inevitable.

Since in a period of such accelerated change parents and children will grow up in literally different worlds, traditions handed from father to son will be among the major casualties. The Talmud describes at length how there will be general dissatisfaction with the values of religion—in such a rapidly changing world, people will naturally be enamored with the new and dissatisfied with the old. Thus, the sages teach that neither parents nor the aged will be respected, the old will have to seek favors from the young, and a man's household will become his enemies. Insolence will increase, people will no longer have respect, and none will offer reproof. Religious studies will be despised and used by nonbelievers to strengthen their cause, the government will become godless, academies will be places of indiscretion, and the religious will be denigrated.

> In the generation when the Messiah comes, young men will insult the old, and old men will stand before the young [to give them honor]; daughters will rise up against their mothers, and daughters-in-law against their mothers-in-law. The people shall be dog-faced, and a son will not be abashed in his father's presence. It has been taught, R. Nehemiah said: In the generation of the Messiah's coming impudence will increase, esteem be perverted. [*Sanhedrin* 97a]
>
> The Wisdom of the learned will degenerate; fearers of sin will be despised; and the truth will be lacking. Youths will put old men to shame. [*Sotah* 49b]

Judaism will suffer greatly because of these upheavals. There is a tradition that the Jews will split up into various groups, each laying claim to the truth, as the Talmud says, "Our truth shall be divided into flocks" (*Sanhedrin* 97a). This will make it exceedingly difficult, almost impossible, to discern true Judaism from the false. This is the meaning of the prophecy, "Truth will fail" (Isaiah 59:15).

Maimonides, in his *Epistle to Yemen* even predicted that many will leave the fold of Judaism completely, without maliciously intending to do harm to the Jewish people, and the nation shall suffer immensely as a result of their actions. This is how our sages interpret the prophecy, "The wicked shall do wickedly, and not understand" (Daniel 12:10).

Of course, there will be some Jews who remain true to their traditions. They will realize that they are witnessing the death throes of a degenerate old order and will not be drawn into it. But they will suffer all the more for this, and be dubbed fools for not conforming to the liberal ways of the premessianic age. This is the meaning of the prophecy (Isaiah 59:15), "He who departs from evil will be considered a fool" (*Sanhedrin* 97a).

One of our important traditions regarding the advent of the Messiah is that it will mark the return of prophecy. In order to counter the terrible social upheaval described above, and the gap between the generations, the Messiah will be preceded by the prophet Elijah, as it is stated, "Behold I am sending you the prophet Elijah before the arrival of God's great day" (Malachi 3:23). There is much dispute with regard to Elijah's function. In a discourse on the subject, Rabbi Menachem Schneerson explains that the purpose of this perennial prophet's materialization before the messianic era is twofold: (1) to uplift and refine the Jewish people, thus preparing them for the messianic redemption—the need for this can be readily appreciated in light of the prophecies of social doom listed above, and (2) to eliminate wrongdoing and heal the rifts of the world through peace, as the prophet foretold that Elijah "shall bring back the hearts of the fathers to the children and the hearts of the children to their fathers" (Malachi 3:24).

The Rebbe explains that in the final analysis, Elijah's endeavors to establish peace among the Jewish people are clearly interrelated with his heralding the arrival of the Messiah. For peace, unity, and brotherly love are the means of hastening the coming of redemption. The sages teach that the exile was caused by unwarranted hatred (*Yoma* 9b; *Gittin* 55b). Undoing the cause of the exile—hatred—will thus erase its effect—the exile itself.

This prophecy of the hearts of the fathers being returned through their children is a clear indication that our generation stands at the footsteps of the messianic era. Who has ever heard of children returning the hearts of their parents to their people and to their God? Clearly, every religion and way of life is propagated from generation to generation only through parents teaching their children of the tradition. But who has ever heard of a tradition going backward? How can it be that children will bring their parents back to Judaism? When a tradition is cut, it usually marks the end of the line. Yet, in our generation we are witnesses to the fact that it is happening. Parents who abandoned Judaism earlier in their lives are suddenly returning to it because of their children. Young inquisitive Jewish minds are embracing Judaism on their own and, after overcoming the usual initial hostility from their parents, they are conveying these eternal truths back to the previous generations, causing them to embrace them, too.

So what we are witnessing is a closing of the generation and a resolution to tremendous social upheaval that has taken place over the last few decades, coming about through the newfound commitment of the children. Society has gone full circle, and if it can continue its course, it will have paved the way for the coming of the Messiah.

Into a world prepared to receive him, the Messiah will then be born. He will be a mortal human being, born normally of human parents. Tradition states that he will be a direct descendent of King David and indeed, there are numerous Jewish families today that can claim such lineage. Some leaders have literally changed the course of history. Evil leaders, like the crazed German butcher Hitler, literally hypnotized entire nations, bringing them to do things that normally would be unthinkable in a civilized society. King Solomon assures in his Song of Songs that for every power that exists for evil, it must certainly exist for good.

Based on the Maimonidean creed, Kaplan envisions the Messiah as a learned, charismatic leader, greater than any other in man's history. He imagines a social and political genius surpassing all others, who, by using the vast communication networks now at our disposal, could spread his message to the entire world and change the very fabric of our society.

Now imagine that he is a religious Jew, a *tzaddik*. It may have once seemed far-fetched for a *tzaddik* to assume a role in world leadership, but the world is becoming increasingly more accustomed to accepting leaders of all races, religions, and ethnic groups. Indeed today there are numerous religious leaders whose opinions are sought by political leaders on all issues. It is not at all far-fetched to picture a *tzaddik* in such a role.

One possible scenario could involve the Middle East situation. This is a problem that involves all the world powers. Now imagine a Jew, a *tzaddik,* solving this thorny problem by adapting eternal truths from the Torah to fit this modern-day dilemma. It is entirely conceivable that such a demonstration of statesmanship and political genius would place him in a position of world leadership. The major powers would have the greatest respect and listen to such an individual. Thus his leadership would transcend demographic politics and he would stand above all of the existing political frameworks. Jew and non-Jew alike would look to this *tzaddik* for guidance in solving the world's ills.

The Jewish people have always had a profound respect for those who assume roles of world leadership. After initial hostility to the concept of a messianic figure due to the amount of suffering caused to the Jews at the hands of false Messiahs, this *tzaddik* would emerge as a leader of unparalleled authority in all Jewish circles. He would make religion respectable by transforming the Jewish religious landscape. Through far-reaching global programs, he would bridge the divide between the Orthodox and non-Orthodox and cause thousands to return to Jewish observance.

It is just possible that all Jewish leaders would agree to name him their leader and confer upon him the Mosaic ordination (see *Mishneh Torah, Laws of the Sanhedrin* 4:11). The chain of this ordination was broken some sixteen hundred years ago and must be renewed before the Sanhedrin, the religious supreme court and legislature of the Jews, can be reestablished. If this *tzaddik* was so ordained by the entire community, he could then reestablish the Sanhedrin. This is a necessary condition for the rebuilding of the Temple: "And I will restore your judges as at first, and your counsellors as at the beginning; afterward you shall be called the city of righteousness, the faithful city" (Isaiah 1:26). Such a Sanhedrin would also be able to formally recognize the Messiah (*Tosefta Sanhedrin* 3:2; *Mishneh Torah, Sanhedrin* 4:1).

In his position of leadership, through direct negotiation, and perhaps with the concurrence of the world powers, this *tzaddik* would regain the Temple Mount for the Jewish people. With a Sanhedrin to iron out the many thorny halakhic questions, it might then be possible to rebuild the Holy Temple.

However, if this is accomplished, we will already have fulfilled the essential part of the messianic promise. It is very important to note that these accomplishments are a minimum for our acceptance of an individual as the Messiah. There have been numerous people who have claimed to be the Messiah, but the fact that they did not achieve these minimal goals proved them to be false.

As both an unparalleled genius and a *tzaddik,* the Messiah will see through the sham and hypocrisy of this world. Thus, the Isaiah foretold, "He will sense the fear of the Lord, and he shall not judge after the sight of his eyes, nor decide after the hearing of his ears" (Isaiah 11:3).

As the Messiah's powers develop, so will his fame. The world will begin to recognize his profound wisdom and come to seek his advice. As a *tzaddik,* he will teach all mankind to live in peace and follow God's teachings. Thus Isaiah foretold:

> And it shall to pass in the end of days that the mountain of God's house shall be set over all other mountains and lifted high above the hills, and all nations shall come streaming to it. And many people shall come and say: Come let us go to the house of the God of Jacob and He [the Messiah] will teach us His ways and we will walk in His paths. For out of Zion shall go forth the Torah and God's word from Jerusalem. And He [the Messiah] will judge between nations and decide between peoples. And they shall beat their swords into plowshares and their spears into pruning hooks. Nation shall not lift up sword against nation; neither shall they practice war any more. [Isaiah 2:2–4]

Although the Messiah will influence and teach all of mankind, his main mission will be to bring the Jews back to God. "For the children of Israel shall sit many days without king or prince. . . . Afterward shall the children of Israel return and seek the Lord their God and David their king . . . in the end of days" (Josiah 3:5). Similarly, "And My servant David shall be king over them, and they shall all have one shepherd, and they shall also walk in My ordinances and observe My laws" (Ezekiel 37:24).

As society reaches toward perfection and the world becomes increasingly Godly, men, with their copious free time brought about by technological advance and lack of war, will begin to explore the transcendental more and more, "for all the earth shall be full of the knowledge of God, as the waters cover the ocean floor" (Isaiah 11:9). More and more people will achieve the mystical union of prophecy, as foretold: "And it shall come to pass afterward, that I will pour My Spirit on all flesh, and your sons and your daughters shall prophesy" (Joel 3:1).

Although man will still have free will in the messianic age, he will have every inducement to do good and follow God's teachings. It will be as if the power of evil were totally annihilated. And as man approaches this lofty level, he will also become worthy of a divine providence not limited by the laws of nature. What is now manifestly miraculous will ultimately become part of the nature of things. This, wedded to man's newly gained powers to bring forth the best that untainted nature has to offer, will bring man to his ultimate destiny, which, according to Maimonides, is a disembodied existence in the World-to-Come. After reaching the highest perfection attainable by man, it will be time for all of mankind to leave their limiting physical existence, and return to the sublimity of spiritual existence in the Garden of Eden.

Yet, notwithstanding the compelling and believable nature of Maimonides' natural, nonmiraculous vision of the future, the Maimonidean view of the messianic age is hotly contested by a host of Maimonides' contemporaries.

23

NACHMANIDES' RADICAL NEW WORLD

A host of assertions of Maimonides pertaining to the messianic era are sharply contested by Nachmanides, Rabbi Moshe ben Nachman. Primarily, he contests Maimonides' allegorical interpretation of the messianic prophecies and the Maimonidean interpretation of the World-to-Come.

Nachmanides devotes all of the final section of his *Gate of Reward* to proving that the World-to-Come is not the Garden of Eden, the place where souls are to be found after their departure from this world. Rather, the World-to-Come, whenever used in a rabbinical context, refers to the epoch of the Messiah. Nachmanides rejects Maimonides' claim that after the resurrection of the dead, the world would continue for several hundred generations, only in order for everyone to die and their souls to return to the Garden of Eden. Nachmanides rather sees the messianic era as the ultimate "reward" promised by Judaism and the highest possible human attainment. While he repeatedly commends Maimonides for his insightful views of the nature of the soul, the Garden of Eden, and the messianic era, Nachmanides sharply contests Maimonides' interpretation of the World-to-Come.

The Rabbi [Moshe be Maimon] of blessed memory has written extensively in Chapter *Helek* and in his Scroll on the Resurrection of the Dead to bring proof that those who attain the

World-to-Come are only the bodiless souls. The matter of *Gan
Eden,* in his opinion, is a selected place on earth in which God
planted trees and various kinds of plants which are greatly
beneficial to man. He will reveal it and disclose it and people
will delight in it. . . . in the era of the Messiah and at the time of
the resurrection of the body, just as [they do] in this world with
its pleasures of eating, drinking, anointing, and washing. Yet
this is not the ultimate reward, as the Rabbi of blessed memory
explained. . . . The world-to-come—that is, the existence of the
soul—is independent thereof, however, and is a natural and
customary way of the world. This however is most surprising.
[*The Gate of Reward*]

But before he subjects Maimonides' approach to rigorous
scrutinization and refutation, he first offers his opinion as to
the radical approach of Maimonides.

The lengthy discussion of the Rabbi [Moseh ben Maimon] of
blessed memory, which was to convince [us] that those inher-
iting the world-to-come will be bodiless, serves two purposes:
He knows that the people of our tradition believe that after the
resurrection, there will be no death. This is in accordance with
the rabbis' interpretation of the verse, "He will swallow up
death forever" (Isaiah 25:8). They state: "The dead that the
Holy One, blessed be He, will resurrect will not return to their
dust" (*Sanhedrin* 92a). According to this opinion, those who
merit the World-to-Come will continue to live in their bodies in
that world. The Rabbi however, abrogated this opinion with all
his strength. Many sages of this generation differed with him on
this matter concerning the meaning of the term *Olam Haba* (the
world-to-come), as you will find in their words. . . .
   As a second objective, the Rabbi further intended to strengthen
[our belief in] the soul itself. He wished to impress upon us that
it is not a body or a power in a body, but a separate intelligence
like the group of angels. Thus, he states in the Scroll of the
Resurrection of the Dead: "The cause for all this [belief in the
body's existence in the World-to-Come] lies in the thinking of the
uneducated masses. They do not believe in a true existence for
anything but the physical body. That which is neither a body nor
a force in a body has no existence according to the opinion of
these common ignorant people. Most of them, therefore,

believe that the Creator is a body, for in their opinion, were He not a body, he would not exist. [*The Gate of Reward*]

But notwithstanding Maimonides' good intentions, Nachmanides demonstrates how ultimately "the Rabbi" had been mistaken and how the World-to-Come can mean nothing save the world in the epoch of the Messiah.

He proceeds to bring scores of rabbinical statements from the Talmud and other sources that prove that the World-to-Come cannot mean the domain of the souls after life on this earth and can only refer to the messianic era. "In any case, concerning the meaning of the World-to-Come, we have learned that the World-to-Come is a world in which the body, the Sanctuary, and its vessels will be present. It is not the World of Souls in which every man receives his due immediately after death and goes either to *Gehinnom* or the Garden of Eden" *(The Gate of Reward).*

One of the simple yet substantial proofs used by Nachmanides is the constant reference throughout talmudic literature that in the future the righteous will be allotted life in the World-to-Come. Now surely the righteous are now in the Garden of Eden and thus, this future event, cannot be referring to their return to the World of Souls. In fact, Nachmanides goes as far as asking why, according to Maimonides, there need even be a resurrection of the dead and a return of the souls of the righteous to the physical world and into a body, only in order to die once again and return to the spiritual domain without a body. Rather, we must conclude that the World-to-Come has not yet been inhabited by anyone, and will only be a future event.

It is quite evident that you will find many places in the Talmud in which the rabbis mention the wicked being in Gehenna. . . . The rabbis also mention that the righteous are presently in *Gan Eden*. However, you will never find anywhere in the Talmud that the rabbis say that no one is presently in the World-to-Come. Instead, they say, "He is destined for life in the World-to-Come". . . . Thus, after the demise of the righteous, the rabbis say of them that "they are allotted life in the

World-to-Come,'' which is their expression indicating the future. You may learn from this statement that when the righteous depart from this world, they go to the Garden of Eden, which is the World of the Souls. They do not go to the world called *Olam Haba*—the World-to-Come, but they are allotted it and destined for it. [*The Gate of Reward*]

Having demonstrated that the world-to-come is a life here on earth, with the soul in the body, Nachmanides must now contend with the various rabbinical statements that imply that the World-to-Come will not involve bodily activity. How can he reconcile his contention that the World-to-Come is the messianic era that will be enjoyed by living humans, with the many talmudic discourses that imply that in the messianic era there will not be life as we know it?

In a radical departure from the naturalistic view of the messianic era adopted by Maimonides, Nachmanides adopts the view of a radical physical transformation of life and the physical world. In doing so, he explains the various prophetic and rabbinic statements about the messianic era according to their literal meaning (Maimonides had taken them allegorically).

Nachmanides explains how human existence in the World-to-Come will be sustained by spiritual sustenance, as opposed to the physical nutrients upon which we are dependent today.

With reference to this world-to-come, the rabbis stated in Tractate *Berakhot* (17a): "Rav often said, In the World-to-Come there will be neither eating nor drinking, neither envy nor hatred nor competition. All [there will be] is that the righteous will sit with their crowns upon their heads, and they will delight in the Glory of the Divine Presence. . . ." This purports to state that the existence of the people who will merit the World-to-Come will be made possible by the light of the [Divine] Glory. This is analogous to the soul's existence in the body in this world being attained by eating and drinking. This concept is akin to the verse, "In the light of the King's countenance is life (Proverbs 16:15)," which was interpreted by the rabbis in *Ve'eileh Shemot Rabbah* as follows: "And they beheld God, and did eat and drink." It was eating and beholding. [*The Gate of Reward*]

Nachmanides adds that there is nothing terribly new or unbelievable about this phenomenon. Indeed, he lists a number of persons who have already experienced this phenomenon of sustenance from spiritual rather than physical sources. "Should we seek to attribute this to a miraculous [and supernatural] act, let the case of Elijah prove [otherwise]. In his living ascent to heaven, he did not cast off the [physical] body and was not separated from the soul. Yet, he still exists since that time and forever" *(The Gate of Reward)*.

The most famous example of a human being existing without the aid of food, water, and other bodily necessities is the forty days and nights that Moses spent on Mount Sinai, to which the Torah attests that he did not eat, drink, or sleep. Nachmanides uses this as yet another reference to what life will be like in the messianic era: "In the messianic era there will be an ascendancy of the soul over the body, which annuls the physical powers, as we have previously mentioned, and causes the body to exist without food and drink, just as the soul exists and as Moses was sustained on Mount [Sinai] for forty days. Nevertheless, the soul will always remain in the body" *(The Gate of Reward)*.

In yet another reference to Moses, Nachmanides maintains that Moses' nonearthly independence continued even after his tenure on Mount Sinai. Rather, his entire sustenance derived from his proximity and communion with Godliness: "Now Moses, whose soul was unique and elevated above those [other] people in the knowledge of his Creator, had no need of that thing [the manna] since his body was made intangible and supported by the Glory of the Divine Presence and his lofty perception [of God]" *(The Gate of Reward)*.

It is for this reason—the divine sustenance the body will enjoy—that eternity and new sublimity of the body are guaranteed. As it will no longer be sustained by finite material objects, the body will not be susceptible to expiration or demise. The infinite spiritual quality that will sustain it will make it indestructible and bestow upon it spiritual qualities thusfar only enjoyed by truly spiritual entities, such as angels and souls.

I have found [the following text] in the *Mekhilta:* Therefore, we believe in the Rabbis' statement: "The dead which the Holy One, blessed be He, will resurrect, will never again return to the earth. You may ask: During that millennium, in which the Holy

One, blessed be He, will be re-creating His world, how will they be sustained? The Holy One, blessed be He, will make them wings, and they will roam over the face of the waters." The connotation of "the wings" is that the soul will be endowed with angelic qualities that the body will enjoy with it. Thus, [the body will] avoid destruction when the elements of the world will be voided [during that millennium]. This is a very familiar and common theme throughout the teachings of the rabbis of blessed memory as they said in the *Midrash* and in the *Gemara:* "That it may be well with you in the world that is all good; and that you may prolong your days in the world that endures for all eternity." That is to say, all who merit that existence will live forever because there will be no death in [that world] . . . [in the world where the resurrected] will never again return to their dust. [*The Gate of Reward*]

Here Nachmanides forcefully argues against the assertion of Maimonides that the resurrection of the dead would be only a temporary matter. He further argues that in that time the body will transcend even the soul because, in addition to the physical virtue it possesses over the soul, it would also acquire the spiritual virtues of the soul. Playing the role of the mystic, Nachmanides introduces a notion that, to the unitiated, is the ludicrous concept of the supremacy of the body over the soul. The human mind almost naturally associates holiness with spirituality and disembodiment. Anything earthly is automatically assumed to be more distant from God than something physical, hence the uniform belief found throughout non-Jewish religions of the inferiority of the body to the soul. Nachmanides understood that one could not accept the argument for the eternity of the body in the messianic era if one did not properly apprehend this principle that the body is not a physical shell, but supercedes even the soul in sublimity. Furthermore, as the normal physiological and biological functions such as digestion and procreation would cease during the messianic era, some other purpose would have to be found for the body:

You may ask [this question] of us: "As the philosophers have said: the body consists of three parts that serve organic functions. They are: the organs of food [digestion], the organs of procreation, and the organs serving the well-balancing of the body. The general purpose of the body's existence, [according to the philosophers], is but for one goal, and that is the consumption of food, which enables the body to exist and to give birth to its like. In the World-to-Come, however, when that goal will be eliminated, inasmuch as there will be neither eating nor drinking then, the body will have no purpose. [Yet, we know] that in God's work nothing is in vain. The answer to all these [apparent contradictions] is that this creation [of the body which will occur] at the time of the resurrection of the dead will be for the purpose of [facilitating] the [biological] services mentioned. The Holy One, blessed be He, does not desire their subsequent cessation. Moreover, there are profound secrets in this formation [of the body] for the [original] creation in this form was not [the result of] some unbridled, meaningless deed. Rather, [the human form was so created] only for the great need and eminent reason, and He Who creates it, blessed be He, desires its [future] existence. If you will press us with the question about the eternal existence of the body that stems from the lower elements, [be advised that] we have already answered you that the existence of the body will [then] be like that of the soul. The existence of the soul will be [effectuated] through its unification with the knowledge of the Most High, and the existence [of the body and soul] will then be assured by that unification. [*The Gate of Reward*]

Nachmanides does not suffice with his insights into the sublimity of the body, but proceeds to criticize Maimonides for failing to see any higher purpose in the body save the execution of its mundane physiological and biological processes.

We wonder, moreover, why the Rabbi of blessed memory found necessary to write the following in the *Scroll of the Resurrection of Dead:* However, the life that is not followed by death is the life of the World-to-Come because it contains no [physical] body. And this is the correct opinion for all knowledgeable people—that those who attain life in the World-to-Come are, like the angels, souls without bodies. The proof for this [belief] is that the body consists of limbs that serve the activity of the soul, and the general purpose of the body's existence is but for one goal. That is to say, consumption of food serves the purpose of sustaining the body procreating its kind so that the generic form can exist. When purpose is removed, there will be no need for [the body] in the World-to-Come. A host of sages have explicitly stated that there will be no eating, drinking, or sexual intercourse in [the World-to-Come]. If their intention is to state that the body will not exist in that world, God, blessed be He, will not bring forth a purposeless thing, and will not create anything except for a purpose. Far be it from His deeds that they should be comparable to those [of the ones who] make the idols. Eyes have they, but they see not; they have ears, but they hear, not. In the eyes of those thinkers, the Creator, too, will create human limbs which serve no functions. Perhaps, according to these people, those [meriting] the world-to-come will not possess limbs at all, but only trunks! Perhaps they will be round or straight as pillars or columns. The opinions of these fools are nothing but laughable to all nations. Oh that they would altogether hold their peace! And it would be their wisdom. All these are the words of the Rabbi, son of Maimon, of blessed memory. . . . We shall now express our surprise at him. . . . What is the sense of these arguments? [*The Gate of Reward*]

The rational and allegorical approach to messianism adopted by Maimonides amazes Nachmanides. He feels that the inability of Maimonides to consign any miraculous nature to the messianic era leads him to misrepresent the essential characteristics of that era. The divide separating the two great scholars seems unbreachable. What is at stake is the entire characterization of Judaism's most awaited epoch. Nachmanides saw a radical and miraculous transformation of the observable world as we know it, while Maimonides, true to his rationalistic approach, saw a far better, but not too different world.

But it is the conviction with which Nachmanides argues his view of the messianic age that enforces the conclusion that he saw his theory as being beyond refutation and that Maimonides, albeit for good reason, had confused the Garden of Eden for the World-to-Come. Nachmanides' argument is methodical, well supported by scores of rabbinic pronouncements, and chronologically sensible. He showed how only through his interpretation could the various stages of the historical process as outlined in the Written and Oral Law fit together:

> We have now explained our intent regarding the reward [observing] the commandments and the punishment for the [transgression]. Let us restate it briefly: The reward of the souls and their existence in the World of Souls is called *Gan Eden* by our rabbis. Occasionally, they call it "the Upper Chamber" or "the Academy on High." After [the World of Souls] will come the era of the Messiah, which is part of this world. At the conclusion thereof, the [great] judgment and the resurrection of the dead will occur. This is the recompense that includes the body and the soul. . . . This is the great principle that is the hope of all who look longingly to the Holy One, blessed be He. It is the world-to-come, in which the body will become like the soul and the soul will be cleaving to the knowledge of the Most High just as it adhered [to that knowledge] in the Garden of Eden of the World of Souls. Now, however, it will be elevated to an even greater [degree of] perception than heretofore, and the existence of all will be forever and ever. [*The Gate of Reward*]

He concludes with an assurance that his view is the most consistent with the statements of the rabbis and the one held by the majority of scholars, despite some significant dissent.

> However, in spite of the fact that Maimonides' theory finds support in the writings of Rabbi Shlomo ibn Gabirol, you should accept our opinion because we have spoken according to the law and have brought proofs to [our] words from those of our Rabbis of blessed memory. I have further found that in his commentary on the Book of Daniel, the Gaon Rav Saadia of blessed memory speaks of the meaning of the term "world-to-come" in accordance with our words. Thus, it is a tradition of the ancients; do not forget their teaching. Still, there is no difference between us with the sole exception of a difference in nomenclature. All, however, agree about the resurrection of the dead and the existence of that time in its general outlines and details, as I have explained. The only [dissenting] opinion is that of Harav Rabbi Moshe [ben Maimon] of blessed memory, who assigned a limited time to the resurrection [of body and soul]

and reverts everything to the World of Souls, as mentioned
above. We, however, declare that the people of the resurrection
will exist forever, from the time of the resurrection of the dead,
to the world-to-come, which is an everlasting world. [*The Gate
of Reward*]

24

RECONCILING THE MIRACULOUS AND THE NATURAL

In the dispute between Maimonides and Nachmanides, one can easily identify the questions of the transcendency and Godliness of the physical compared with the spiritual, the body compared with the soul, material existence compared with ethereal existence, the earthly compared with heavenly, and so on. Superficially it would seem fair to assume that Maimonides comes down clearly in favor of the supremacy of the spiritual over the physical, while Nachmanides, with his mystical insights, recognizes the sublimity in the physical over the spiritual.

However, matters are not quite that simple. One should always be weary of jumping to early conclusions when studying Maimonides. Glaring inconsistencies in his messianic approach must be reconciled. Maimonides bases his messianic sketches entirely on rabbinic pronouncements about the messianic era, yet these statements do not seem to support him.

As pointed out by Nachmanides, on the surface there are a great many *midrashim* that would appear to contradict the Maimonidean principle that the era of the redemption will not inaugurate a new and miraculous world order. For example, the Talmud maintains that "ultimately all the shade trees in Israel will eventually bear fruit, as it is written, 'The trees will bear fruit and the vine and the fig trees will give forth their strength' (Leviticus 26:4)" (*Ketubot* 112b).

To do justice to the Maimonidean approach, one must give latitude for the allegorical meaning of this passage. Surely the term *fruit trees* could be interpreted as a reference to Torah scholars and *shade trees* to the unlearned, since in another passage the Talmud uses similar references when speaking of the sages and the masses (see *Taanit* 7a). Yet, the abundance of rabbinic exegesis suggesting a radical transformation in field production as we know it makes many of Maimonides' allegorical interpretations untenable. For instance, yet another rabbinic insight into the same verse quoted above maintains, "The earth will not give forth produce as it does now, but rather as it did in the time of Adam, the first man. On the very day he sowed, crops were produced" (*Ketubot* 112b; *Torat Kohanim*).

The rejection of literalism in the messianic prophecies, which is stubbornly maintained by Maimonides, led many other commentators, aside from Nachmanides, to reject the former's approach. Case in point, Rabbi Avraham ben David, known as *Raavad,* living up to his reputation as archnemesis of Maimonides, argues with his relegation of all prophecies to allegory. "Behold," he warns, "the Torah writes, 'And I will remove predators from the earth,' implying that this prophecy is surely not an allegory, but rather a description of what will actually take place that God would transform the predatory nature of many wild animals."

An interesting approach to reconciling Maimonides with the miraculous rabbinic pronouncements about the messianic age is taken by Rabbi Dovid ben Zamra, *Radvaz,* in his response to the comments of *Raavad.* He states that the verse about the neutering of wild animals does not represent a contradiction. Just as the other verses are allegories, so is this.

> What one should believe is the following: The [prophecies] will be fulfilled in a literal manner in the land of Israel. This is implied by the verse, "They shall do no evil, nor shall they destroy throughout My holy mountain, because *the land* [i.e., the land that is best known] will be full of knowledge." Similarly, it is written, "I will remove predators *from the land.*" In other lands, in contrast, "the world will continue according to its pattern." [In these lands] the prophecies will be fulfilled in an allegorical sense, as it is written, "Nation will not lift up sword against nation, nor shall they learn war any more." [Isaiah 2:4]

But in the land of Israel the prophecies will be fulfilled in both a literal and an allegorical sense.

Upon closer examination, however, this reconciliation of Maimonides is found wanting. Maimonides was of the opinion that there would be no supernatural innovations inside or outside Israel and states as much in his pronouncements: "One should not entertain the notion that in the epoch of the Messiah any element of the natural order will be nullified, or that there will be innovations in the work of creation." Surely, the institution of a miraculous order within the land of Israel would constitute an "innovation in the work of creation."

Further proof to this effect can be brought from Maimonides' pronouncement to the effect that the Messiah need not work miracles or resurrect the dead in order to qualify as the Jewish redeemer. Maimonides brought proof to his assertion from the fact that Rabbi Akiva accepted the validity of Bar Kozeba's messiahship in spite of the fact that he had not performed any wonders or signs. Now, since the Bar Kochva revolt took place in the land of Israel, it would appear that Maimonides maintains that the natural order will continue to prevail during the era of redemption, even in the holy land.

Of the many commentators who attempt to reconcile the allegorism of Maimonides with the literalism of the sages, the proposition by Rabbi Meir ben Gabai, author of *Avodat Hakodesh,* seems perhaps the most plausible. Nature as we perceive it today is not the same as it was at the time of Adam in the Garden of Eden. As a consequence of his sin in the Garden, the earth was punished along with Adam and Eve. But in the messianic era, all creatures will return to the nature with which they were originally endowed at the beginning of creation, prior to the sin of the tree of knowledge. Thus, Maimonides' affirmation of a constant in the world order can still accommodate a return to the *original order* of nature. Before the sin of the tree of knowledge, all trees bore fruit, and there were no predators. But the sin corrupted the spiritual matrix of the world and the result was these negative consequences. The messianic redemption, however, will bring perfection back to the world, and God's original intention for the order of the world will be restored.

But upon closer examination, this too must be rejected. Maimonides' rejection of any innovations in nature is not merely referring to changes in potential form, but in the *actual,* observable world around us. It does not seem to matter exactly *when* the potential for fruit-bearing was taken from certain trees, nor when certain beasts were endowed with a predatory nature. What does matter is that their nature has since changed, and Maimonides emphasizes that it will not change again even in the messianic age.

To be sure, it is highly desirable to reconcile the position of Maimonidean rationalism with rabbinic supernaturalism concerning the epoch of the Messiah, in order to emerge with a unified front regarding the future.

This need for reconciliation is especially acute since Maimonides himself seems to teeter between outright allegorism and the embracing of profound supernaturalism. Two examples of this will suffice.

First, there is a debate in the Talmud as to whether a man is permitted to walk in the street on *Shabbat* carrying a sword, bow, or some other militaristic object. The debate revolves around whether these articles are regarded as ornaments, in which case they possess the same law as jewelry and are thus not considered as carrying. The majority opinion in the Talmud, with which Maimonides concurs, is, "They are not ornaments. They are shameful, for it is written, 'And they shall beat their swords into plowshares and their spears into pruning hooks . . . and they shall not learn war any more.' " In other words, were these articles considered ornaments, they would not have to be transfigured in the messianic era.

Thus it seems that Maimonides rules that a physical transfiguration of these war objects will take place in the messianic redemption and the world will never know war. This prophecy is taken quite literally.

But even more important, Maimonides lists as one of the Articles of Jewish Faith that after the advent of the Messiah there will be a resurrection of the dead! What kind of occurrence could there possibly be that is more radical, and more greatly defies today's natural world, than this? How could Maimonides relegate all of the messianic prophecies to the realm of allegory with the promise that the natural world would be preserved, and still accommodate an affirmation of the resurrection of the dead?

Rabbi Menachem Schneerson supplies the answer. The position of Maimonides is that there will be two periods within the era of redemption. The former will be associated with the arrival of the Messiah, at which time the world's natural order will be kept intact, but subsequent to this stage a time will arrive when extraordinary occurrences will take place that defy the rules of nature. It is in this latter sequence that the resurrection of the dead will take place.

In this context is the cross-reference made by Maimonides between the proposed messiahship of Bar Kochva and that of the ultimate redeemer, both of whom need not perform any miracles in order to substantiate their candidacy. With this reference Maimonides wishes to clarify that the coming of the Messiah will not bring in its wake a new world order; hence, whether or not the Messiah himself will be a miracle worker is irrelevant to his role among the Jewish people.

Maimonides defines the role of the Messiah in normalistic terms, with emphasis on the nationalistic aspects of his achievements and their direct bearing on the spiritual character of the nation. The Messiah will restore the Jewish monarchy, rebuild the Temple, and gather in the Jewish exiles from all corners of the globe. By doing so, he will create an environment in which the Jewish people will be able to observe the Torah and its commandments in a perfect manner. Furthermore, the Messiah will remove any obstacles to the worship of God, such as war and hunger, in the world at large. As a consequence, the world's inhabitants "will be free to involve themselves in Torah and its wisdom without any pressures or disturbances. At that time there will be neither famine nor war . . . and the occupation of the entire world will be solely to know God." Thus, amid the natural everyday running of the world, the world's inhabitants will be elevated to a perfect state of Godly knowledge and practice. The restoration of the world to God constitutes the primary focus of the Messiah's mission.

This conception of the monarchy found full expression with the first of the Davidic dynasty, Kind David himself. He united the Jewish people under one banner and completed the conquest of the land of Israel, thus securing peace for the nation. He then undertook the preparations for the building of the Temple in Jerusalem. Likewise, his direct descendant, the messianic king, will oversee this process until its completion. This explanation sits well with the overall purpose of a Jewish monarch as outlined by Maimonides: "A king's purpose and personal objective should be to elevate the true faith" (*Laws of Kings and Wars* 4).

Thus Maimonides begins his discussion of the messiahship with these words: "In the future, the messianic king will arise and renew the Davidic dynasty, restoring it to its original sovereignty." Next Maimonides indicates that this will make possible the complete observance of the Torah and its *mitzvot*. "He will rebuild the Temple and gather in the exiles. . . . Then the observance of all the laws will return to their previous state . . . offer sacrifices . . . sabbatical and jubilee years according to all their particulars mentioned in the Torah." All the elements of Jewish religious observance that were absent in the exile because the Jews were outside Israel and lacking a Temple will be restored.

To further emphasize this point, Maimonides adds a law, directly following this one, discussing the establishment of three new cities of refuge for those accused of manslaughter: "Similarly, in regard to the cities of refuge, it is stated, 'When the Almighty shall expand your borders . . . you shall add three more cities' (Deuteronomy 12:20). This command was never fulfilled. Surely, the Almighty did not give this commandment in vain, and thus the intent was that it would happen in the epoch of the Messiah." Thus, not only would the *mitzvah* of establishing cities of refuge, which had been absent from Jewish life since the advent of the exile, be resumed, but it would be done in a much more complete and perfect manner. The same rule applies to all other *mitzvot*.

Since the purpose of the Messiah is to bring about a perfect state of religious observance, it cannot be expected that he must necessarily be a miracle-worker. If anything, changing the natural order of the world is somewhat in contradiction to the concept that "this Torah, with all its statutes and laws, is eternal.'' Thus, the original era that will be ushered in with the arrival of the Messiah will not be a miraculous one.

However, there will follow a truly miraculous period in which God will "remove predators from the earth" and cause trees of shade to bear fruit. These prophecies speak of the era of redemption as a whole and need not be interpreted as allegories. They will be fulfilled in a literal sense in the latter period of the redemption, in which the dead will also arise from their graves.

Rabbi Menachem Schneerson admits that this approach remains somewhat inadequate. Since the advent of the Messiah will not necessitate a departure from the natural order, which event is it that will? If it is not the messianic era itself, what cause is there that will lead to the resurrection of the dead and fundamental transformation of the world as we know it, to the point where miracles will dictate the order of the day?

A further difficulty presents itself from the writings of Maimonides himself. In his *Letter on the Resurrection,* Maimonides writes that his own statements in the *Mishneh Torah*— that the prophecies concerning the redemption are allegorical in nature—do not represent a definite and final ruling on the matter. Indeed, it is quite possible that the prophecies will be realized in a literal sense.

But if the purpose of the Messiah is to bring about a state of redemption that finds expression in the complete observance of the Torah and its commandments within the context of material existence, then a new and miraculous world order would seem to contradict this.

In the final analysis, Rabbi Schneerson explains that a true reconciliation of Maimonides with the opinion of Nachmanides, as well as the rabbinical messianic expectations, hinges on an important talmudic pronouncement regarding the messianic era:

It is written: "Behold, one like a son of man came on the clouds of heaven" (Daniel 7:13); however, it is also written, "Your king will come like a poor man riding on a donkey" (Zechariah 9:9). If the Jewish people are found worthy of the redemption, then the Messiah will come "on the clouds of heaven" (Daniel 7:13); if they do not merit, he will come "like a poor man riding on a donkey" (Zechariah 9:9). [*Sanhedrin* 98a]

What the Talmud introduces is that there are two possible paths of conduct for the Messiah. If the Jewish people are found sufficiently meritorious, then the messianic era will come via the high road. But if their merits are found lacking, then the Messiah will follow the ordinary route.

This concept the messianic era being dependent on the righteousness of the Jewish people is also used by the sages in reference to when the Messiah will come. The redemption will come about in either of two ways. Isaiah says, concerning the redemption, "The little one shall become a thousand, and the smallest a mighty nation. I, the Lord, will hasten it *in its time*" (Isaiah 60:22). Whereupon, the sages hasten to resolve the apparent discrepancy between the words *in its time* and *I will hasten it*. They state as follows: "If they are worthy, 'I will hasten it'; if they are unworthy, it will come 'in its appointed time' " (*Sanhedrin* 98a; *Taanit* 1:1 [p. 3a]; *Yalkut Shimoni* II, Isaiah, sec. 503; *Song of Songs Rabbah,* end; *Zohar* 1:117b).

On yet another verse in Isaiah, Rashi clarifies this more fully: "Unto Me, one calls from Seir; Watchman, what of the night? The Watchman said: 'The morning comes, also the night. If you will desire, desire you. Return come again' " (Isaiah 21:11–12). Following the explanation of the Talmud in *Sanhedrin,* Rashi clarifies these enigmatic words as follows:

> The Almighty said: "The Prophet cries out to Me from under the yoke of Edom. 'O Guardian of Israel, What will come of this night and this [great] darkness [of exile]?' " Whereupon, the Almighty replied, "I can cause the morning to arrive for you, and also the night, which is destined to come upon the wicked at the end of the days. If you truly seek to hasten the arrival of the Final Redemption—Repent!" [Rashi, *Sanhedrin* 94a]

Yet another example of the different forms that redemption can take, depending on Jewish merit, is the dispute found in the Talmud regarding the building of the Third Temple. Rashi and other commentators, based on the Babylonian Talmud, maintain that the Third Temple will descend from heaven. It will not necessitate human construction. The Jerusalem Talmud, however, maintains that the Third Temple will be built by the Messiah. Although the latter opinion is adopted by Maimonides, if the Jews are found worthy, they will be granted a heavenly Temple, and if not, the Temple will necessitate a mortal effort.

Now in his halakhic compendium, *Mishneh Torah,* where Maimonides' intention is to ultimately convey what will surely be fulfilled, he details the latter scenario. After all, who is to say that indeed the Jews will be found sufficiently worthy to deserve a miraculous messianic deliverance? The entire people has free will, and assurances of that sort cannot be made in a work of Jewish law, where everything must be accurate and precise. Therefore, Maimonides lists that the natural order will continue to prevail. The possibility remains, however, that the collective spiritual attainments of the Jewish people will bring about a miraculous world order.

Based on this understanding, we can already understand what will lead to the advent of the second period in the era of redemption. Once "the occupation of the entire world (including the non-Jewish nations) will be to know God" and the Jews will have achieved perfection in their commitment and observance to God's law, then we will be in a position to merit the advent of a miraculous world order, including the resurrection of the dead.

Thus, in *Letter on the Resurrection,* Maimonides adds that the Jews can in fact "merit" the materialization of all of the messianic prophecies in their literal form, not only at a later stage in the messianic process, but at the very beginning of the redemption (*Likutei Sichot,* vol. 27, *Behukotai;* vol. 18, Balak).

With this the Maimonidean and Nachmanidean visions of the messianic future may be reconciled, but only in regard to the epoch of the Messiah itself.

However, the dispute as to the exact definition of what the World-to-Come is remains. According to Maimonides there will be an era that will follow even that of the Messiah, in which all people will die and then enter the World-to-Come, which in the opinion of Maimonides is the Garden of Eden, a world of souls only with no bodies. Nachmanides, of course, identifies the World-to-Come as the messianic era and the resurrection of the dead and foresees this as being the culmination and climax of the entire historical process.

Indeed, these differences seem irreconcilable. The Tzemach Tzedek dwells upon the vast difference that separates the two great sages in his work, which deals with the esoteric reasons for the *mitzvot—Derekh Mitzvotecha.* In elucidating the mystical angle of the *mitzvah* of *tzitzit,* he resolves that there can be no question that the overwhelming Jewish view, especially that held in the mystical circles of the Kabbalah and *Hassidut,* follows that of Nachmanides. It is here that we may begin to appreciate all that we have gained through our lengthy explanations of how the physical world in general, and the resurrection of the dead in particular, serves as the very culmination of the creative process and the greatest single revelation of Godliness possible.

As this, the simultaneous revelation of God's infinite Essence and the preservation of the borders and limitations of the world, constitutes the highest possible supernal manifestation, there can be no doubt that this represents the culmination of everything that is and the highest communion there can be between Creator and created. Everything, including the lofty spirituality of the Garden of Eden, pales into insignificance compared to the revelation that will take place in the messianic era and the resurrection of the dead. This era will be eternal. Nothing will supersede it.

Epilogue

Personal Thoughts about the Messiah: Toward a Community of Communities

There must be a practical side to the messianic era. In the final analysis, the Messiah must come as a result of human initiative. It is insufficient to await the arrival of the Messiah. We must actively engage in bringing him. How is this done? What does a world preparing itself for the coming of the Messiah look like? Most important, how can humankind as a whole work together toward the arrival of the Messiah? Is there a dimension to messianism, amid its sublime philosophical overtones, that is both practical and human?

In March 1990, our Oxford University L'Chaim Society invited Elie Wiesel to address the students of Oxford University. It was our wish for this great humanitarian to address a large Jewish and non-Jewish audience and thus we staged the lecture at the Oxford Union Society. Thus it was that speaking before a crowd of 1,500 students, many of them non-Jews, he was asked what makes a human being a good person. Responding to the question with regard to Jews, he said something incredibly courageous and controversial: "In my opinion, a Jew is only a good person if he is a good Jew."

In my customary post-L'Chaim Society event assessment, I encountered many students who felt indignant about the remark. While they highly applauded his overall address, this statement seemed to touch a raw nerve. Is the world indeed better off with *Jewish* Jews? And if it is, can this truth be portrayed in a manner in which the pivotal human values of the equality of all men and the brotherhood of nations is preserved?

For over two hundred years the Jews were enslaved to a mighty empire, Egypt. The Almighty had promised to take them out. A strong leader would be needed, one who embodied many diverse qualities. He would have to be noble, so that the Jews would respect him. He would have to be compassionate, so that the Jews would cherish him. He would have to be charismatic, so that the Jews would follow him. And he would have to be exceptionally wise, so that he could serve as an intermediary between God and the Jews.

The leader found was Moses. But his selection was not based on the possession of the above virtues. Rather, the *Midrash* relates a story that depicts the virtue for which Moses was selected the Jewish redeemer.

Moses served as shepherd to the flock of his father-in-law, Jethro. Once, when bringing the flock back from a day of grazing, he noticed that a small straggler had been left behind because it could not keep up with the stronger, swifter sheep. Moses temporarily abandoned the entire flock and returned to gather in the straggler. When the Almighty saw how he had equated the straggler with the entire flock by showing it the same care as the rest of the flock, He declared, "He shall be the leader of my people."

Ostensibly, the story seems to merely indicate that Moses' care for each and every individual found favor in God's eyes. But the significance of his action goes far deeper than just that. Moses didn't return for just any sheep, but for the smallest and weakest. He displayed how he felt the flock to be lacking without it. Not because he thought that one day, if fed properly and looked after, this sheep would grow to be the pride of the flock, big and strong like its counterparts. Rather, the sheep, even in the miserable state it was, was an indispensable member of the flock. Moses recognized that without this straggler, the *entire flock* was flawed.

Stated in other words, Moses did not return for the sake of the *straggler,* but for the sake of the *flock.* He didn't only return because it would be a shame if the little creature would die of starvation or thirst. He returned because as the shepherd, he had been entrusted with a flock, not a collection of individuals. That flock consisted of this little sheep as well. Even supplanting this sheep with another would not have served to compensate for its loss.

Moses was unlike the social worker who helps troubled individuals because, whether the world needs them or not, he believes that every person is important and is entitled to life and happiness. This belief in the rights of the *individual* was not what motivated him to protect the straggler. Rather, it was his obligations to the *community* that made him understand the value of every component part. He was a leader. He had a collective perspective. He looked after the individual because the nation was incomplete without him. By putting the entire flock at risk for the sake of the straggler, Moses demonstrated his recognition that in the quest for building a greater mass, not even the most insignificant component part could be ignored.

The Almighty desired a leader who acknowledged that without the integration, participation, and contribution of every individual member of the nation, the nation would be deficient. Someone who saw that the diversity inherent in creation between nations, people, animals, and things, be they big or small, was a blessing and made for a more glorious whole, a better qualified organization.

In today's society people have progressed beyond the bias and prejudice of the past. They pride ourselves on their *tolerance*. They believe in every man's inalienable right to be different. They have learned to allow those opinions that do not necessarily concur with their own, and we silence no one for expressing such opinions.

On many occasions I have watched in wonder how bitter opponents debate at the Oxford Union Society. Although they usually disagree with each other's every point, they are still relatively congenial to one another. Their differences are usually never resolved. Yet, they publicly show each other respect. Basically and very gentlemanly, they *agree to disagree*. So that is their secret. They believe that each participant is entitled to an opinion, and they respect that right. (Similarly, the protocols of England's House of Commons calls for each member of the House to refer to a colleague as "the honourable member" or "the right honourable gentleman," even amid scorching attack.)

But is this really progression? Tolerance is really a repugnant state of mind. Rather than find any redeeming virtue or positive element of another person's or party's differences or assessments, one *tolerates* or *bears* it. One swallows hard. One stomachs, or suffers, their right to be different.

There is something immoral about this approach. It is one thing to *tolerate* one's right to be different. It is quite another to recognize a virtue that can be extracted from his distinctiveness. To tolerate another person implies that while one allows his opinions or differences today, if tomorrow he would disappear from the face of the earth, it would make no difference whatsoever. One would not so much as recognize his absence. There is nothing to be learned from his conflicting opinion or differences, and his absence will in no way compromise or impair one's own state of being. One existence is totally independent of his. They are different, and their differences, far from benefiting either of them, are merely a source of contention and regression, not harmony and advancement.

Imagine a country in which all are pacifists. How long could it last? Would it not become prey to a belligerent neighbor. Conversely, imagine a country in which all citizens are hawks. What would prevent them from crossing the line of legitimate defense to inhuman aggression and even massacre? There is an inherent beauty and perfection in the divergence of human opinion. But in order for that beauty to be manifest, one must go beyond tolerating one's colleagues, and even one's rivals' existence, to realizing that it is their existence and differences that allow us to maintain our own position and identity.

The Jewish world seems deeply divided. Unfortunately, this is not a new phenomenon. What is new about the divisions is that they are largely political. In Israel the country's inhabitants are deeply torn between those who would trade land for peace and those who feel that this would only invite further aggression encouraged by indefensible borders. The amazing thing is not that they disagree, but the sharp antagonism, even hatred, that exists between the two groups. Can none see that if they were all of one mind, the country might either degenerate into the inhuman dictatorships of its Arab neighbors or weaken itself to the point where another holocaust would be possible? The country's present stalemate is not due to conflicting views. Every country has that. It is due to the inability of either side to see the necessity for the other and to reach a realistic consensus based on the present situation.

A certain Jewish student who was heavily involved in an important Oxford society once told me how proud he was that as a Jew he had risen to high office. He accused the Presidents of the Jewish and L'Chaim Societies of priding themselves on trivial, parochial accomplishments and urged them to get involved in larger, more secular groups. I asked him, "Suppose there was no one interested in running these societies. Would you still have put all your time into your present society? It is only now that they function properly and have devoted people running them that you criticize. Had this not been so, you would probably have felt the need to do something about the lack of activities for Jewish students. Because these societies and students exist, you can do what you're doing today. So you should be applauding them for keeping the torch of Judaism alive, while they should be applauding you for succeeding in non-Jewish circles while remaining fully committed to your Judaism."

Why can we not learn from our teacher Moses, not merely to *tolerate* the existence of a different sheep in our flock, but to recognize the absolute necessity of that sheep for the wholesomeness of the remainder.

A famous talmudic dictum declares, "Saving a single individual is like saving the entire world." God created a complete world, a world in which each individual, along with his/her intrinsic differences, added to its perfection. When one individual is missing, there is suddenly a gross imbalance in Creation, an imbalance that might serve to compromise the uniqueness of each of the earth's inhabitants.

And here the magnitude of murder comes into perspective. The enormity of the offense is not confined to the violation of the sanctity of human life, but to adversely affecting the entire world. When God created the world, this individual was an irreplaceable component of its perfection and equilibrium, and yet the murderer chose to disrupt that fine tuning and throw the world into imbalance. Murder is thus the ultimate statement of arrogance. It is one man's actualization of his belief that another man serves no purpose on this earth.

Note the symbolism inherent in the sacrificial service in the Temple. Any animal disfigured in even the most unimportant way, such as a cut in its eyelid, was disqualified from being brought up as a sacrifice. This is because it is a *blemished animal.* It made no difference where the imperfection lie. The animal remained imperfect.

The Bible teaches that the greatness of Moses and his ability to make insights as to the worth of every individual lie in his unparalleled humility: "And the man Moses was the humblest of all the people that were on the earth" (Numbers 12:3). Now how was this possible? After all, as an individual Moses had the powers of a king and was in constant conscious communion with God. How could he have been humbler than the water-carrier?

The answer is that, when looked at as an individual, Moses was far greater than other individuals. But Moses defined himself in reference to the whole of the Jewish nation, and not as an individual. Moses still saw his role as only one among many. As every individual was essential to the integrity of the entire people, he was one among equals. It made no difference that his role was more exalted than that of the other Jews. Thus in spite of his obvious elevation above the entire nation, Moses remained the humblest of all men. He regarded himself as just one cog in the massive machinery of the Jewish nation. Had the water-carrier been missing and Moses present, the nation would still be imperfect.

The world has a similar saying. "Who is an important person? One who makes others feel important." No person is perfect. Although every human possesses personal virtue, there are bound to be many vital properties lacking from one's personality. An important person, therefore, is someone who recognizes what can be learned and acquired from every other person, even the lowliest of people, and thus looks at everyone as being on an equal plane. It is only then that one may absorb what others have to offer, enhance one's character, and elevate oneself to importance. An important person therefore is someone who recognizes that on some level every person is important.

While in New York I once met a prominent rabbi from Israel. Among other things, he had a reputation for being extremely friendly and unassuming. After introducing myself and saying how honored I was to meet him, the rabbi launched into a detailed account of his accomplishments and renown within society. For a moment I was taken aback and told him how, with such lengthy accounts of himself, one might get the impression that he is a braggart and a show-off. "I am," he replied. "But the difference between myself and other show-offs is that I leave room for you and everyone else to be a show-off, too." This was his secret.

Humility does not mean that one feels lowly and has nothing to offer, and tolerance does not mean that one is willing to put up with another's differences. Rather, humility means that while one is fully aware of one's gifts, that does not preclude one's recognition of someone else's virtues either! The world is big enough for all of us to be special. And tolerance means that one feels the need to learn from, and absorb the qualities of, the different members of society and use them to one's mutual advantage in harmony.

In this age of egalitarian and liberal thinking, how can Jews still promote what is to many intellectuals a shameful and vainglorious sentiment of being the chosen nation? How can Jews preach to the world that they are better than everyone else?

Understanding the concept of chosen nation as arrogant behavior on the part of the Jews is a gross misrepresentation. On the contrary: it is a humbling motif. The Jews were not merely chosen as God's special people, as if the Almighty was playing favorites. *They were chosen for a mission.* And that mission was to spread the knowledge of the creator and His expectations of man to all nations. Thus, God's choosing the Jewish people was a calling that would forever remind them that alone they are insufficient. If the Jews wanted to believe for even a moment that so long as they served God justly and lovingly, God would be satisfied, He made the purpose of their being on this earth to tell the other nations that they are important, too. God is not satisfied with the contribution of the Jews alone, but desires the service and participation of all nations.

This is what being chosen means and the responsibility it entails. Can anyone think of a greater humbling device than a nation whose whole existence is dedicated to teaching the other nations that God loves and needs them, too?

It is for this reason that Judaism discourages Gentile converts. It is not because Jews feel they are part of an elite club and no outsiders are allowed. Quite the contrary! Judaism does not invite converts because it is a fallacy to believe that one need be a Jew in order to enjoy closeness to God or lead a fulfilled life. The way God created each and every one of us is the way in which He wanted us to serve Him. For a Gentile to believe that he must be Jewish in order to "upgrade" his existence is not only erroneous, but it can be extremely damaging. By becoming a Jew, he might neglect to make the contributions to society in the way in which he was meant to do! The world needs him the way he is, which is why God created him that way. What God does expect, however, is that he develop his inner potential for what he is within the divine scheme of things, to his greatest potential. In this way, Jews and Gentiles alike can benefit from what he makes of himself within the parameters of God's will.

A Jewish neighbor of mine who survived the Holocaust but converted to Catholicism after emigrating to England ("We did it because we were tired of being persecuted") visited Auschwitz with a Catholic group. They prayed in one corner, and a Jewish contingent that was also visiting prayed in another. He approached the Jewish worshipers, an Orthodox group from Boston, and asked if they would join the Catholics for a joint prayer service. They thanked him but declined. "Could you imagine," he said to me, "that even in a place like Auschwitz we are still divided and cannot even get together for a joint prayer. Have all of us become like Nazis?"

"No," I replied. "The Nazis believed that everyone had to conform to a certain ideal, everyone had to be the same. If you had brown eyes instead of blue, if you had black hair instead of blonde, you were inferior. Thank God we live in a world where we can not only respect, but even thrive on each other's differences. The fact that we can pray in one corner and you in the other, and no one derides the other for saying the wrong prayer or not having the right to pray at all, is proof that we have progressed beyond the Nazi ethic.''

Another person, this one a member of the Oxford Jewish community, invited me to a monthly meeting, an encounter between Jews, Christians, and Muslims. The purpose was to enhance mutual respect through mutual understanding. I declined. Notwithstanding the nobility of the cause, I rejected its underlying premise. Why is it that mutual respect can only come through understanding each other? If we don't understand each other's differences, or if they are so sublime as to transcend rational explanation (as many religious tenets are), can there then be no respect? Is human nature so naturally biased that one cannot learn to *thrive* on each other's differences, even if they appear strange or unacceptable?

What is it about the human mind that it cannot accept differences as a blessing, but a curse? Why is it that even when one speaks of ''tolerating'' differences, the tolerance is spoken of as a necessary evil?

To our great misfortune, we live in an age which not only does not appreciate differences, but actively seeks to obliterate them. On the contrary, equality in today's society seems to mean that there must be an indistinguishable, homogenous mass where all things are equal by virtue of their being similar. Pluralism and multiculturalism are difficult to achieve. While most decent societies promote the concept, those who have to live being different still feel like outcasts. This is due to two factors.

This first is a weakness of identity on the part of the minority groups. At the end of the day if an individual is not strong about what he is, what he represents, and why it is important that he continue, then even in the most tolerant of societies he will want to acculturate and be like everyone else.

I made this point to a progressive rabbi on a television program. We were part of a panel devoted to the subject of ''Multiculturalism in Modern Society.'' The rabbi entered into a long discourse of how one Sunday of every month he takes his children to church in order for them to grow up informed and tolerant of other faiths. This way he hopes that just as his child will grow up accepting people for what they are, his son will be able to be Jewish and accepted by society as well. He then added that for this reason he is opposed to Jewish schools because they promote segregation and a lack of understanding.

I was indignant and asked him how often he took his child to Synagogue. He said about the same: once a month. I told him that to the best of my knowledge Oxford is a tolerant society, yet I know of many students who come to the University and after a few months take off their Yarmulkas. This is not because people treat them differently, but because they feel different. And everybody's ambition is to fit in. "What do you do to ensure that your child will not only want to be Jewish, but have the backbone to implement it at University and work later in life?" I asked him. The beginning of tolerance is people feeling good and confident about what they are. Miserable people treat other people miserably.

The other reason for the failure of true multiculturalism is that modern society does not like differences. In Judaism the word holy actually means "distinct" or "removed." Something is holy by virtue of it being dissimilar to something else. Thus, a human being becomes holy when he acts differently than animals. Instead of eating whenever, however, and whatever he likes, a Jew eats kosher food, and not by sticking his head into a bowl. When a person does eat without human etiquette, we say that he behaves like an animal. Human beings are holy by virtue of their being different.

Similarly, God is holy because He is not like man. He has no body, limitations, or other corporal description. *Shabbat* is holy because it is different than the other days of the week. To treat it like any other day of the week is to deny its holiness. Judaism teaches man to be sensitive and appreciative of differences.

But in modern society, man is increasingly obliterating all differences. New-age thought teaches that all men are gods. Stores are open seven days a week so that there is no day of rest. Men and women are encouraged to believe that aside from physiological variations, there are no real differences. And science today has taught man that for all practical purposes he is no different than other animals.

It can be appreciated that with this kind of thinking rampant, the differences between nations and peoples are also being obliterated. The Jewish people are gradually disintegrating through intermarriage, and many young people even feel repulsed by parents who try to encourage them to marry within the faith. They do not believe that they are different and are frightened of the very thought.

One of the reasons people are reluctant to accept or admit to existing differences is because many nations have been downtrodden and abused because they were different, by other nations who felt themselves to be superior. But if one can encourage a world-view that acknowledges every nation's, indeed every person's, ability to benefit from diversity and multiformity, that cannot happen. It is only arrogance that allows us to believe that we are sufficient on our own.

If we applied this ideal to life and even politics, we might find solutions to ongoing problems. Take South Africa as an example. In our effort to abolish apartheid, we should be appealing to the South African government's sense of ambition rather than their obviously deadened sense of humanity. We should emphasize to them that if their policies continue as they now stand, they will never be a great nation. So long as they believe that such a large element of the population, as the blacks represent, can make no significant contribution to the advancement of their society, they shall always remain pathetic. Their isolation of the blacks and their separation of them from mainstream life in South Africa signifies not only a denial of basic rights, but a belief on the part of the white community that their society cannot benefit from black integration. They have convinced themselves that they have nothing to learn from the blacks, and this is the real tragedy.

The belief that from everything in this world something positive can be extracted, even those things that appear negative at first, has always been a cornerstone of Judaism. One of the greatest examples of the implementation of this outlook on life was Maimonides. In his celebrated philosophical treatise,

Guide to the Perplexed, Maimonides writes that what people usually refer to as "the evil inclination" is not essentially evil. Rather, it is an impulse, an undirected impulse. He saw the evil inclination as an intensity of energy so potent that it could overtake man's sense of forward direction and goodness, and lead him astray. But energy is precisely what man requires to rise to the challenge of worthy achievement. So, instead of viewing man's propensity for evil as negative and distancing oneself from it, one should look to manipulate and cultivate it—put a harness on it and thrive on its immense energy.

Hasidism developed this concept further by describing man's evil inclination as "the animalistic soul," in contradistinction to the good and "Godly soul." While the good soul may be Godly, it is not as energetic or as driven as the animal soul, which, like its name implies, possesses the raw power of a beast. Using the analogy of an ox, which the Talmud says "can churn out and plough much wheat" so long as it is harnessed, man must use his intellectual faculties to saddle his animal soul. If he is successful, it will be the animal soul dragging the Godly soul to the service of God, and not the reverse.

Maimonides saw a divine purpose in Christianity and Islam. He wrote how both of these religions had brought the knowledge of God and the Messiah to distant isles so that there is now a universal familiarity with the concept of the messianic era. Where before in the history of religious debate has any theologian of universal renown written of the divine purpose played by other religions? Maimonides saw in every historical occurrence a way forward toward a better time that would be shared and enjoyed by all peoples.

It was also Maimonides who wrote in his celebrated *Laws of Repentance* that every individual should always picture the world as if on a scale, teetering between guilty and virtuous. If the individual should do one positive act, he saves the entire world; one wrong move, and the world has had it. One should never underestimate the power of a single good deed, and never overlook every individual's ability to bring salvation to mankind, Jew and Gentile alike.

Of course, all of the ideas laid out thusfar can only work

within a sound, moral framework. Otherwise, who is to say that the thief, the bigot, or the Nazi don't make a positive contribution to their environments. Ultimately, it is the Almighty alone Who can determine which contributions lead to the enhancement of society and which to its collapse. It was He who created all nations ethnically different, and it is He alone Who knows what serves the public good.

The world cannot be run at human whim. It needs an ultimate plan and a regulator who can determine whether it is progressing or regressing. This is the role of the Torah, the divine law, which puts each of one's contributions into perspective. It teaches that while contributions of compassion and justice by all peoples lead to the betterment of civilization, murder and bigotry lead to its destruction.

It also teaches that different people have different roles. Jews have the commandments of the Torah to observe. Non-Jews have the seven Noachide laws to observe, among which are the prohibitions of theft, murder, adultery, cruelty to animals, blasphemy, and the precept to establish courts of justice. The same Torah teaches that the failure of the non-Jew to keep his commandments is equally as detrimental as the failure of the Jew to keep his. Both are indispensable. Both need not assume the other's role to be deemed worthy. Through the contributions of both the world maintains a healthy balance and equanimity.

This idea of dual roles in creation is exclusive to Judaism. No other group is so adamant of the inexclusive right of one group to the truth. The only one with a copyright on truth is the Almighty, and He spelled out different routes for different groups to attain it. He even set out different avenues for men and women to realize their full potential and made it clear that it is harmful for women to choose men for their role model. He went as far as giving women specific commandments that would serve to enhance their precious gifts of femininity.

For the entire world to be just male, or just female, would be insufferable. The same would apply if the entire world had been only Jews or Gentiles, or if all people looked the same or had only the same ideas. By using each other as role models of what we should be in place of learning from each other's virtue, we deny the world the perfection it could attain through diversity.

What the world needs in order to achieve a higher degree of perfection is Jewish Jews and non-Jewish non-Jews, meaning that each group should adhere to the disparate codes of conduct designated for them by the Almighty.

This is the beginning of a messianic world, a world in which contention, jealousy, and war can never play a part for each nation. Each individual would see God's wisdom in creation and, by extension, the perfection that exists in the whole of creation. A messianic world is one where all the people of the earth, while retaining their intrinsic identities, come together to create a better world. This is radically different from the homogeny usually found within the doctrines of secularist utopian states. Marx and Stalin had visions of the workers of the world uniting to create a fairer, more just world. Hitler tried to achieve the same utopia through other means. But both argued for a single race, a single class. It seems that perfecting the world always seems to necessitate everyone becoming the same. The result of those doctrines, though, was a far cry from utopia. They ended with Auschwitz and the Ghulag Archipelago.

The reason is simple. The epoch of the Messiah is a time when the unity of God will be seen in our world. The world that God created will once again be reclaimed as His. But in Judaism, unity never means homogeneity. Rather, unity means taking different parts and demonstrating how they all comprise a greater whole. Unity in marriage is not when a husband puts on his wife's dress, or when a wife tries to please her husband by joining him in a night out with the boys. Rather, unity in marriage means that people who are essentially different, as different as male and female, come together and through loving one another prove that essentially they are one. Thus, when they have a child together, their unity is demonstrated in the form of a single, indivisible, entity, which makes for an incredible equation of unity: $1 + 1 = 1$.

This is the equation that sums up the messianic era. Many different 1's, in the form of nations, people, and ideas focusing together to serve and reunify the ultimate 1—God Almighty, creator of heaven and earth, whose infinite power and essence is reflected in the great diversity in creation, which all emanates from Him. The manifestation of that unity is the goal of the messianic era.

There is, however, one fundamental proviso to all of the above. In order to come about, it requires leadership. For example, a car consists of millions of different parts, but without someone to put it all together, it remains just an odd collection of incongruent pieces. Once it is assembled, through leadership, it not only stands as a complete unit, but it can move. It can progress.

The same is true of humanity. While the role of each and every nation is indispensable, all of their contributions are ultimately worthless unless there is some party who can orchestrate it together meaningfully. This is the role of the Jewish people, who were entrusted with a divine revelation at Sinai and commanded to teach the nations of the earth their laws and the rules by which they can make a meaningful contribution. The Jews were entrusted with the message of monotheism, which they have fulfilled faithfully, the testament to which is the existence of Christianity and Islam, the daughter religions of Judaism.

But this was not the end of their responsibility. The Jews were also entrusted with ensuring that the world comes to-gether to *serve* that one God, according to the universal code of morality that is binding on all of mankind. The Jewish respon-sibility did not end with teaching the world to leave their idols and embrace God. Rather, the meaning of being a "light unto the nations" is to teach them how God wants to be served, as well as which patterns of behavior develop the Godliness of the world and which patterns counteract it. When that teaching is complete and all nations will serve God in unison and under-stand how God desires all people of the earth to serve Him, with no one left behind, we will have reached the messianic future. Everyone will strive to work together instead of against each other.

Often in Oxford I am confronted by students who refuse to come to the Orthodox Jewish activities, based on the predominant Jewish religious refusal to negotiate a land-for-peace settlement. Many are members of the Peace Now movement. I tell them that firstly, I cannot comprehend how they could reject the entirety of Judaism, all the good things that even they admit Judaism incorporates, for the sake of one facet of *halak-hah*. But more importantly, I tell them that religious Judaism and *Shalom Ahshav* represent the exact same ideals. We say, *"Moshiah* Now!" and they say "Peace Now!" There is nothing more rudimentary about a messianic era than the fact that it will be an era of peace and there is nothing new about crying our for peace. These political activists have been preempted by two-and-half thousand years by the Jewish prophets who foretold of a time when all war and strife would cease.

Peace cannot exist in a vacuum. War will not leave the earth until the causes of war—jealousy, hatred, and contention—leave the earth along with it. By educating the world and bringing them to higher moral values, and teaching the world about a God who created man and commanded him to pursue justice, one is preparing the way for the Messiah. God said that we should do whatever we can, and He will add the final finishing touches by sending the Messiah.

The Jewish people are in need of a leader, a wise leader, a leader who can once again seize the initiative, grab hold of the Jews by the collar, and tell them to get moving to bring the world with all its inhabitants toward the ultimate destination. This leader will be the Messiah himself. He will be someone who will awaken the Jewish and non-Jewish world to their ultimate purpose. He will once again establish God as the king over both the heavens and the earth. Like Moses, the first redeemer, he will take a nation out from the throes of acculturation and Godless society, and give them new life as the chosen nation who must in turn arouse the world at large from their slumber.

The book *The Day America Told the Truth* is an extensive study of the change in American social attitudes. It was based on thousands of interviews with people from all walks of life. One of the major themes it dealt with was what was described as "a general decline in moral and ethical standards." It seems that the vast majority of all those interviewed agreed that society was not as virtuous as it once was. And while this information should serve as no great surprise, the majority opinion on the cause should be surprising: a lack of leadership. The nation felt that there was no longer anyone to look up to. We had lost all of our heroes. This is why the world is riper and more ready now for the advent of a messianic leader than ever before in history.

Gone from the landscape are the charismatic political leaders of just a generation ago—the Churchills, the Roosevelts, the De Gaulles, the Kennedys. And people are looking to fill the void. This sets the stage even more for the arrival of the Messiah, a universal leader.

It is for this reason that in order to be a good person, or a good citizen, a Jew must first be a good Jew. If he does not live the life of a Jew, if his identity is sunken beneath Gentile values and a Gentile life-style, he offers the world nothing that it does not possess already. He takes but does not give. And while he may go on to offer the world great inventions, cures for disease, and solutions for war, there is still an integral part of his personality that remains undeveloped, from which the world could and must benefit.

The world has a fascination with the Jewish people that cannot be ignored or explained away trivially. At times this fascination has led to gross atrocities against the Jewish people. It seems as if the world knows, by some supernatural means, that they need us. On the other hand, they might prefer to live without us. One thing is for sure. The world cannot ignore the Jews. It is as if the Jews have become the conscience of the world.

For nearly two thousand years the Jewish people were unable to make a Jewish impact on the world. How could they? They were not part of mainstream society. They lived in ghettos. Some were forced upon them by their Gentile neighbors, others were self-imposed. Many communities were frightful of full integration because of the dangers of assimilating. They took steps to remove themselves from the outside world, thus insuring that their children would be immune to Gentile influence. At the same time, they also rendered themselves impotent to influencing society in a uniquely Jewish way. And the Jewish nation slumbered.

While the world fought religious battles, murdered, pillaged, went through a dark age, fought battles of empire on distant shores, the Jewish isolation insured that they would not do the same. Of course, it also insured that the Jewish teachings of "Thou shalt not kill," even in the name of God, was heard by no one. Similarly, the Jewish teaching of "Who is rich? He who is satisfied with his lot" went untaught, as did the Jewish propensity for study as the guide to a life of moral and ethical excellence. The Jews could have taught much to medieval man, but all remained quiet, either forcibly, or by choice.

This state of affairs changed drastically in the first part of the eighteenth century. With the French Revolution and German emancipation, the Jews were granted equal social rights, rights that enabled them to fully integrate into secular society. The Jews responded with great enthusiasm, the age-old fear of assimilation giving way to golden new opportunities. To be sure, certain groups responded with caution. "New [societal adaptations] are forbidden from the Torah" was the motto of their champion, Rabbi Moshe Schreiber, the *Hatam Sofer*. But most embraced the opportunity to rejoin the larger world.

Here at last was the opportunity to make a Jewish stamp on the world. The opportunity to contribute to a world that had been so dominated by the influence of other nations up to that time confronted the Jews. How did they respond?

They largely failed. As Jews they made an impact, but not a Jewish impact. One group, headed by Moses Mendelson, argued that "one should be a person in the street, and a Jew at home." A compartmentalized Jewish identity is what they favored. The world was either not ready or could not appreciate a true Jewish imprint.

Others, notably Abraham Geiger, argued for the transformation of Judaism. The essence would have to be preserved, but it should be repackaged in a way that would make it more appealing to the enlightened masses. A traditional Jewish identification would be too overwhelming. A more digestible Judaism was the answer. Of course, when one begins to tamper with age-old truths, it is difficult to draw the line between the trivial and the essential. It was not long before the new ameliorated Judaism bore little resemblance to the original.

Still others maintained that there was no room for the Jew in
Gentile society, even in the postemancipation enlightenment.
Jews should move to Israel. And while the Zionists justifiably
argued for the need for Jews to reinhabit their homeland, they
seemed oblivious to the important contributions the Jews could
make in their native societies. The European continent and
other residences of the Jews at that time were perceived as
having been the scene of too much persecution; too much
blood had been spilled. Hence the Jewish hesitation to contribute anything to their benefit.

The result all round was a lost opportunity. Although Jews
contributed to every major field—philosophy, science, the arts,
and government—it was the mark of a Jew that they left, not a
Jewish mark.

And this neglect has largely continued to this very day. And
yet, this is the generation that will bring the Messiah. How long
will it be before the role of Jewish teacher is assumed? Can one
continue to starve the world of pivotal Jewish teachings that
could improve the lot of all of mankind. Why is it that the
average non-Jew's impression of the Jewish nation and the
Jewish religion remains bagels, shmaltz herring, and circumci-
sion?

The world is ready for a Jewish presence. Every nation has
had their chance. We as Jews have benefited from what they
have offered. Til this very day we remember their wise men.
We have learned much from what their sages offered. Should
we not reciprocate and teach them of ours?

The world learns of how the Greeks philosophized, how the
Romans dominated the earth, and how the Egyptians built
pyramids. Yet, the only thing they seem to learn of the Jews is
how they died. Can we communicate nothing aside from the
fact that Jews are the world's perennial victims?

The Jewish people must refocus their priorities. While com-
batting anti-Semitism is of great significance, it falls far short of
the obligation to bring the Messiah. The Jews are the nation that
cannot shirk the responsibility of the prophets. For two thousand years the voice of Isaiah has been heard and his vision has
been inspiring. He foretold of a world in which there would be
no anti-Semitism, because there would be no hatred. No Jews

would be killed because there would be no war. Jews are the bearers of these dreams, and it is the Jews who bear the responsibility to make them a reality. The non-Jewish fascination with the Jews continues. It is growing ever steadily. The subjects of Israel, Jewish businessmen, and anti-Semitism still dominate the media. While the Jews have the world's attention, it is time to seize the moment. Jews cannot know whether this opportunity will ever rise again. They literally have the opportunity to bring the Messiah. All it takes is action.

Living on the threshold of the messianic age should be a most exciting experience for any Jew. Other generations have expected the Messiah's imminent appearance on the basis of the forced interpretation of one or two prophecies, whereas Jews today are living through the entire range of messianic tradition, often coming to pass with uncanny literalness. If one keeps one's eyes open, one can almost see every headline bringing Jews a step closer to this goal.

But as also predicted, it is a time of great challenge. These are times of snares and temptations lying in wait for the unwary, drawing them away from the truth. The world has much to offer, which can detract Jews from their mission. But is it eternal?

The voice of the prophet Jeremiah can still be heard. It is lamenting the fall of Jerusalem and the burning of the Temple. It is overpowered, however, by the sound of the non-Jewish prophet Balaam, "A star shall rise forth from Jacob" (Numbers 24:17).

The non-Jews yearn for the Messiah as much as the Jews.

The world yearns for leadership. Never before has mankind been so divided as to its prospects for the future. There are some pessimists who say that mankind is approaching its end. They predict that mankind will either pollute the entire planet or overpopulate to the barest marginal existence. Others see man doing the job more quickly, bringing his civilization crashing down on his head in a nuclear war.

On the other hand, there are optimists who predict a utopian future for mankind. They see unlimited energy being generated by thermonuclear furnaces, the conquest of man's most dread diseases, and the solution of all the social problems, leading to a world beyond one's fondest present dreams.

Never before has mankind been faced with such a wide range of possibilities. Never before has it had such tremendous power at its disposal, to use for good or evil. And never before has there been such a great need or demand for leadership to help guide and transport man to the glorious destination that awaits him.

While the perfection of society has forever been an elusive and almost impossible dream, this generation no longer tolerates war, injustice, inequality, the poisoning of our environment, or any of the other evils that were once felt to be inevitable. There is a sudden global change of conscience that seems to be shaking the very roots of civilization. More and more, people are coming to the conclusion that the evils of society are not merely the natural consequences of civilization, but diseases that call for a cure. The only thing that is lacking is for someone to orchestrate all of the efforts and good will together within a divine plan.

In the summation of his speech at the Oxford Union, Elie Wiesel related how, while conversing with the president of an African nation, the president accused the Jews of controlling the world, everything from the banks to the media. "No, that is inaccurate," Wiesel replied. "We do not, and have not, controlled the world at all. We've played quite a small role in the world up to now. But this is something that I wish the world would allow us to do. I don't want to control the whole world. What I ask is that you give us the world, give us your children, for just one generation, and let us show you what we can teach it. I promise, we will give it back in a better condition than when we took it."

The world is ripe for a Jewish contribution. It will come from those who do not shy away from being different and try, to the best of their ability, to lead Jewish lives. All Jews have earned the right to play the part. Our parents never lost it. Now it is time to live it. Hundreds of generations look anxiously to us as they pass on the baton. Dare the nation of Israel fail them?

Index

About the Author

Shmuel is the rabbi and director of the Chabad House of Oxford University and the L'Chaim Society of Oxford, the university's third largest student organization. He studied at Toras Emes Rabbinical College in Jerusalem, the Rabbinical College of Sydney, Australia, and the Central Lubavitch Yeshiva in New York. Rabbi Boteach lives in Great Britain with his wife and three young children.